RACHEL'S CRY

PRAYER OF LAMENT AND REBIRTH OF HOPE

Kathleen D. Billman and Daniel L. Migliore

UNITED CHURCH PRESS
CLEVELAND, OHIO

United Church Press, Cleveland, Ohio 44115
© 1999 by Kathleen D. Billman and Daniel L. Migliore

Library of Congress Cataloging-in-Publication Data

Billman, Kathleen D. (Kathleen Diane), 1950–
    Rachel's cry: prayer of lament and rebirth of hope / Kathleen D.
Billman and Daniel L. Migliore.
        p. cm.
    Includes bibliographical references and index.
    ISBN 0-8298-1353-5 (pbk. : alk. paper)
    1. Laments in the Bible.   2. Rachel (Biblical matriarch)   3. Mary,
Blessed Virgin, Saint.   4. Suffering—Religious aspects—Christianity.   5. Hope—
Religious aspects—Christianity.   6. Theology, Doctrinal.   7. Pastoral theology.
I. Migliore, Daniel L., 1935– .   II. Title.
BS1199.L27B55 1999
242'.72—dc21   99-30816
                                                                    CIP

For our students and colleagues,
families and friends,
who have helped us understand
the deep relationship between lament and hope

CONTENTS

Prayer of pain + protest -
resource for healing
linked w/ capacity for praise
[hope]
Holism + integration
Where has prayer of lament been in
Bible? Christian trad?
Where is it today?
How can that help people +
congregations?

PREFACE

This book is the fruit of a long conversation about prayer that began between the two of us several years ago and gradually expanded to include more and more people, not only those who have spoken to us from the printed page and in scholarly conversation but also those who have spoken in classrooms and from church pews. As we entered more deeply into this conversation, we became convinced that the prayer of lament, or what might also be called the prayer of pain and protest, is vital to theology and pastoral ministry today, that it is a profound resource for personal and corporate healing, and that it is inseparably related to the capacity for hope and praise. Without the resistance and protest that are expressed in the prayer of lament, Christian life, worship, and ministry can quickly become shallow and evasive.

When we decided to collaborate on this project, it was not because we considered ourselves experts on prayer. We were, and continue to be, more learners than teachers in this subject. But as theological educators we are frequently asked to address the quest of many students for a spiritually centered life and ministry and to answer questions about topics that often cut across the boundaries of our disciplines.

As a pastoral theologian, Kathleen regularly encounters urgent questions arising from ministry with suffering people. Among these questions are: How do I respond to a person's experience of devastating grief in a way that fosters hope? How do I minister to someone whose understanding of God leaves no room for expressions of pain? How do I pray with someone who is chronically depressed? How do I minister to others when I am myself experiencing the absence of God? Theological, psychological, and cultural questions arise from immersion in ministry, calling for careful assessments of sufferers and their different contexts, an exploration of the dynamics of healing and the resources of the Christian faith, and a willingness to critically examine one's own assumptions about ministry.

As a systematic theologian, Daniel finds that seminarians, pastors, and laity are eager to explore ways in which the deep and abiding affirmations of Christian faith intersect and illumine life and ministry. Such explorations sometimes unsettle familiar beliefs and long-held pieties and prompt many pressing questions: Why is there so much suffering in the world? Does God intend for us to suffer? What is the meaning and purpose of prayer in the face of suffering and loss? How honest can we be in prayer? What guidance does the Bible and the theological tradition give us regarding the inclusion of lament as well as praise and thanksgiving in prayer?

Although the starting places for theological inquiry are often different in our respective disciplines, each of us wants to consider Christian life as a whole and to assist in the integration of belief, practice, ministry, and prayer. Our collaboration on this volume is based on the conviction that crossing the disciplinary boundaries of academia, while not without risk, is imperative. We decided that the risk was worth taking if it might lead to a deeper understanding of Christian prayer and a stronger ministry of the church.

Every book has its life context, and ours is no exception. Although the contexts of our schools are quite different (Princeton and the South Side of Chicago), the centrifugal forces that fragment the lives of seminarians, professors, pastors, and laity are powerfully at work in both contexts. Since we experience these forces in our own lives, this book addresses our questions as well as those others have asked of us.

Readers will hear early on in this book the worry that much of what is called "spirituality" today converges all too easily with a consumer-oriented culture. As a commodity, prayer is sold as an antidote to burnout, a buffer against the world's brokenness, or a guarantee of inner peace and calm no matter what is happening around us. Christian prayer, we contend, is neither denial nor distraction. It allows distress and alienation to come to voice.

Of course, not all efforts to express alienation and distress are generative of new life. Not all protests against what is happening inside us and around us are constructive. Nevertheless, the mystery that lies at the heart of the biblical story is that God is at work precisely in the places where dis-ease and yearning are most acute and where the starkest, most fearful truths are told. It is at such points that one also glimpses the mystery of how the people of God may become agents of resistance, hope, and transformation.

This book attempts to enter these mysteries. We do not seek to glorify the prayer of lament per se, but to explore the deep link between lament and hope. Our concern is not only with the question of how the prayer of lament has functioned in the biblical witness and in the Christian theological tradition, but where it may be found today and how it might enrich the life of individual Christians and congregations tomorrow.

ACKNOWLEDGMENTS

If we acknowledged by name all those who have contributed to this book, the list would be very long. We are grateful to our respective institutions—Princeton Theological Seminary and the Lutheran School of Theology at Chicago—for sabbatical leaves during which most of the book was written. We are indebted to our colleagues Christie Neuger, Patrick Miller, Connie Kleingartner, Herbert Anderson, Barbara Rossing, Tina Krause, Mary Pellauer, and Lois Livezey for reading parts of the book and offering helpful comments.

We also want to express our thanks to many other colleagues and friends with whom we have had engaging conversations on topics related to the book; to the many students in our classes who listened and responded to our ideas in their initial stages and who in some cases read early drafts of our work; and to those church leaders and members of congregations who were so generous and courageous in sharing their stories of lament and hope and who reminded us over and over that this was a project needed by the church.

Special thanks to Timothy Staveteig, editor of The Pilgrim Press, for his encouragement and wise advice; to Ed Huddleston and others on the Pilgrim/United Church Press staff for their prompt and cheerful help; and to our research and technical assistants, David Norwood, Jennifer George (PTS), and Michele Ports (LSTC).

Not least, for support and understanding throughout the project, we are deeply grateful to our spouses, Jim and Margaret, and to our families, Adam, Mark, and Rebecca.

Finally, we are grateful to each other for the challenges and joys we have experienced in coauthoring this book.

INTRODUCTION:
MEDITATION ON PRAYER

Prayer has many voices and many seasons. There is jubilant prayer and plaintive prayer, summer prayer and winter prayer. When the psalmist cries, "Let everything that breathes praise God!" (Ps. 150:6), we hear the summer voice of prayer. It is the voice of Christmas, Palm Sunday, Easter, and Pentecost. Its colors are white and red, and its music as exultant as Handel's "Hallelujah Chorus." The summer voice of prayer is the glad response to the gospel, and it is vital to Christian faith and life.

But there is also a winter voice of prayer: "Out of the depths I cry to you, O God" (Ps. 130:1). The winter voice of prayer is the voice of Israel in bondage, wandering in the wilderness, and mourning in exile. It is the voice of Hagar, Hannah, Rachel, Jeremiah, and Job, the voice of Jesus in Gethsemane and on the cross. In the church year, the winter voice of prayer is heard especially on Maundy Thursday, Good Friday, and Holy Saturday. Its color is purple, and its music agitated and sorrowful as in the African American spiritual "Were You There When They Crucified My Lord?" Like the Easter voice of prayer, the Good Friday voice of prayer belongs to the biblical drama of salvation and to the life and worship of the church. The summer and winter voices of prayer cannot be separated without damage to the life of faith.

As we have pondered these seemingly contradictory voices of prayer and wondered how they are related in the biblical tradition and in Christian life and ministry, our imaginations have come to focus increasingly on two women of the Bible, Rachel and Mary. They have become for us powerful metaphors of the wholeness of prayer and spirituality that needs to be reclaimed by Christians today.

RACHEL'S LAMENT

Rachel is remembered above all for her lamentation. In one of the most poignant passages of scripture, the prophet Jeremiah describes her inconsolable grief because her children have been slain or carried into exile. "A voice is heard in Ramah, lamentation and bitter weeping. Rachel is weeping for her children; she refuses to be comforted for her children, because they are no more" (Jer. 31:15).

It is Rachel's refusal to be consoled that rivets our attention. She does not remain silent while facing the loss of her children. She weeps and laments, and her weeping is bitter. She resists the comfort extended to her because she refuses to be reconciled to the injustice and violence of her world.

Rachel's cry and her bold refusal of solace bring two aspects of her suffering to voice. The first is that she weeps for herself and anguishes over her loss. Rachel's children are gone, and she weeps because she can no longer see them, hold them, hear their laughter, or comfort their tears. All that might have been is no longer possible.

The second aspect of Rachel's cry is her anger and resistance. "She refuses to be comforted for her children, because *they* are no more." Rachel's refusal of comfort reflects not only her own anguish but her rage at the senseless slaughter of children. It is not only that she does not have them, but that they are no more. Although the children's cries have been silenced by death, Rachel continues to cry out on their behalf, to remember their suffering, and to resist consolation while such outrages continue.

There follows in the text a startling promise of God. While we are not explicitly told that Rachel laments before God, that her cry is a prayer of lament, the text nevertheless reports that God hears her cry and responds to it with a promise: There is hope; your children shall come back to their own country; justice and peace will reign on earth.

The portrait of Rachel weeping and refusing consolation on account of her terrible loss is etched in the imagination of the believing communities nourished by the biblical witness. The figure of Rachel gives voice to the grief of countless Jewish mothers over many centuries and indeed to the inconsolable grief of all humanity in its afflictions. Rachel does well to weep, and she does well to refuse consolation. Her resistance to all easy comfort registers a powerful protest to outrageous suffering and injustice. It is a protest so deep that it must become a prayer, for only God can provide the needed hope that justice will prevail and that the future will be different.

Rachel's bold, disturbing, and prophetic cry has made her a revered figure of the Jewish community. The prophet Jeremiah and later Jewish tradition clearly understand her crying and her resistance as expressions of faithfulness. From biblical times to the present the traditional grave of Rachel has been an important site of Jewish pilgrimage. In refusing to accept easy consolation, Rachel does what is right. Her resistance is both a protest to and a waiting on God. In her own way, Rachel holds open the possibility of again praising the God of justice and new life.

The story of Rachel, however, has not been nearly as influential in the life and worship of the Christian church. Rachel remains, in important ways, an outsider to Christian spirituality. At best, she stands on its margins. Like Job, she is a resister, a protester who refuses the consolations of orthodox theology and conventional pastoral care. Most Christians are certainly not inclined to think of Rachel and Job when they look for models of prayer and piety.

MARY'S HOPE

Forgetful of Rachel and her lament, the church has been inclined to look to another biblical woman for its model of prayer: Mary, the mother of Jesus. More specifically, many Christians find their exemplar of prayer in Mary's response to the angel Gabriel: "Let it be to me according to your word." The contrast seems stark: Rachel refuses, Mary accepts; Rachel weeps, Mary rejoices; Rachel loses her children, Mary is given a child; Rachel expresses rage, Mary is serene. The piety and prayer of the church have been far more like Mary's than like Rachel's.

But the truth is not as simple as this neat contrast suggests. Rachel's lament paradoxically makes room for the new. It keeps open the possibility of once again praising God, not falsely or mechanically, but from the heart. Only when longing for redemption from the ravages of sickness and war is intense can the seeds of renewed hope for the coming reign of God's justice and peace take root. Rachel's lament is not contrary to praise but the precondition of authentic, honest praise.

Also contrary to many conventional portrayals, Mary's prayer is far from a naive acceptance of things as they are. In the Magnificat, Mary's great prayer of praise, Mary rejoices that God has overturned the injustice of this world, has lifted up the poor and satisfied the hungry.

> My soul magnifies God, and my spirit rejoices in God my Savior. . . . God has brought down the powerful from their thrones, and lifted up the lowly; God has filled the hungry with good things and sent the rich away empty. (Luke 1:46, 52–53)

If Rachel's lament is an act of faithfulness making room for authentic doxology, Mary's praise is steeped in prophetic faith. If Rachel's lament and her refusal of consolation await the time of new praise of God, Mary's praise and exultation are fully aware of the reality of pain and loss. For Mary, like Rachel, will lose her child, and the sword of grief will pierce her heart too. So the evangelist Matthew weaves together the griefs of Rachel and Mary. While their son is still an infant, Mary and Joseph flee with him to Egypt to escape the genocidal policy of Herod. As the evangelist tells the story of their flight, he reminds us of Rachel's cry: we hear her voice once again weeping bitterly and refusing all consolation (Matt. 2:16–18).

Rachel and Mary are thus bound together as sisters of faith in the biblical tradition. Even though the church has often remembered Mary but forgotten Rachel, the two belong together in the prayer and practice of Christian faith. Together they remind us that the danger of praise without lament is triumphalism, and the danger of lament without praise is hopelessness.

PRAYER OF LAMENT AND REBIRTH OF HOPE

As we will emphasize throughout our study, we affirm the importance of thanksgiving, praise, confession, petition, and intercession in Christian prayer. We suspect, however, that many Christians are inclined to exclude their own deepest cries and the profound cries of other people from their understanding and practice of prayer. What has happened to the prayer of lament, protest, and contention with God in Christian prayer, and what are the consequences of its loss for Christian life and ministry?

Rachel's cry needs to be reclaimed in Christian prayer, the liturgy of the church, and pastoral ministry. Christian prayer is whole and strong only when it includes both Rachel's cry of sorrow and protest and Mary's cry of joy and praise. That is the theme of this book.

Our study begins with a description of the loss and recovery of the prayer of lament within mainline American churches (chap. 1). We then examine the importance of the prayer of lament in the biblical tradition (chap. 2) and trace how it has been received in the Christian theological tradition (chap. 3). Next we explore what use has been made of the lament prayer in modern pastoral theology (chap. 4). With this background, we venture a pastoral theology of the prayer of lament (chap. 5) and offer vignettes of ministry that provide glimpses of the embodiment of the prayer of lament in corporate worship, pastoral care, the struggle for justice and reconciliation, and theological reflection in congregations (chap. 6).

Prayer, we are convinced, is a practice of the freedom that is born of the Word and Spirit of God. We hope this book on the prayer of lament will help others discover, as we have discovered, how remarkable that freedom is.

CHAPTER ONE

THE LOSS AND RECOVERY OF THE PRAYER OF LAMENT

Pain—is missed—in Praise.
—Emily Dickinson

The practice of prayer is being renewed today both inside and outside the church. Growing numbers of small groups meet for prayer and Bible study in local congregations, schools, and workplaces. Congregations in search of a pastor hope to find someone who will offer spiritual leadership as well as helpful sermons and sound management. In virtually every theological school there is lively discussion about the role of spiritual formation in the training of ministers. Clearly, there is a burgeoning interest in spirituality within Christian churches today as people look for deep resources to live with meaning and purpose in a complex and often chaotic modern world.

Within the wider society, too, the interest in spirituality and prayer is strong. Movements like Promise Keepers and other religious gatherings fill sports stadiums and convention centers with story, song, prayer, and calls for renewed commitment to God, family, and community. In addition to these widely discussed movements and events on the current religious scene, interest in Eastern religious traditions continues to rise. Church members as well as those unaffiliated with any church are exploring the spiritual heritages and devotional practices of other world religions. New Age literature and music fill the shelves of bookstores and music shops. Retreat centers flourish, spiritual guides offer their wisdom on street corners and in shopping malls, and numerous TV programs instruct their viewers on the way to robust spiritual health. All this suggests a real spiritual hunger in contemporary American society.

To many thoughtful Christians, the recent turn to spirituality in both church and society is at once encouraging and unsettling. On the one hand, the new openness to and longing for deeper spiritual life presents the church with opportunities for proclamation and ministry missing only a few decades ago. After a time when even theologians declared the demise of religion and the triumph of secularity, the recent wave of interest in prayer and other spiritual disciplines seems enormously promising.

On the other hand, there is reason to wonder whether the new popularity of prayer and spirituality automatically translates into a real deepening of relationship with God and others. Questions can be raised about the vagueness of the new interest in spirituality, the superficial optimism and faddishness that often attend it, and the frequent disconnection of the spirituality boom from the deep social crises of our time. Like so much else in our market-driven culture, all religious practices, including prayer, can be co-opted by market forces and packaged in a way that will guarantee a quick sell and large profits.

The present study takes its place in the context of the recent surge of interest in spirituality and prayer but pursues a largely unfamiliar and possibly unpopular question. It asks whether our understandings and practices of prayer take honest account of the radical evil and suffering that scar the lives of so many people, whether our spirituality and our prayers heed the words of the American poet Emily Dickinson quoted at the beginning of this chapter: "Pain—is missed—in Praise." Commenting on Dickinson's words, Kathleen Norris speaks of the "treacherous journey" between pain and praise that must be traveled if a sentimentalizing of both pain and praise is to be avoided.[1] Are we disturbed by prayer as well as comforted? Is a voice of anguish and protest heard in our prayers, and what difference does it make if that voice is present or absent?

In this introductory chapter we will define what we mean by the prayer of lament and will explore a few instances of pastoral ministry that suggest the potential of the lament prayer for contributing to spiritual growth and the rebirth of hope. We will then note the extent to which the prayer and worship of the mainline Christian churches often seem to reflect the attitudes of the wider culture rather than challenging these attitudes. After identifying some of the questions that might be raised about the proposal to incorporate honest lament and protest more fully in prayer and worship, we conclude the chapter by presenting the primary aims of our book.

WHAT IS MEANT BY THE PRAYER OF LAMENT?

By the prayer of lament we mean that unsettling biblical tradition of prayer that includes expressions of complaint, anger, grief, despair, and protest to God. We encounter such prayers above all in the Psalter, but we find them in many other books of the Bible as well. While these prayers often make us uncomfortable, they are clearly an important part of the biblical tradition of prayer. Contrary to what we may assume, the Bible makes room in the life of faith for daring complaint to God rather than declaring such prayer off limits.

As we are using the term, the prayer of lament is distinguishable from the more familiar penitential prayer. In the penitential prayer, or prayer of confession, there is a strong sense of guilt and remorse for sins that have been committed and a plea to God for forgiveness and renewal. Such prayers are of great importance in the biblical tradition and in all Christian life and worship rooted in this tradition. As we will see, however, the primary emphasis of the prayer of lament is not on the grievous sins of those who pray but on their misery, their sense of suffering unjustly, and their feeling of being abandoned by friends and even by God.

A number of theologians, led by Old Testament scholars, have underscored the importance of the prayer of lament. In fact, in recent years we have seen a veritable explosion of study of the lament psalms of the Old Testament. Reflecting on the results of his detailed and influential research on the place of lament in the prayer life of ancient Israel, Claus Westermann states: "It would be a worthwhile task to ascertain how it happened that in Western Christendom the lament has been totally excluded from human relationship with God, with the result that it has completely disappeared above all from prayer and worship."[2]

Among American biblical scholars, Walter Brueggemann has led the way with his extensive and penetrating writings on the prayer of lament.[3] He speaks of the "costly loss" of this form of prayer in the life and witness of the church.[4] The studies of Brueggemann have been a constant source of insight for this study. Substantial books on prayer in the Bible by Patrick Miller, Samuel Balentine, Denise Dombkowski Hopkins, and others have also added significantly to our understanding of the prayer of lament.[5]

In a poignant passage, Balentine describes his own personal experience of the loss of the lament and protest tradition of prayer that dares to address God boldly and honestly.

> The church taught me how to pray and, more subtly, how not to pray. One was to praise God, but not protest; to petition God, but not interrogate; and in all things to accept and submit to the sometimes incomprehensible will of God, never challenge or rebel. Yet when life's circumstances would not permit either such passivity or such piety, this advocacy of a rather monotonic relation to God seemed destined to silence if not exclude me and, I suspected, other struggling questioners from the ranks of the truly committed, the genuinely faithful. "You must not question God." If one cannot question God, then to whom does one direct the questions?[6]

While the new interest in the prayer of lament has been led by Old Testament theologians, scholars in other fields have also explored the topic. Among pastoral theologians, Donald Capps, Herbert Anderson, William Hulme, Eugene Peterson, and Denise Ackermann have made important contributions.[7] So too have David Power, Elaine Ramshaw, and others in the area of liturgics and theology of ritual.[8]

The prayer of lament requires theological interpretation that explores the connection between prayer and the central affirmations and practices of the Christian church. Hence the writings of theologians and philosophers on prayer,[9] suffering and hope,[10] atonement,[11] reconciliation,[12] and Trinity[13] are also important resources for our study.

Our work draws freely from many of these sources, attempts to integrate a number of their insights, and seeks to advance the discussion of the pastoral and theological significance of the prayer of lament by contributions of our own.

THE EXPERIENCE OF LOSS AND THE PRAYER OF LAMENT

An occasion of the prayer of lament familiar to believers in all ages is the experience of sickness, loss, death, and bereavement. The death of a loved one—especially the premature death of a family member or close friend as a result of disease, accident, or violence—often precipitates a spiritual struggle for the person of faith who has been deeply wounded by what has happened and wants desperately to understand why.

When Ann Weems, widely read author of poetry, stories, and meditations, lost her twenty-one-year-old son, Todd, in tragic circumstances, she was devastated. "The stars fell from my sky," she writes.[14] While Weems's experience of grief was not unlike that of countless others who have unexpectedly lost a loved one, that knowledge did not lessen her pain. Caring people kept in touch with her and offered what help they could. One of her friends, Walter Brueggemann, called and told her he was working on the book of Jeremiah. Referring to the passage in that book where Rachel is described as mourning for her children and refusing to be comforted, Brueggemann asked Weems if she thought Rachel will find comfort. Weems answered: "No, Rachel will not be comforted. Not here, not now, not in the sense of being ultimately comforted. Of course, those people who are surrounding me with compassion are doing the work of angels, and I bid them come, but Rachel will be comforted only when God wipes the tears from her eyes."[15] Brueggemann then suggested that Weems compose her own psalms of lament. Her book *Psalms of Lament* was the eventual outcome of that suggestion.

Weems's prayers are honest, poignant cries of pain and faith. They could not have been written by someone who did not believe in God. Neither could they have been written by someone who had never experienced the absence of God in the midst of terrible loss, abuse, or injustice. In one of her psalms Weems writes:

O God, what am I going to do?
He's gone—and I'm left

with an empty pit in my life. . . .
How could you have allowed this to happen?
I thought you protected your own!
You are the power:
Why didn't you use it?
You are the glory,
but there was no glory in his death.
You are justice and mercy,
yet there was no justice, no mercy for him. . . .
O Holy One, I am confident
that you will save me. . . .
You are the power
and the glory;
you are justice
and mercy.
You are my God forever.[16]

Weems's bold and bracing prayers deviate from much conventional piety. They bear witness not to serenity but to struggle. No smooth talk to cover grief is provided, no simple solutions offered for the terrible loss experienced. The acute pain is honestly acknowledged in the presence of God.

Another mark of Weems's psalms is that, both individually and collectively, they remain in a certain sense unfinished. This is no oversight or deficiency in her work; the psalms are left unfinished because the grieving is unfinished and probably will never be fully finished this side of the completion of God's promises. Even in the last psalm of the book, Weems confesses that her tears are still hot and her pain cannot be scrubbed away.

Nevertheless, there is movement in Weems's prayers. The author journeys haltingly, circuitously from pain to praise, yet without ever denying the reality of the pain of the loss she has experienced. She yearns for peace but experiences it only in fleeting moments. In the meantime, she finds that "anger and alleluias" often careen around her.[17]

Finally, the reader of these psalms recognizes that while Weems's experience is intensely personal, it is also remarkably universal. Brought to God, her experience of pain, loss, and protest somehow reverberates with the groaning of the whole creation. The intensely personal suffering takes on social and cosmic dimensions. In the preface to her book, Weems says her psalms are not for everyone; in one sense this is true, yet in another sense the prayers she writes are spoken on behalf of all who have experienced or may yet experience affliction.

For Weems the prayer of lament is no exercise in self-help and her book no how-to-do-it manual. When faced with terrible loss, we need help far beyond ourselves. "Our only hope is to march ourselves to the throne of God and in loud lament cry out the pain that lives in our souls."[18]

Prayers like Weems's are difficult for many Christians to read or hear. They certainly do not conform to the prayers with which most churchgoers are familiar. Is it really appropriate for Christians to pray in this questioning, unaccepting spirit? Would we not show stronger faith if we quietly resigned ourselves to whatever happens as the will of God? Might not prayers of protest like those of Weems be the first step in a process of losing one's faith and if included in any form in public worship result in the weakening of the faith of the church as a whole? What place does the prayer of lament have in Christian faith and worship? Should it be honored or forgotten or simply viewed with suspicion and pushed to the farthest margins of spiritual life?

THE SEARCH FOR JUSTICE AND RECONCILIATION AND THE PRAYER OF LAMENT

Prayers of lament and protest are not only voiced by bereaved parents and other wounded individuals who have experienced wrenching personal losses. They are also voiced by entire peoples who have been ravaged by war or have suffered poverty, hunger, oppression, and humiliation for long periods of time. They are the prayers of those in Nazi death camps; the victims of religious and ethnic conflicts in Kosovo, Northern Ireland, Rwanda, and other lands; the homeless; the inner-city poor. They are the prayers that arise from situations like the apartheid system in South Africa and its aftermath.

In the wake of the dismantling of the system of apartheid, South Africa now faces the enormous task of rebuilding a truly multiracial nation in which people respect and trust each other. Reconciliation of the races in South Africa will be an arduous process. One instrument intended to facilitate this process is the Truth and Reconciliation Commission appointed by the new government and led by Bishop Desmond Tutu. Its task is to give those who suffered under apartheid a chance to tell their stories and to call to confession those who perpetrated injustices.[19]

Not surprisingly, the commission has been the focus of considerable controversy. Critics want the commission to do its work as quickly as possible so that attention can be focused on the rebuilding of the nation. Survivors of abuse under apartheid, however, want the chance to tell the stories of what actually took place during the apartheid regime and how much suffering they endured. They remain deeply ambivalent about the granting of amnesty to perpetrators.[20] How do Christians pray in such a situation?

In the service of dedication and blessing of members of the Truth and Reconciliation Commission held at St. George's Cathedral in Cape Town in 1996, the litany combined several kinds of prayer.[21] It included prayers of repentance for the reign of terror during the apartheid era, involving torture, maiming, and murder of women, men, and children. It also included prayers of lament for the loss of loved ones, for opportunities of life snuffed out, and for the terrible feelings of bitterness with which so many survivors were left to struggle. Finally, the litany included prayers for healing and new life and prayers of thanksgiving to God for the promise of new beginnings.

The litany used in this service of dedication intentionally combined both penitential prayer and prayer of lament. Alongside the confession, "We repent," was the lament, "We mourn." Many in the congregation, and in the wider society, were especially in need of praying for forgiveness of wrongs done, and many others were especially in need of lamenting the abuse and losses they unjustly suffered during the apartheid regime. No doubt many were in need of praying both forms of prayer. In postapartheid South Africa, as in other situations where the church addresses victims and perpetrators with the message of judgment and hope, prayers of repentance and prayers of lament necessarily intertwine.

Despite the effort at inclusivity, the prayer used in this dedication service doubtless raised many questions in the complex context of South Africa today. Would critics of the commission be right in seeing a prayer like this as too provocative and serving only to worsen the resentments and hatreds within the society? Would victims of the apartheid system be right in seeing this prayer as timid and lacking in honest expressions of anger and outrage for all the horrors that were experienced under apartheid? In the search for justice and reconciliation in contexts of racial, ethnic, and religious strife, pastors and church leaders in South Africa, the United States, Yugoslavia, Northern Ireland, Rwanda, and other countries around the world will no doubt frequently face the practical and theological question of what place prayers of lament and the spirituality they represent have in Christian life and worship. What role does honest lament have today in the process of healing, reconciliation, and renewal in the life of a community or even of entire nations such as South Africa, Yugoslavia, or the United States?

QUIET DESPAIR AND THE PRAYER OF LAMENT

The need and appropriateness of the prayer of lament are not always readily evident. When parents experience the loss of a child as a result of disease, accident, or violence, or when an entire people experiences the terrible destruction of war and despoilation, we are not surprised to hear the voice of Rachel lamenting her loss. Yet there are also life situations in which grief, anger, and despair are veiled in secrecy. Experiences of emptiness, loss of meaning, betrayal, abandonment, and quiet despair are realities for countless people, and these experiences have the power to shake confidence in self, others, and God.

For many middle-class Americans—perhaps especially American men—work gives life much of its zest and meaning. Many men often find great joy in their work because it gives them a sense of identity, a feeling of belonging, and a sense of significant accomplishment. Not surprisingly, then, when work goes sour,[22] or when people find themselves out of work because of downsizing or economic downturn, they often face not only a financial crisis but a deep spiritual crisis as well.

One pastor describes the spiritual struggles of men in his congregation this way: "Men used to bring relational issues to me for care, especially issues around family and spouses. But over the past eight years or so the major issue has been around jobs and their various stresses—especially, loyalty, meaning, and security. As one of my parishioners said, 'Everything I used to believe is no longer true. I was taught by my father that if you worked hard and stayed loyal, you would get ahead. I now know that this is no longer true.'"[23]

The comments of this pastor are confirmed in a recent study by the sociologist Robert Wuthnow. According to Wuthnow, both the emptiness of work and the fear of unemployment are suffered quietly by many people today at all levels of society, and the church is not helping as much as it should to minister to these needs. One priest reported that he sometimes preached sermons extolling the virtues of hard work but had to admit that four men in his parish had committed suicide the previous year because they had lost their jobs.[24] Another pastor reported that a high-level executive in his parish had lost his job and was so ashamed that he was afraid to walk in his neighborhood during the day for fear that people would start talking about him. His very sense of identity was threatened, and he did not know how to ask for help.[25] Commenting on the widespread anxieties about work today, Wuthnow writes: "Picking up the pieces when people's lives have been shattered by the pressures, strains, and disappointments of the workplace is . . . one of the significant ways in which the churches can minister to the middle class."[26]

A question not raised by Wuthnow or by the pastors he interviewed is whether the unemployed or those deeply troubled by their jobs would find a safe place in their churches if they sought help there in giving expression to their disappointment and anger. Is a Bible study or a prayer group the place to ask questions like "Is it fair that I am put out of work after years of faithful service?" and "Must things be this way?" Does the church's understanding of prayer and spirituality make room for the questions and protests of those who feel defeated, abandoned, and left to quiet despair?

AMBIVALENT ATTITUDES TOWARD LAMENT IN WORSHIP AND LITURGY

These brief portraits of loss, anger, and despair suggest a crucial test for every Christian spirituality and practice of prayer in our time: Are they bold enough and strong enough to include the prayer of lament as well as prayers of thanksgiving, confession, and intercession? When we pray, do we evade the hard realities of our own painful experiences and the sufferings of others, or do we honestly name things as they really are? Do our prayers acknowledge our anger and despair over injustice and violence as well as our joy and gratitude for experiences of love and beauty?

One way of diagnosing the spiritual health of congregations is to examine their liturgies. What we are likely to discover is that the prayer of lament is noticeably absent in the worship of many congregations. In a recent article, Lester Meyer argues that the lament psalm is "underrepresented" in the church's use of the Psalter.[27] In particular, he examines the *Lutheran Book of Worship*, the Episcopalian *Book of Common Prayer*, and *Lectionary for Mass: The Roman Missal*. The Lutheran *Book of Worship* includes 122 of the 150 psalms in its Psalter. Of the 28 omitted psalms, "twenty (71%) are lament psalms while another five (18%) have lament-like qualities."[28] In the lectionary for Sundays and principal festivals, 60 of the 150 psalms are omitted, with 43 (72 percent) being laments or "lament-like."[29]

The Book of Common Prayer includes the entire Psalter, but the lectionary readings for Sundays and major festivals omit 67 psalms, of which 55 are laments and 11 are related to the laments (a total of 72 percent). The *Lectionary for Mass: The Roman Missal* omits 78 psalms from the Sunday readings, with 68 percent of the omitted psalms being lament or lament related.[30] Following up on Myers's study, we have discovered that, with one exception, the same lament psalms are omitted from the *United Methodist Hymnal* and the *Presbyterian Hymnal* as are omitted from the Lutheran *Book of Worship*. Lament psalms are also noticeably absent from many funeral liturgies. So too are prayers that acknowledge feelings of anger and confusion.

While statistics can sometimes be misleading, we think the above data suggests that the psalms of lament are poorly represented in the worship books of most mainline denominations. With notable exceptions, it would appear that prayer and worship in many Christian congregations fail to make room for the experiences of lament, protest, and remonstration with God. It is not the lament psalms but the penitential psalms and the psalms of praise that are chosen for inclusion in worship.

If we ask what has happened to the prayer of lament in the history of Christian worship, the answer is too complex to be handled satisfactorily within the scope of this study. We will have to leave to more competent historians the task of a thorough history of the prayer of lament. We can say, however, that the psalms of lament were not always absent in Christian liturgies. For example, Heinrich Schütz, who lived during the Thirty Years' War, set many of the lament psalms to the music of his time.

It is true, of course, that Christian worship and theology have had different accents in different periods. As Paul Tillich explains, this is because the meaning of salvation has been understood and experienced somewhat differently depending upon the experienced negativities from which rescue has been sought.[31] It is understandable, therefore, that in some periods of Christian worship the focus on sin and guilt has been very pronounced, and the use of the penitential psalms has supplanted all other forms of lament. Traditional eucharistic liturgies, both Roman Catholic and Protestant, have often reflected this penitential tone. The liturgical renewal movement of the 1960s, on the other hand, attempted to recover earlier forms of eucharistic celebration, with the result that an emphasis on thanksgiving, celebration, and victory over sin and death replaced the earlier severe emphasis on contrition and penitence.

We believe that the swing of the pendulum in the twentieth-century liturgical renewal from penitence to celebration in Christian worship has been a valuable and much needed corrective. Nevertheless, the new liturgies are themselves in need of reform to the extent that they omit the prayer of lament and protest.

The ambivalence and suspicion that surround the lament prayer in Christian worship and spirituality register the discomfort of the tradition with attitudes and behaviors that seem overly aggressive, insubordinate, and negative. The true believer, especially in the practice of prayer, is expected to exhibit compliance rather than resistance. As a result, instead of providing space for protest and grief, what churches often offer are worship services that are "unrelentingly positive in tone."[32] The exclusion of the lament screens out people who find the services shallow or harmful and provides no theological and liturgical way to come to terms with disturbing human experiences. A clear consequence of banishing the many moods of the psalms of lament—among them, anguish, remorse, fury, protest, even hatred—is that we lose an essential resource in confronting the very emotions that terrify us, in a context where we might receive some help in admitting them, understanding them, and coping with them. In a society and world with many volatile tensions and violent conflicts, this is a serious failure of ministry.

AMBIVALENT ATTITUDES TOWARD LAMENT IN AMERICAN SOCIETY

If Christian piety and worship are ambivalent about the acceptance and use of the prayer of lament, this no doubt reflects, at least in part, wider cultural attitudes toward negative emotions.

Attempting to portray the salient features of contemporary American culture, especially in broad brush strokes, is hazardous. Every culture is complex and contains many diverse and even conflicting characteristics. Portraits of a majority culture will not necessarily be accurate descriptions of all of its members or of all subcultures within it. Nevertheless, it seems safe to say that within American culture there are deeply conflicting attitudes toward expressions of grief, rage, and other negative emotions. On the one hand, there is the oft-noted tendency in our culture to cover up experiences of loss and failure in both personal and public life and to uphold what has been called official American optimism. On the other hand, there is a strong counterpressure in therapeutic American society, often encouraged by the mass media, to "let it all hang out," to demand that all emotions be immediately and publicly vented.   Catharsis

Our century has certainly provided ample reasons to lament. Two devastating world wars, the holocaust of six million Jews, "ethnic cleansing" in the Balkans, numerous other genocidal wars, the use of nuclear weapons and anxiety about their potential future use, the continuing reality of racism and sexism in our society and in other lands, the plight of our inner cities, the scourge of famine in Third World countries, the abuse of the environment, the worldwide spread of incurable diseases like AIDS, the millions of political refugees—these belong to any description of the terrors of this century. While a surface optimism continues to reign in North America, especially when the economy is strong, beneath the surface there is widespread fear of social disintegration. We hear of the breakdown of the family, the alarming loss of respect for government officials and agencies, the fear that environmental damage is severe and growing. Some inner-city residents describe their neighborhoods as war zones and random acts of violence erupt in supposedly safe suburban and rural areas. Terrorist acts in New York and Oklahoma City and recent armed assaults on school children by their schoolmates have exposed the precarious nature of social cohesion in America as in the rest of the world. Moreover, the gap between rich and poor continues to grow, and the possibility of serious outbreaks of ethnic, racial, and religious conflicts in the years ahead looms ominously at the start of the twenty-first century. The litany need not be extended. We have ample reasons to lament.

These facts notwithstanding, the dominant culture of North America often minimizes the place and importance of expressions of lament. We are a people reluctant to grieve our failures, especially our corporate and public failures, limitations, and losses. Cultural critics like Ernst Becker and Robert J. Lifton have analyzed the American penchant for denial of experiences of failure, negativity, guilt, powerlessness, loss, and death.[33] Theologians like Douglas John Hall, noting the difficulty many North Americans have in dealing with negative experiences, have underscored the virtual incomprehensibility of a theology of the cross within the mainline churches.[34] In face of lamentable realities—whether the bombing of Hiroshima or the continuing racism of our society—we are adept at "psychic numbing" and theological cover-up.

Countless diversions are available, of course, to hide the underside of our experience, not the least of which is round-the-clock entertainment via television, Internet, and computer games. Also, there are abundant outlets for complaint, anger, and hatred on radio and TV talk shows and in the secrecy of the Internet. We thus live in a culture of bizarre contradictions: told, on the one hand, to stop complaining and address our problems with positive thinking, American inventiveness, and faith in the future ("If we can go to the moon, we can do anything"); bombarded daily, on the other hand, with apocalyptic images of social disintegration, poverty, disease, violence, and material and sexual seduction. Side by side with the appeals of advertisers, politicians, and some popular preachers to the longstanding optimism of Americans are the many signs in our common life of an underlying sense of powerlessness to confront the intractable negativities of our personal lives and corporate history. The rage that boils within the experience of powerlessness is often exploited by the mass media and leads only to increased feelings of alienation.

We live in what many call a postmodern world in which the vision and presuppositions of the Enlightenment, such as faith in continuous progress, the rule of reason, the celebration of the independent self, and a culture of civility now seem exhausted. We seem bereft of intellectual and spiritual resources to cope creatively with the experience of loss of power and prestige or the burning resentment that persists after experiences of abuse and oppression.

When great losses are experienced and hope is eclipsed, what are the conditions of the emergence of "hope beyond hope?" Walter Brueggemann's answer to this question is on target: "Only grief permits newness."[35] Without lament, hope is stillborn. The point is not, of course, that lamenting guarantees the rebirth of hope. Only the grace of God does that. It does mean, however, that God's grace undergirds the freedom and courage not only to confess sin but also to refuse premature consolation and to persist in protesting injustice while awaiting the coming of God's justice and peace.

QUESTIONS UNDERLYING RESISTANCE TO THE LAMENT PRAYER

Suspicion about or even strong resistance to any proposal to reclaim the prayer of lament in Christian life and ministry might be prompted by a number of legitimate concerns. We do well, therefore, to identify some of these questions at the beginning of our study.

1. An obvious first question is whether use of prayers of lament would simply feed what has been called our present "culture of complaint." Do we really want to encourage childish whining and the habit of blaming others for whatever hardships and failures we experience? According to some critics of North American life, we have become a culture in which everyone desires victim status and few are willing to assume personal responsibility for their situation. Today, the criticism goes, victims are invented with the same passion that some past cultures have cultivated and celebrated their heroes.

In *The Culture of Complaint: The Fraying of America*, Robert Hughes contends that debates about subjects like multiculturalism, Afrocentrism, radical feminism, and affirmative action are saturated with the spirit of chronic complaint.[36] The spirit of complaint suggests we are all victims of our parents or other authority figures; we all come from dysfunctional families, and our schools, our churches, our political institutions have betrayed us. The litany of complaint is endless. Even the white American male, says Hughes, now demands victim status. All of this complaining generates an unhealthy "us" versus "them" mentality and passes all responsibility to others. A culture of complaint undermines accountability and shatters all connections beyond the circle of one's fellow victims. Equally disturbing, complaint is a calculated game of power. "Complaint gives you power—even when it's only the power of emotional bribery, of creating previously unnoticed levels of emotional guilt."[37]

Let it be clear from the outset that our interest in the retrieval of the prayer of lament has nothing in common either with the "culture of complaint" or with the ideological critique of complaint. On the contrary, as we shall argue, the prayer of lament, properly understood, does not undermine but strengthens the sense of personal responsibility, and it supports rather than attacks the sense of solidarity with others.

2. A second question is closely related to the first, only now posed not from the standpoint of the dominant class but from the viewpoint of the marginalized: Would not the prayer of lament simply foster a victimization consciousness and thus drive people further into the depths of powerlessness and helplessness? This is an important question. Those who have experienced marginalization or abuse, or who have counseled and worked with the abused, know how difficult it is to break free of victim consciousness. One of the terrible wounds that is created by oppression and abuse is that persons begin to think of themselves in a way that mirrors the treatment they have received. They have been treated as mere passive objects, and after a period of time they begin to see themselves in that way. A simplistic classification of people as victims can have the unintended effect of further robbing them of their capacity as agents and their resources for responding to their condition.

As we hope to make clear, we understand the prayer of lament as giving voice to something very different from mere victim's consciousness. In our judgment, the lament prayer does not wallow in the experience of powerlessness but is already the beginning of renewed agency and the affirmation of self-worth in the presence of God.

3. Still another question is whether lament prayer is likely to give support to the cult of individualism and subjectivity which is rampant in modern culture. According to Hughes, one of the characteristics of the culture of lament is its subjectivism, its fixation on my feelings and my story. The cul-

ture of complaint turns inward and is no longer able to see objective reality outside the self. Hughes quotes Goethe: "Epochs which are regressive, and in the process of dissolution, are always subjective, whereas the trend in all progressive epochs is objective."[38]

In the course of our study we will show that there is a "subjective" dimension to the lament prayer, but this by no means disqualifies it as authentic prayer. We insist that the experience of affliction cannot be viewed by the subject in an attitude of pure objectivity. This is not to say, however, that the one who laments is necessarily caught in a prison of subjectivity. Attention to the subjective dimension of life and experience is not identical with subjectivism.

4. A fourth question prompted by any reclaiming of the prayer of lament is whether it might pose a serious hazard for those who do not have the resources to name and deal with their pain. The afflicted may fear that if they begin to lament and weep for their wounds and losses, they will never be able to stop. Isn't denial safer than utter despair? The pastor often faces the question of the value of denial in some circumstances. Refusal to lament may be a necessary temporary defense against total collapse in face of overwhelming loss. The value of such resistance as a coping mechanism must be acknowledged. But as we shall argue, it is the wisdom both of the biblical witness and the modern helping sciences that there can be no lasting recovery from serious trauma unless the pain is named and lived through.

5. Moving to more explicitly theological issues, it might be asked whether lament manifests a lack of strong faith and trust in God's goodness and wisdom. If God knows best, is not our task to submit without protest to the divine will? This is perhaps the most frequently encountered theological ground of resistance to including prayers of lament in Christian life and worship. We contend that this argument is based on certain assumptions about God and humanity that are deeply problematic both from the standpoint of the biblical witness and the testimony of human experience. Faith and lament are not antithetical. In circumstances of distress, lament may well be the only possible form of faithfulness to God.

6. Another possible theological objection is whether lament prayer presupposes an attitude of self-righteousness and thus undermines the importance of the confession of sin and the prayer for forgiveness. Does the lament prayer foster resentment, anger, and hatred, and even raise these to a new and dangerous level of intensity by including these feelings in the very act of prayer? As already stated, we fully affirm the importance of recognizing and confessing sin and praying for God's forgiveness. But in calling for the freedom to bring anger and bitterness to God, it by no means follows that attitudes of hatred and acts of violence are sanctioned.

7. A final question is whether the prayer of lament contradicts Christian belief in the resurrection of Jesus Christ and necessarily erodes Christian joy,

hope, and praise. This question seems to assume that the resurrection of the crucified Jesus has removed all suffering and affliction from the world. Such an assumption clearly contravenes the witness of the New Testament that the Christian community, together with the whole creation, lives between the time of the resurrection of Christ and the coming consummation of all of God's purposes for humankind and the created cosmos. This in-between time is a time of mission and service, a time of hope and groaning for the redemption of all things. In this in-between time there is sorrow as well as joy, lament as well as praise. Within Christian prayer, there is not only an Easter voice but also a Good Friday voice.[39]

AIMS OF A RECOVERY OF THE PRAYER OF LAMENT

Having reviewed in this chapter the suspicion of lament in contemporary society and its eclipse and possible recovery in the prayer and worship of the church, we conclude with three summary theses to help clarify the aims of our work and avert possible misunderstandings.

First, reclaiming the prayer of lament is aimed at the recovery of the wholeness of Christian life and the wholeness of Christian prayer. We do not seek to focus on the lament prayer because we are gloomy or pessimistic persons, or because we seek to reduce Christian life to tears and groans. Nor do we seek to exaggerate the importance of lament at the expense of other forms of Christian prayer. Our contention is that there is prayer of surrender and prayer of resistance; prayer of praise and prayer of lament; prayer of joy and prayer of sorrow. We do not speak of the prayer of sorrow, complaint, and resistance in order to displace or weaken the prayer of surrender, praise, and joy. On the contrary, we seek not less but deeper joy in Christian life and worship; not a reduction but a strengthening of doxology. We do not wish to narrow or fracture Christian prayer but to reaffirm its breadth and wholeness. We believe this wholeness is yearned for and needed by all people of faith, whether they be in the academy or the congregation, the sanctuary or the street corner.

Exiled from much Christian piety and worship yet audible in many places of suffering both inside and outside the church, the prayer of lament and protest must find its place in Christian prayer if it is to be honest and robust. That is our thesis. Without the prayer of lament the other important elements of prayer—praise, thanksgiving, confession, intercession—atrophy and ring hollow. How can praise be free and joyful if the realities of broken human life are not named and lamented? How can heartfelt thanks be given for healing if the wounds are denied? How can confession of sin be sincere if we turn all sorrow into guilt? How can intercession be strong if our language does not reflect knowledge of the real sufferings of those for whom we pray?

Second, recovery of the prayer of lament aims to be responsive to the realities of human experience and the struggles of Christian life and thereby to enrich the practice of pastoral care. It is neither good theology nor good pastoral ministry to ignore the realities of experience or to impose certain doctrinal interpretations on experience that obscure what is actually happening. Our argument is that good theology and good pastoral practice mandate that we remain open to and learn from the prayer of lament. In particular, we think it is essential to avoid the tendency in the Christian tradition of prayer and worship to collapse the lament prayer into penitential laments. As previously stated, we believe that confession of sin is a vital part of Christian life and worship, and we have no desire to minimize or overlook its importance. Yet we believe there is suffering and pain that cannot be dealt with if lament is associated primarily with repentance for sin. We believe that pastoral wisdom includes recognition of the need both for confession of sins and for lament and protest against injustice, abuse, and devastating loss. Among the necessary skills of pastoral ministry is the ability to discern when and how these two forms of lament are to be given voice.

Third, recovery of the prayer of lament is not only true to human experience and required by pastoral care but also faithful to the biblical witness and consistent with the basic pattern of classical Christian doctrine. The core doctrines of Christian faith are hospitable to the prayer of lament.

Christians believe in the goodness and justice of God who wills life rather than death for creation. When life in relationship is damaged or lost, there is cause for lament.

Christians further believe that human beings are created in the image of God and are embodied beings. While a dualistic philosophy that is disdainful of the body might discredit lament for bodily harm and loss, Christian faith refuses to do this because of its affirmation of the integrity of the person as created by God and its hope in the renewal and fulfillment of embodied life.

Most decisively, Christians believe that the incarnation, death, and resurrection of Jesus Christ constitutes God's unequivocal Yes to humanity. The gospel proclaims that God does not remain aloof from humanity's brokenness and pain, that no human experience is strange to the life of the creator and redeemer, that God enters into utmost solidarity with humanity, even into the terrible experience of godforsakenness.

Furthermore, Christians affirm the doctrine of justification by grace through faith. We do not become acceptable to God by good works or noble piety. We are not justified by the beauty or correctness of our prayers or by our success in suppressing our anger and grief when we confront the persistence of evil in the world and in our own lives. The freedom to lament is consistent with the confession of justification by grace through faith.

Finally, Christians confess belief in the church as the people of God and the body of Christ. We do not believe that Christians are religious virtuosos who should be able to overcome suffering and loss by themselves. The freedom to lament is an opportunity to acknowledge our dependence on God and others and to open ourselves to unexpected help from beyond ourselves.

Our aim in writing this book is to be helpful to all our readers and especially to pastors and the congregations they serve. We have no interest in scoring debating points. We contend that the prayer of lament is experientially, pastorally, and theologically important. It is consistent with a theology of the incarnation and a theology of the cross; it is prayer bold enough to name the events and powers that threaten the goodness of the creation and the promises of the gospel. It is no modern invention, no easy accommodation of theology and church life to the whims of contemporary culture. On the contrary, it is deeply embedded in the biblical tradition of prayer. Exploring that tradition is the task to which we now turn.

Prayer of lament · bringing anger, grief, despair, protest to God!
    Ex: appropriate in loss, anger, despair.
But seems to have lost its place in most mainline
    Christian churches. Reflects cultural trends.
Some of the resistance to lament comes from a s q
        complaint vs responsibility
        victimization vs power
        subjectivity
        despair - not able to control it
        faithfulness
        self righteousness
        eroding joy
But answers to each!
Main points in recovering prayer of lament -
        wholeness?
        Enriches pastoral care
        True to bible, Christian doctrine

See pgs 12, 16

CHAPTER TWO

THE PRAYER OF LAMENT
IN THE BIBLE

How long, O God? Will you forget me forever? How long
will you hide your face from me?
—*Psalm 13:1*

T here is always an underground Bible awaiting discovery. Indeed,
the history of the church is replete both with new interpretations
of biblical texts and with rediscoveries of the central message of
the Bible in new contexts. Unexpectedly, dimensions of the biblical witness obscured or even entirely hidden by all too familiar ways of
reading and hearing its message have come to light.

Over the past several decades, Christians in many poor countries of Latin
America, Africa, and Asia have read the Bible through the lens of their own
experience. They have found in it a story of God's "preferential option for
the poor" that is disturbing to many Christians in North America and
Europe. The theme of God's solidarity with the weak and the abused has
been present in the Bible all along, but for many Christians in relatively
affluent societies this aspect of the biblical witness has remained underground and out of sight.

Similarly, in recent years Christian women around the world have also
been discovering an underground Bible. They too have been reading the
Bible through different eyes and have been finding unexplored dimensions
of its message. Many of these women approach the Bible with suspicion of
its largely patriarchal framework and the male-dominated traditions of biblical interpretation. At the same time, the suspicion of women readers of the
Bible is often coupled with a robust confidence in the Bible as a powerful
source of new life and liberating hope for women and men alike.

We contend that the Bible remains an underground book for many
Christians today in still another respect: its depiction of the boldness and
honesty of prayer. This strand of the biblical witness is often absent in the
teaching and practice of many Christian churches. Every pastor could tell
stories of members of congregations who felt obligated to be submissive and

resigned in the wake of tragedy. While readily using the Bible for comfort, instruction, and praise, Christians may seldom if ever look to it as a resource to voice their pain, grief, and anger. This suggests an attitude toward prayer and piety that seriously underestimates the role of lament and protest in biblical faith, that no longer hears the voice of Rachel in both Old and New Testaments, and that diminishes Christian life and ministry by silencing honest lament.

In this chapter we offer a brief outline of the meaning and history of the prayer of lament in the biblical witness. Our sketch is dependent on the work of biblical scholars and makes no claim to completeness. Nevertheless, by our venture into the large and rapidly growing scholarly literature on the prayer of lament in the Bible, we hope to establish an essential point of reference for our subsequent chapters and for the overall argument of our book.

THE MANY VOICES OF THE BIBLE

The Bible contains many different voices. Walter Brueggemann proposes the courtroom as the most apt image for understanding the interplay of the different voices of the Old Testament. There are voices that constitute Israel's core testimony to the character and purposes of Yahweh; there are also voices of countertestimony that dispute the accuracy of the core witnesses; and there are the unsolicited voices of Israel's neighbors. When we read the Bible, we must attend to the diversity and even clash of voices within it rather than forcing its many voices into a single monotone.[1]

Paul Ricoeur makes a similar point in his analysis of the wide variety of literary forms in the Bible. Ricoeur argues that a hermeneutics of revelation must consider carefully "the variety of discourses within which the faith of Israel and then of the early church is inscribed."[2] Among the literary forms of the Bible that Ricoeur identifies are prophetic discourse, narrative, moral commands and exhortations, wisdom literature, and hymnic discourse used in prayer and worship. Each form has a distinctive function in conveying some aspect of the revelation to which the Bible bears witness. The central point of Ricoeur's analysis is that "the literary genres of the Bible do not constitute a rhetorical facade which it would be possible to pull down in order to reveal some thought content that is indifferent to its literary vehicle."[3] On the contrary, modulated by the diverse literary forms in which it is expressed, biblical revelation is "polyphonic" and rich in meaning.[4] By offering a multiplicity of discourses that serve different purposes, scripture enables us to participate in the many aspects of covenantal life with God.

In recent decades, biblical studies and theology have devoted considerable attention to the narrative genre of scripture. One important function of narrative for a community of faith is that it offers a comprehensive framework within which the entire range of experience, including times of terror and

chaos, can be contained. Although Ricoeur has been one of the major con-
tributors to a deeper understanding of the importance and function of biblical narrative in witnessing to revelation, he emphasizes that other literary
genres of scripture are equally indispensable. In particular, he contends that
wisdom literature, including the book of Job with its bountiful laments, is
of great importance in sustaining the life of faith. According to Ricoeur, the
wisdom tradition serves to challenge the totalistic tendencies of narrative
theologies in face of experiences of tragedy, radical evil, and the suffering of
the innocent. For the wisdom theologians, the ambiguity, brokenness, and
pain of life are too great to be resolved within some overarching narrative
framework. In other words, the wisdom tradition knows that lived experience is sometimes like a broken vase whose shards cannot be easily reunited
rather than like a puzzle whose pieces can be neatly fit into a unified design.

Ricoeur includes the prayer of lament in his catalog of literary forms of
the Bible. We agree with his judgment that this form of prayer, however "dis-
quieting, paradoxical, and almost scandalous," is an irreplaceable expression
of biblical faith, no less than narrative, moral imperative, or other literary
forms of the Bible.[5]

If attention to the diversity of voices and literary forms is one of the essen-
tials of responsible biblical interpretation, of equal importance for the recovery of the prayer of lament in theology and pastoral ministry today is the
awareness of the hermeneutical significance of the social location of both
text and interpreter. Modern biblical study has long taken for granted that
the biblical texts must be understood in their own historical contexts.
Increasingly, interpreters of the Bible also recognize that every reading of
these texts takes place in a particular context and is shaped by the experiences
and understandings that the interpreter brings to the text. The interpreter is
not a tabula rasa on which the Bible imprints its message. As Hans-Georg
Gadamer argues, "prejudices," or preunderstandings, are not only
inescapable, they are productive in the process of understanding.[6] The particular experiences and questions we bring to the interpretative task, while
always in need of correction and reformulation, open dimensions of the text
that might otherwise be overlooked or undervalued.

Attention to the context of the interpreter need not lead to relativism in
interpretation, as some fear. It does, however, underscore how important it
is for the church to be open to unfamiliar readings of familiar texts. On
numerous occasions the church has discovered that those who read the Bible
from the context of suffering, or from the location that Dietrich Bonhoeffer
called the underside of history, may see and be moved by things that others
who do not share that context may miss. More specifically, the voices of
lament present in scripture have been more noticeable and of greater importance to some readers than to others.

An example of the difference context makes in the reading of the Bible is given by Emil Fackenheim in his comparison of the differences between Christian and Jewish readings of Jeremiah 31. Fackenheim points out that whereas Christians assign primary significance to the promise of the new covenant (31–34), Jews are drawn to the verse earlier in the chapter that recounts the lament of Rachel who refuses to be comforted because her children are no more (15). Fackenheim writes: "Just this [passage] is most moving for Jews, or for all who ever mourned, or thought of mourning, at the wall in Jerusalem, weeping with Rachel for children, exiled still."[7] Speaking out of the history of Jewish suffering, Fackenheim insists that the Bible must not be read solely as a book of promise and comfort; the divine promise in the biblical witness must not be separated from the voices of lament, like Rachel's, that resist all easy consolation.

There are many voices in the Bible: voices of joy and voices of anguish; voices defending God and voices questioning God; the Magnificat of Mary and the cry of Rachel; the graceful Gospel of Luke and the disturbing Gospel of Mark; psalms of praise and psalms of lament. The temptation to hear the joyful voices and dismiss the anguished voices among the biblical witnesses tempts us again and again. When the church succumbs to this temptation, the result is always the impoverishment of Christian life and ministry. We grow in our reading of the Bible as we allow its diverse emphases and perspectives—reflected in the sometimes disturbing interpretations of biblical texts that arise out of contexts quite different from our own—to challenge, enrich, and correct our familiar readings.[8]

LAMENT IN THE OLD TESTAMENT

Prayer is a basic element of Israel's religious life. The God of Israel is a personal God who has chosen a particular people for a special mission in the world and has summoned them to worship and obey God alone. As the living, covenanting God, Yahweh addresses Israel in both mercy and judgment: "I will walk among you and will be your God, and you shall be my people" (Lev. 26:12). Because Israel has been elected to covenantal relationship with God, prayer is a natural expression of Israel's freedom and responsibility within the covenant. The relationship between God and Israel is dialogical. It is like an ongoing conversation: God speaks and Israel responds; Israel speaks and God responds.

The richness of Israel's prayer includes expressions of radical dependence, basic trust, remorse for transgression of divine law, and thanksgiving for the undeserved and unfathomable goodness of God. Yet among the most distinctive marks of the prayer of Israel is the bold inclusion of prayers of lament, protest, and argumentation with God. Indeed, according to the Old Testament scholar, Claus Westermann, Jewish spirituality, with its vigorous prayers of protest, differs sharply from much Christian spirituality that often extols the virtues of submissiveness and passive acceptance of suffering.[9] In prayer, Israel is completely, even stunningly, honest with God. "No holds are barred, no questions or feelings taboo."[10]

Consider a few examples. Devastated because "God had closed her womb," Hannah weeps bitterly as she prays to have a child (1 Sam. 1:1–20). Driven from home, alone in the wilderness with her child, and out of water, Hagar— Abraham's "slave woman"— hides the boy under a bush and desperately prays she may at least be spared having to witness his death (Gen. 21:8–21).

The prophet Jeremiah complains to God: "You will be in the right, O God, when I lay charges against you; but let me put my case to you" (Jer. 12:1). Job, having lost children, health, reputation, and possessions, cries to God:

I will give free utterance to my complaint;
I will speak in the bitterness of my soul.
I will say to God, Do not condemn me;
let me know why you contend against me. (Job 10:1–2)

Prayer in the Hebrew Scriptures freely expresses feelings of distress, anger, and abandonment. Israel cries to God, boldly questions God, complains that God is far off, argues with God in prayer.

The most familiar of Israel's prayers are, of course, the psalms. In these texts we hear the many voices of Israel's rich life of prayer: the prayers of individuals and of the entire community; prayers of confidence and fear; prayers of hope and despair; prayers of praise and lament.

Brueggemann divides the psalms into three groups according to how they may have functioned in the piety and liturgy of ancient Israel. He names these groups respectively psalms of orientation, disorientation, and reorientation. In psalms of the first group (of which Psalms 1, 8, and 119 are well-known examples), life is experienced as basically stable and well ordered; the ways of God in the world are praised as coherent and reliable. In psalms of the second group—the lament psalms (Psalms 13, 22, 88, 137 are good examples)—life is experienced as being in disarray. What is prominent is not the order of life but its disorder; not well-being and prosperity in life, but pain, alienation, injustice, humiliation, and death. In the third group (Psalms 30 and 138 are representative), life is experienced as open to surprise and unexpected grace. Such psalms bespeak a sense of God's new presence and activity that brings joy where before there was only despair.[11]

It is in the psalms of lament that we find the most remarkable expressions of Israel's audacity in both personal and corporate prayer.

How long, O God? Will you forget me forever?
How long will you hide your face from me? (Ps. 13:1)

My God, my God, why have you forsaken me?
Why are you so far from helping me, from the words of my
groaning? (Ps. 22:1)
Rouse yourself! Why do you sleep, O God? Awake, do not cast us off
forever! (Ps. 44:23)

According to biblical scholars, the psalm of lament has a definite structure with several elements: the opening address, the complaint, the confession of trust, the petition for help, and the vow of praise. While not all of
these elements are found in every lament psalm, they are all present in Psalm
22, which has been aptly described as the lament psalm par excellence.[12]

Address: "My God, my God . . . (22:1a)
Complaint: "Why have you forsaken me? Why are you so far from
helping me, from the words of my groaning?" (22:1b)
Confession of trust: "Yet you are holy, enthroned on the praises of
Israel. In you our ancestors trusted; they trusted, and you delivered
them." (22:3–4)
Petition: "Do not be far from me, for trouble is near and there is no
one to help." (22:11)
Vow of Praise: "From the horns of the wild oxen you have rescued
me. I will tell of your name to my brothers and sisters; in the midst
of the congregation I will praise you." (22:21a–22)

While analysis of its structure is illuminating, even more important is the
question of what is going on theologically and spiritually in the lament
prayer. Brueggemann finds three salient elements in these prayers: (1) Israel
complains of the incongruity between the promises of Yahweh and lived
experience; (2) In voicing its complaint and calling on Yahweh to respond,
Israel takes the initiative in the covenantal relationship; and (3) Israel's complaints often, though not always, move Yahweh to answer and save.[13]

Our purpose in this chapter is to identify those characteristics of the
lament prayer in the Old and New Testaments that have important implications for theology, spirituality, and pastoral care. Since we are not biblical
specialists, we refer interested readers to the excellent works of Walter
Brueggemann, Claus Westermann, Patrick Miller, and Erhard Gerstenberger
on biblical prayer.[14] We begin with the Old Testament.

1. *The Old Testament prayer of lament is a bold and disturbing form of prayer.*
So intense and passionate is the lament prayer and so extraordinary the freedom that it displays in relation to God that it may strike many Christians as
excessive and even breathtaking. "How long, O God, will you look on? . . .
Wake up! . . . Bestir yourself" (Ps. 35:17, 23). Yet, as Westermann notes, "In

the Old Testament there is not a single line which would forbid lamentation or which would express the idea that lamentation had no place in a healthy and good relationship with God."[15]

Biblical scholars debate whether the laments should be viewed primarily as supplications or as complaints. The distinction is not always easy to make, but it is important. Viewing lament as essentially supplication would mean that in lament the one who prays urges God into activity to bring about change, while viewing lament as complaint would mean that the one who prays takes issue with God because of God's apparent inactivity. We agree with Miller that "both dimensions are present in the lament psalms."[16] By contrast, much of the theological tradition of the church has tried to soften or ignore the complaint dimension of these prayers because it has been thought to violate an assumed prayer etiquette.

2. *The biblical prayers of lament have particular life contexts.* One of the goals of scholarly research on the lament prayers of the Bible is to establish, as far as possible, their *sitz-im-leben,* their life context and their particular uses in ancient Israelite religious practice. The psalms clearly contain both laments of individuals and communal laments, and each form grows out of particular fears and dangers. Individuals may complain of severe illness, old age, misfortune, false accusation, or abuse by a neighbor, friend, or even family member. The entire community may lament corporate disasters like drought, disease, or threat of military defeat. Some of these prayers were no doubt part of corporate worship; others may have been used in more intimate worship contexts.

Two points regarding the life contexts of the biblical prayer of lament are worth underscoring. First, while the prayers of lament arise out of very different dangers and disasters, common to them all is the perceived dissonance or "incongruity" between the promises of God and experienced reality.[17] In these prayers Israel is honest with God and with itself.

Second, these prayers are quite different from an attitude of resignation or submission to given social circumstances or dominant social forces. They represent a voice of opposition to the given social reality. They are a factor for change in their context and not merely a reflection of it.

Brueggemann argues, for example, that Psalms 9–10 cannot be understood apart from the background of oppressive social relations in which the "poor" and the "helpless" are exploited and murdered by the "wicked" and the "greedy." At the same time, Brueggemann contends that Psalms 9–10 represent a prayerful "practice of alternative politics," "an act of political imagination," in which the voice of the poor, the needy, and the afflicted counters the ideology of the rich and the powerful by insisting that the power of Yahweh redefines and changes social realities. Brueggemann's point, of course, is not that the prayer of lament is simply a disguised form

of political rhetoric. The point is that genuine prayer is also an act of political imagination. "The God-question is situated exactly in a social dispute
between the wicked who say 'There is no God' and the poor who say 'God
has forgotten,' and yet who voice an urgent imperative to that same God
who has forgotten. The dispute about God is clearly not an innocuous religious question, but a life-and-death dispute about the nature of social reality,
social power, and social possibility."[18]

3. *Many of the lament psalms implicitly or explicitly reject the idea that all
suffering is caused by sin.* "Hear a just cause, O God; attend to my cry; give
ear to my prayer from lips free of deceit" (Ps. 17:1). There are, of course,
well-known psalms of lament for personal or corporate sins that are familiar
to most Christians. These so-called penitential psalms (6, 32, 38, 51, 102,
130, and 143) are regularly used in Christian liturgy. Penitential psalms,
however, represent a distinct minority of the lament prayers in the Psalter.
Far more frequent than penitential psalms are laments to God motivated by
such experiences as sickness, misfortune, unjust treatment by others, and
personal or communal distress. In such cases the believer may wonder
whether God is indifferent or even unjust.

In defending their innocence the psalmists are not claiming to be free
from all sin. Rather, they are pleading innocence of some specific wrong
with which they have been charged or complain of the disproportionate
severity of their suffering. Miller states clearly the theological issue that this
aspect of the lament psalms raises. "Traditionally [these psalms] have been
seen as reflecting the human condition of sinfulness before God, a condition
that is directly attested in the so-called penitential psalms . . . and inferred
from the association between sickness and judgment that may be discerned
in various Old Testament contexts. In contemporary interpretation of the
psalms, that view is being recognized as much too simple, if not misleading.
Most of the psalms either do not identify the plight of the lamenter with sin
or at least are ambiguous on that score."[19] In registering the complaints of
those who uphold their innocence and cry out for salvation from their distress, the lament psalms point to the need of expanding the meaning of salvation to include deliverance from suffering as well as forgiveness of sin.

4. *Old Testament prayers of lament often include expressions of raw anger and
cries for vengeance against enemies.* Some of the thoughts and imagery contained
in the prayers of lament are harsh and even violent. The psalmist curses his
enemy: "May his children wander about and beg; may they be driven out of
the ruins they inhabit" (Ps. 109:10). Burning for revenge, the psalmist cries,
"O daughter Babylon, you devastator! Happy shall they be who pay you back
what you have done to us! Happy shall they be who take your little ones and
dash them against the rock!" (Ps. 137:8–9). Such prayers are ferocious; their
blisteringly hot anger and deep hatred are completely undisguised.

While it is common practice simply to remove such outbursts of rage from prayer books and liturgies, we will argue later that such a strategy is evasive. We agree with Bonhoeffer that for Christians "the crucified Jesus teaches us how to pray the imprecatory psalms."[20] At the same time, we contend, also with Bonhoeffer, that prayer that is zealous for the reign of God may understandably explode in outrage against such evils as genocidal wars, the abuse of children, or willful disdain for the poor.

5. *The tradition of biblical lament juxtaposes trust and doubt, lament and praise in sometimes extreme tension.* One side of the dialectic of lament and praise is that God is assumed to have the power to save the person or community experiencing distress; the other side is that the one who prays boldly complains that God has withheld this saving power or is even the cause of the suffering being experienced. Thus the lamenter complains passionately, "Why have you forsaken me?" but directs this complaint to none other than "My God."

In the Bible, lamenting before God and trusting in God presuppose each other. Old Testament lament does not exist in a vacuum; it is always part of a history of relationship with the God of the covenant whom Israel praises. Westermann is emphatic: "There is not a single Psalm of lament that stops with lamentation. Lamentation has no meaning in and of itself."[21] Even if Westermann's remark must be judged an overstatement, since at least Psalm 88 does indeed "stop with lamentation," his basic point is valid. Because of its covenantal context, Israel's lament is never simply an emotional outburst or an exercise in self-pity. It is a cry for relief from suffering so that God may once again be praised.

If it is true that for Israel there is no lament without praise, it is equally true that for Israel there is no true praise divorced from lament. The praise of Israel is rightly understood only in its close relationship with experienced pain. "Praise," Westermann states, "can retain its authenticity and naturalness only in polarity with lamentation."[22]

Samuel Balentine elaborates on this inseparable relation of lament and praise for the Old Testament believer: "For doxology to be authentic it must be sung 'back down to pain, where hope lives; to hurt, where newness surfaces; to death, where life is strangely given.' When this movement back down to lament does not occur, when the reason for praise is sacrificed, muted, or abstracted, when to the summons, 'Praise the Lord' one cannot give an answer to the question 'Why?' then praise is on the way to being co-opted by self-interested officiants for ideological, and ultimately idolatrous, purposes."[23] In Israel's prayer there is no lament that does not anticipate renewed praise; no praise that does not presuppose that lament is an appropriate response to the radical evil that threatens God's purposes for human life and the whole creation and that only God is capable of overcoming.

6. *The prayer of lament sometimes includes the element of protest in which the one who prays enters into intense, even angry, argument with God.* While there are examples of the protest prayer in the narrative and prophetic literature of the Old Testament, it is in the psalms of lament and, above all, in the book of Job that we meet the most uncompromising piety of protest.

In some of the psalms we find not only expressions of anger, despair, and hate but also arguments why God should act on behalf of the sufferer. The one who prays gives reasons why the given situation is intolerable and why God should act to rectify it. As Miller observes, such argumentative prayers are a kind of counterpoint to the arguments God gives in support of obeying the law. The one who prays "can urge reasons upon God for acting in behalf of the one in need, just as God, in giving the law, urges reasons upon the people for responding and obeying."[24] No more impressive evidence could be given of the genuinely dialogical character of biblical prayer.

The freedom to argue with God comes to fullest expression in the book of Job. This book is among the most remarkable expressions of faith in all religious literature. In the poetic sections of the book, lament takes the form of fierce argumentation with God. Not only does Job lament his terrible physical, familial, and financial losses; not only does he curse the day on which he was born; Job accuses Yahweh alternately of indifference, hostility, and faithlessness. Job dares to put God on trial. As we shall note later, this tradition of arguing with God has a long and eloquent history in Judaism, even if its boldness has always made the defenders of orthodoxy shudder.

7. *The prayer of lament presupposes an awareness of the freedom and hiddenness of God.* The ways of God are mysterious and unfathomable. Although Yahweh has entered into covenant with Israel and has promised to be faithful to the covenant, the hard facts of experience do not always confirm these promises. Israel's acknowledgment of the mystery and hiddenness of the God who is revealed in the covenant with Israel is vividly described in the story of Moses' request to see God only to be told that only God's backside may be seen: "You shall see my back, but my face you shall not see" (Exod. 33:23). Israel holds to the faithfulness of God in the wilderness and unpredictability of lived experience. Yahweh is just and faithful, steadfast in love and never capricious. At the same time, Israel does not pretend to greater knowledge than it has. It can only cry that there are times when it experiences not God's justice but injustice and undeserved suffering and thus the hiddenness of Yahweh's face. In such times there is a faith-threatening discrepancy between the promises of God and the lived experience of Israel. In this terrible hiddenness of God, Israel cries out, "How long, O God?" (Ps. 13:1) "My God, my God, why have you forsaken me?" (Ps. 22:1).

8. *In the same biblical tradition that contains prayers of lament there is testimony that God also laments, that God mourns along with the people of Israel*

because of their sin and suffering. God not only tolerates the prayer of lament but also instructs the people to lament that they may be healed: "Hear, O women, the word of God, and let your ears receive the word of God's mouth; teach to your daughters a dirge, and each to her neighbor a lament" (Jer. 9:20).

In some of the most moving passages of the prophets, God goes beyond instructing Israel to lament. The God who calls the people to lament participates in their lamentation.

> How can I give you up, Ephraim? How can I hand you over, O
> Israel? . . . My heart recoils within me; my compassion grows warm
> and tender. I will not execute my fierce anger; I will not again
> destroy Ephraim; for I am God and no mortal, the Holy One in your
> midst, and I will not come in wrath. (Hos. 11:8–9)

Talk of the suffering and lamentation of God may offend certain orthodox conceptions of the divine nature. But for Israel this way of speaking of God is unavoidable. Related to Israel in covenantal faithfulness, Yahweh "is directly affected by the misfortune and failure of this people."[25]

9. *In the prayer of lament, Israel remembers in order to hope.* Remembering in order to hope takes at least two different forms in Old Testament prayer. Most prominent, of course, is remembering the mighty deeds of God. The canonical Psalter includes prayers rehearsing God's mighty deeds of the past as well as prayers of hope for the coming of God's redemption. Memory and hope are intertwined in the prayer and worship of Israel. Even within the same psalm, memory and hope are often tightly bound together. Psalm 22 is again the classic example. Crying out of the depths of loneliness and abandonment, the psalmist recalls the time when Yahweh was close by and offered protection. The hope-inspiring memory of the psalmist is both communal and personal.

> In you our ancestors trusted;
> they trusted, and you delivered them. . . .
> it was you who took me from the womb;
> you kept me safe on my mother's breast. (Ps. 22:4, 9)

Drawing upon both personal and corporate memory of God's covenantal faithfulness and love enables Israel to hope that the presence and help of God will become manifest again.

> If my father and mother forsake me,
> God will take me up. . . .

I believe that I shall see the goodness of God
in the land of the living. (Ps. 27:10, 13)

But in addition to the memory of God's mighty deeds, there is another
form of memory to which Israel holds in order to hope. It is paradoxically
the memory of unredeemed suffering. There is a poignant instance of this in
the story of Jephthah's daughter (Judg. 11:30 ff.). This is not only the story
of a foolish vow and a tragic surrender; it is also the story of the faithfulness
of the women of Israel in remembering and mourning the lost life of a child.
Like Rachel, the women who befriended the daughter of Jephthah refused
to be comforted. "So there arose an Israelite custom that for four days every
year the daughters of Israel would go out to lament the daughter of Jephthah
the Gileadite" (Judg. 11:39–40). In this strange form, too, Israel remembers
in order to hope.

To summarize: There is a "voice of pain" (Brueggemann) that is heard in
Israel's prayer. To separate the songs of praise from this voice is to distort the
bold piety of the Old Testament. The voice of pain keeps prayer anchored in
real life experience and prevents it from drifting off into make-believe and
empty phrases. Israel's faith and hope are all the more remarkable for refusing to stifle the voice of anger, pain, and despair. While the lament tradition
of Israel cannot be described as the central or core tradition of Israel's prayer
life, it is nevertheless an enormously important "countertradition."[26] Without
attention to this countertradition, repetition of the mainstream tradition
becomes fraudulent and incredible.

LAMENT IN THE NEW TESTAMENT

When we turn to the New Testament practice of prayer, we find remarkable
continuity with the prayer of the people of Israel but also distinctive elements.[27] As heirs of the Old Testament tradition of faith, Jesus and his fol-
lowers considered prayer an indispensable part of life in the service of the living God and in expectation of God's coming reign. As in ancient Israel, so
in the New Testament community, prayer was experienced as communion
with a personal God, a God who is not an It but a Thou. While the New
Testament community is often described as gathering for prayer, and while
the New Testament writers urge constancy in prayer, they do not provide us
with nearly as many actual prayers as are found in the Old Testament. It is
important to remember, however, that the Hebrew Scriptures continued to
be the holy book for the early Christian community.

The central question for our purposes is: What happens to the prayer of
lament and protest in the New Testament? Westermann puts the question
sharply: Does the loss of lament in the prayer and worship of the Christian
church have its basis in the New Testament itself?[28] While we cannot provide

a comprehensive answer to Westermann's question within the scope of our study, we can point to some passages that counter the idea that the New Testament is inhospitable to the prayer of lament and protest. Our thesis is that while not as prominent as in the Old Testament, strands of the prayer of lament and protest are not only present in the New Testament but are found at decisive points in the story that it tells. In our discussion we will follow the same outline as in the previous section on lament in the Old Testament.

1. *New Testament prayers, including the Lord's Prayer, are full of passion and a sense of urgency.* Some might argue that the prayer Jesus taught his disciples fuels the suspicion that the prayer of lament disappears in the New Testament. Where, it might be asked, is the evidence of lament in the Lord's Prayer? While it cannot be denied that this prayer lacks explicit elements of the lament prayer tradition, nevertheless it is far from being the safe or undisturbing prayer that it has unfortunately too often become for too many of its users.[29]

The Lord's Prayer is filled with passion for the cause of God in the world: for the honoring of God's name, the coming of God's reign, and the doing of God's will. It also contains impassioned petitions for those things that are necessary for human life: daily bread, forgiveness of sins, and strength to withstand the forces of evil (Matt. 6:9–13/Luke 11:2–4). However familiar the words of the Lord's Prayer may be to us, there is nothing routine about its petitions; they are passionate cries for the triumph of God's life-giving grace in the world in the face of the threatening powers of death and destruction. Commenting on the Lord's Prayer from the perspective of the poor of Latin America, Leonardo Boff says that we must learn to listen to all the "overtones" present in the supplications of this prayer. The cry "thy kingdom come" springs from a radical hope that the poor often see contradicted; the petition "thy will be done" is a matter of urgency for the poor since their very lives are in jeopardy should God delay in bringing justice to the earth.[30]

If we consider the petitions of the Lord's Prayer with sensitivity to the staggering misery and suffering in our world, we should have no difficulty in grasping Boff's point. The words, "Let your reign come! Let your will be done!" are a cry, not a dispassionate request. We are to pray these words with a sense of urgency and with passion and longing because the justice, peace, and fullness of life that God wills are so painfully absent in the world as we experience it. Likewise, the cry "Save us from evil" (that is, from the forces of evil within and around us that threaten us with destruction and death) echoes the urgent cries of the psalms. Rightly understood as the anguished cry of those in need and in distress, the Lord's Prayer shares the passion of the rich prayer tradition of Israel.

2. *Like the prayers of lament in the Old Testament, New Testament prayers also have their particular life contexts.* The prayers of the earliest Christians are

prayers of a beleaguered and persecuted minority. As the testimony of Paul reminds us, the dangers of being an ambassador for Christ were considerable. Paul lists imprisonments, floggings, stoning, shipwreck, danger from opponents and bandits, sleepless nights, hunger, and thirst as among the hazards he endured for the sake of Christ (2 Cor. 11:23 ff.). On top of this, he speaks of a personal "thorn in the flesh" that tormented him and for whose removal he prayed three times (2 Cor. 12:7 ff.). No doubt Paul had far more than his own personal experiences in mind when he speaks of the Spirit helping us in our weakness and interceding on our behalf "with sighs too deep for words" (Rom. 8:26), but his own experiences would surely have been included.

The life context of early Christian prayer was, however, social and political as well as personal. If the prayers of the Old Testament have a sociopolitical setting, so also do the prayers of Jesus and the New Testament witnesses. Prayer in the New Testament does not glorify powerlessness and abandon the hope for justice and peace throughout God's creation. To pray for the hallowing of God's name, the coming of God's reign, and the doing of God's will is to envision a new world very different from the social realities and power arrangements of a world in which the poor are neglected and the powerful control everything for their benefit. What Brueggemann says of Psalms 9–10 could also be said of the Lord's Prayer: each time it is boldly uttered, precisely as prayer to God, it also "redefines power relations" and creates a possibility "for energy, courage, hope, and imagination that orders political power differently."[31]

3. *In the New Testament, prayer includes but is not reduced to the petition for forgiveness of sins.* The Lord's Prayer includes a plea for forgiveness as one of its several petitions. Yet neither in this prayer nor in other teachings of Jesus is there any suggestion that if we are hungry or in danger it is because we have sinned. Jesus explicitly repudiates the idea that all who suffer are receiving the consequences of their sins. When the disciples ask Jesus whether the blind man or his parents have sinned, he replies that neither is the case. What is certain is that God intends that the blind man be healed (John 9:1–3).

The ministry of Jesus was wider than a ministry of forgiveness of sins. Many people came to Jesus for healing of various kinds of infirmity and sickness. In some cases the person was healed with a word of forgiveness (Mark 2:5). In other cases, however, Jesus responds to a cry for healing without mentioning sin or forgiveness (Mark 5:21–43). As Miller writes, "The active ministry of Jesus clearly had to do with human suffering. Jesus of Nazareth heard and accepted the lament of the people around him and acted to deliver them from their particular experiences of suffering. While forgiveness of sins was also a central part of Jesus' ministry and often took place in the context of healing, it did not happen in place of healing."[32] We draw two conclusions

from the petitions of need to which Jesus responded in his ministry of healing. First, it is inappropriate to reduce the lament that arises from suffering
to the plea for forgiveness. Second, the salvation and healing which Jesus
brings in his ministry and in his death and resurrection are a deliverance
from inexplicable suffering as well as from human sin.

4. *While the cry for vengeance against enemies is far rarer in the prayer of the
New Testament than in the Old, its presence reminds us of the seriousness of evil
and the reality of divine judgment.* In the book of Revelation we find prayers
that resemble the plea for vengeance on enemies present in some of the Old
Testament psalms of lament. The seer hears the cries of those who have been
slain for the word of God and pleads that their blood be avenged (6:9). Some
critics of Christian faith have seen this as evidence that the spirit of resentment and vengeance was not conquered by the gospel message. We agree
that from a gospel perspective, many serious questions are raised by such
prayers, whether found in the Old Testament or the New, and we will
address some of these questions at a later point.

Two facts seem to us incontrovertible. The first is that the decisive New
Testament word regarding our attitude toward the "enemy" is the teaching
and practice of Jesus: "Love your enemies and pray for those who persecute
you" (Matt. 5:44). The apostle Paul teaches the same: "Bless those who persecute you; bless and do not curse them" (Rom. 12:14). Christians are not
to avenge themselves but are to leave wrath and judgment in the hands of
God. The second fact is that if it is antigospel to demonize enemies or to take
the judgment of God into one's own hands, it is also a mistake to pretend
that there are no enemies of God or that there is no judgment of God on
evil. As Eugene Peterson observes, Jesus did not call his disciples to be "wit-
less when we pray 'deliver us from evil.'"[33]

5. *As is evident in the prayer of Jesus in Gethsemane and in the apostle Paul's
prayer for the removal of his "thorn in the flesh," prayer in the New Testament
can involve profound struggle.* The prayers of Jesus are the norm of prayer for
the Christian community: the prayer that he taught his disciples and Jesus'
own prayers that are recorded in the gospel tradition. The relatively few
recorded prayers of Jesus include not only a prayer of thanksgiving to God
for the power at work in his ministry (Luke 10:21), an intercessory prayer
for the unity of his disciples (John 17:20–21), and a prayer of commitment
of his life work into the hands of God (Luke 23:46), but also prayers of
struggle and lament. For a proper understanding of the relationship of New
Testament prayer to the lament prayer of the Old Testament, the
Gethsemane prayer of Jesus and his cry of abandonment on the cross are of
special importance.

In the Garden of Gethsemane Jesus prays for the cup of suffering to be
removed from him (Luke 22:42). We are told that he sweat blood as he

entreated God to spare him from the agony he was about to face (Luke 22:44). A number of Christian exegetes, embarrassed by this portrayal of Jesus' struggle in prayer, have tried to explain it away in some fashion, but it is hard to make human sense of the Gethsemane prayer without assuming a real struggle and the raising of hard questions. The Gospel of John already shows difficulty with the Synoptic account of the Gethsemane struggle. Whereas in the Synoptic tradition Jesus prays in agony that the cup of suffering be removed from him, the Johannine Jesus asks rhetorically, "Should I pray, 'Father, remove this cup from me?'" and answers, "No, for it was just for this reason that I have come" (John 12:27).

We believe that the Gethsemane prayer is properly understood only if we take as seriously the plea "Remove this cup from me"—which Jesus repeated three times, all the while "distressed," "agitated," and "deeply grieved" (Mark 14:33–34)—as we do his final consent, "Yet not what I want, but what you want" (Mark 14:36). In the juxtaposition of Jesus' cry of distress and his trusting commitment to God we have a precise parallel to the tensive co-presence of lament and trust in the lament prayers of the psalms. No disguised docetic Christology should be allowed to obscure this participation of Jesus in the profound struggle of prayer characteristic of the Old Testament lament tradition.

As mentioned earlier, struggle in faith and prayer was also familiar to the apostle Paul, who reports that he was given a "thorn in the flesh" to keep him from boasting. He prayed to God three times to remove this thorn, but his request was not granted. Instead he was told, "My grace is sufficient for you, for my power is made perfect in weakness" (2 Cor. 12:8). Like Jesus, Paul prayed in anguish (three times emphasizes the intensity and persistence of the prayer) only finally to consent to God's will. It is important to note that in the case of both Jesus and Paul the consent to God's will in the midst of suffering was connected to a specific vocation. It was for the sake of faithfulness to this divinely given vocation that consent was given. Consent was not a result of some general principle of acquiescence governing every instance of suffering.

6. *While the prayer of lament and protest is evident in relatively few Gospel narratives, some passages, often overlooked, breathe its spirit.* A cry analogous to the Old Testament prayer of lament is found in the story of the storm at sea, when the disciples urgently questioned the sleeping Jesus: "Teacher, do you not care that we are perishing?" (Mark 4:38). After stilling the storm, Jesus asks the disciples in turn: "Why are you afraid? Have you still no faith?" (4:40). In this passage the implication is clear that the disciples' urgent questioning of Jesus' apparent unconcern arose from a lack of faith.

In other New Testament passages, however, the spirit of protest and argumentation with God receives commendation. Take, for example, Jesus' parable of the widow and the unjust judge (Luke 18:1–8). The widow keeps bothering the judge with her demands for justice until he does something about them. At the conclusion of the parable, Jesus asks whether in the end times faith will be found on earth. A number of commentators have puzzled over this question and have concluded that it is unrelated to the parable Jesus has just told about the widow and her refusal to accept the triumph of injustice. However, we think that, read in context, Jesus' final question points to the inseparability between genuine faith on the one hand and passionate prayer and activity for justice on the other. God will be faithful to the end. The question is whether the faithfulness of God will be met by the faithfulness of God's people as exemplified by the widow's zeal for God's reign of justice in the world and her refusal to accept injustice as the final word. Israel's tradition of the prayer of lament is very much alive in this parable of Jesus.

Another provocative text is the story of Jesus' encounter with the Canaanite woman who begs him to heal her daughter. When Jesus refuses to offer help because his ministry is directed first to God's chosen people, the woman counters with the argument that even dogs under the table are allowed to eat the crumbs that fall to the ground (Mark 7:28). This is a truly remarkable text for several reasons. Not only is the plaintiff a Gentile; not only is she a woman; but most astonishing of all is the fact that this Gentile woman dares to argue with Jesus and triumphs in the exchange. As Susan Lockrie Graham notes, women's speech is rarely recorded in the Gospel of Mark. In this instance, however, a woman not only comes to speech but uses language to argue her case with Jesus, and her daring remonstration is recognized as an expression of authentic faith.[34] Thus while this text has often been celebrated as a vindication of the church's mission to the Gentiles and as a demonstration of the high place assigned to women in the New Testament community, it should also be noted that we have in this passage a ratification of the tradition of lament and protest. For the New Testament the Canaanite woman is an exemplar of authentic, bold, risky prayer. Gail O'Day makes this point forcefully: "The very boldness of the woman's stance before Jesus has its roots in Israel's bold stance before God in the laments. The form which helps readers understand Matt. 15:21–28 is neither miracle story nor apophthegm [wisdom saying], but the psalm of lament. Matt. 15:21–28 is a *narrative embodiment of a lament psalm*."[35]

7. *Acceptance of the lament prayer in Christian prayer is irrevocably ratified by Jesus' cry of abandonment on the cross.* Most powerfully, the Old Testament lament tradition finds expression in Jesus' use of Psalm 22 in his awful cry of abandonment on the cross, "My God, my God, why have you forsaken me?" (Mark 15:34). By itself this text would provide reason enough to declare that the prayer of lament belongs in Christian prayer. The experience of the hiddenness of God is part of the drama of the incarnation as well as being part of the drama of Christian life.

In the history of Christian theology the cry of abandonment has frequently been muted or explained away in order to avoid the embarrassment
of ascribing a prayer of lament to Jesus. Some commentators have proposed
that this word of Jesus from the cross was spoken only for the benefit of his
hearers; others have suggested that it was intended to demonstrate the full
humanity of Jesus and is not to be attributed to his divine nature; still others have contended that when Jesus quoted the first verse of Psalm 22 he
would have thought of the whole prayer that includes praise to God.

We would take issue with such exegetical efforts insofar as they are
attempts to blunt the edge of the gospel witness. Jesus' cry of abandonment
confirms the fact that he shared to the utmost depths the pain and suffering
of humanity. Classical Christian doctrines of atonement have been one-
sidedly Pauline in orientation and have not taken with sufficient seriousness
"either the implications of the story of the Passion's being told in terms of
the lament of Psalm 22 or the relationship of the death and resurrection of
Jesus to the ministry of Jesus."[36] Among the profound meanings of the suffering and death of Christ "for us" is his awful lament to God as representative of all who suffer and are crushed by the forces of this world. The cry of
Rachel and all other cries of the distressed are present in the cry of Jesus.

8. *Because the New Testament community sees Jesus in the most intimate relationship to God, the lament of Jesus becomes the basis of Christian affirmation
that God also laments.* The New Testament has no explicit references to the
mourning and grieving of God as does the Old Testament. Nevertheless, it
does record Jesus' lament for Jerusalem because it did not recognize the way
that leads to peace (Luke 19:41–44), his weeping when he is told that his
friend Lazarus is dead (John 11:35), and above all, his lament from the cross
(Mark 15:34). Although traditional Christian theology sometimes resisted
the implications of its own trinitarian faith and spoke of the divine attributes of impassibility and immutability, recent trinitarian theology from
Barth, von Balthasar, and Moltmann to Third World and feminist theologies
have affirmed the suffering of God and have found new depths of meaning
in the grief and mourning of God in relationship to a groaning creation.[37]

9. *In New Testament prayer, memory and hope are closely bound together.*
The classical New Testament expression of this bond is Romans 8:18 ff. In
this passage, Paul contrasts the sufferings of the present with the coming
glory of the children of God. He sees Christian prayer taking place between
the times of the coming of Christ in lowliness on the one hand and his coming in glory on the other. When we are overwhelmed by the power of evil
and suffering, the Spirit helps us pray with sighs too deep for words.

For Paul, the groaning of the Spirit in our prayers is a groaning of anticipation as well as a groaning of pain. The love of God manifest in the cross
and resurrection of Jesus Christ and actively present in the community of

faith by the power of the Spirit offers certitude that nothing in heaven or on earth "will be able to separate us from the love of God in Christ Jesus" (Rom. 8:39).

Even this brief survey of New Testament prayer shows that it is far more hospitable to the prayer of lament than is often assumed. It is undoubtedly true that the prayer of the New Testament community is significantly shaped by the theology of the cross. In particular, this means praying for those who inflict suffering rather than crying out for vengeance, and subordinating one's own pain and suffering to the needs of others.[38] All the same, the prayer of lament, while it undergoes important changes in the New Testament, is not lost. Indeed, it is notably present at both the beginning and ending of Matthew's telling of the Gospel. At the beginning of his Gospel, Matthew recalls the weeping of Rachel for her children as he relates the story of the holy family's flight from Herod and the genocidal decree that all Hebrew children two years or under be slain. At the climax of this Gospel we are told of Jesus' passion and his cry of desolation from the cross (27:46).

Despite the evidences of the persistence of the lament prayer in the New Testament that we have presented, there can be no denying that some passages of the New Testament show a tendency to mute the lament tradition. We have already seen evidence of this in the Johannine version of the Gethsemane prayer. It is also apparent in passages of the New Testament where Christians are counseled not to lament but to show patience and endurance in face of suffering (James 5:7–18).

Still, we would argue that, at its center, the New Testament like the Old acknowledges the reality of evil and suffering and gives voice to the mourning of the afflicted and the longing for justice and renewal of life. Furthermore, like the Old Testament, the gospel tradition refuses to equate suffering with sin. In addition, the New Testament like the Old includes lament in tensive juxtaposition with the praise of God rather than as an end in itself. Finally, the faith of both Old and New Testament envisions a God who without ceasing to be God shares the lamentation of a groaning creation.

LAMENT IN POST-BIBLICAL JUDAISM

The power of the "countertradition" of prayer embedded in the lament prayers of the Bible is attested in the long history of *hutzpa k'lapei shamaya*, or bold, even defiant, prayer, in Judaism that has helped sustain a people in times of terrible suffering.[39]

Anson Laytner tries to retrieve the motif of arguing with God for contemporary Judaism. In the post-Holocaust era, it is essential that "contemporary Jews not only learn of the continuous heritage of doubt and protest and acquire a vocabulary through which to express the present mood, but also gain a sense of assurance that the present spiritual crisis, far from being unique in history, has analogies and precedents in other times and in other places of Jewish history. Beyond this, knowledge of the motif may help to reawaken or reanimate a sense of the dynamism of prayer by revitalizing and reevaluating the divine-human relationship."[40]

Laytner shows that there was great tension between praise and lament in the rabbinic tradition just as there was in the biblical tradition. The reality of suffering was predominantly dealt with by counseling submission to the inscrutable will of God. Rabbi Akiba held that Job was wrong to question God and rebel against his suffering. According to a later rabbinic source, had Job not rebelled against God, today the Amidah (the Eighteen Benedictions of the Jewish liturgy) would begin by an address to "The God of Abraham, Isaac, Jacob, and Job." Nevertheless, this approach was never wholly accepted by the rabbis. In "law-court prayers," God was argued with and the divine judgment questioned. "The Rabbis encouraged popular acceptance of Akiba's teaching on suffering while at the same time reserving for themselves the right and responsibility of arguing with God when the need arose."[41]

The Jewish way, Laytner argues, is one of "creative discontent." "We are called Yisra-el, one who struggles with God. It is our task to struggle continually with God just as we struggle against many idols of our own making."[42] Laytner documents this struggle with God in post-Holocaust Jewish poetry. He cites, for example, the poet Kadia Molodowsky, who pleads with the God of Israel to choose another people. Israel, says the poet, is tired of corpses, and she has exhausted all her prayers. "We have no more prayers," Molodowsky writes, but as Laytner observes, "despite its hostile tone, Molodowsky's poem is, in fact, one more prayer."[43]

In the post-Holocaust era, Elie Wiesel has continued this tradition of lamenting and arguing with God in powerful novels, essays, and plays. Among his many books is a drama entitled *The Trial of God*.[44] The drama takes place in the midst of a pogrom in Shamgorod, Poland, on February 25, 1649. A handful of surviving Jews, hiding in the village inn, decide to hold a trial of God for allowing these terrible events to occur. Berish acts as the prosecuting attorney, but no one wants to be the defense attorney until a stranger named Sam appears and volunteers for the job. Sam defends God and calls upon the Jews to submit to God's will however unjust it may appear. "Endure. Accept. And say Amen," Sam demands. While the other Jews are taken in by Sam's arguments, Berish refuses to submit. "I'll use my last energy to make my protest known," he says. In the denouement of the drama, Sam's demonic identity is revealed, and the drama ends in darkness and the sound of murderous roars.

But true to the biblical tradition of lament, Wiesel does not simply abandon or curse God. Complaining of the absence and silence of God, Wiesel nevertheless longs to "make up" with God and experience God's parental care and companionship again. On the occasion of the observance of the Jewish holy days in 1997, Wiesel composed a moving prayer of lament. "Where were you, God of kindness, in Auschwitz? What was going on in heaven, at the celestial tribunal, while your children were marked for humiliation, isolation and death only because they were Jewish?" Wiesel confesses that fifty years after the Holocaust, these questions still haunt him. Yet over the years gratitude has replaced bitterness. "At one point, I began wondering whether I was not unfair with you. After all, Auschwitz was not something that came down ready-made from heaven. It was conceived by men, implemented by men, staffed by men. And their aim was to destroy not only us but you as well. Ought we not to think of your pain, too? Watching your children suffer at the hands of your other children, haven't you also suffered? . . . Let us make up, Master of the Universe. In spite of everything that happened? Yes, in spite. Let us make up. . . . It is unbearable to be divorced from you so long."[45]

RECOVERING BIBLICAL LAMENT IN THEOLOGY AND MINISTRY

Even our very limited synopsis of the complex biblical traditions of lament should be sufficient to show that in the biblical understanding and practice of prayer, both praise and lament, doxology and complaint, adoration and anger are held in tensive unity. As noted in the first chapter, however, in many churches today this strand of prayerful lament and protest found in the biblical prayer tradition has virtually disappeared. Our survey of representative hymnals and liturgies concurs with the judgment of Walter Brueggemann that in the worship services of most mainline churches "the lament psalms simply do not exist."[46] This neglect, Brueggemann suggests, inevitably conveys the message that anger, outrage, and protest do not belong in Christian prayer or worship: "If you feel this way, or want to pray this way, do so elsewhere."

Such an attitude, even if only implicit in our worship services and understandings of ministry, undermines the vitality of our practice of prayer. A church that has forgotten or feels uncomfortable with this dimension of prayer is to that extent alienated from the biblical tradition, cut off from the cries of suffering people in our congregations, society, and around the world, and deaf to the groaning of the whole creation so gravely endangered today by human abuse and exploitation.

Consistent with our survey of the biblical witness, we suggest that there are several important contributions that a reclaiming of the biblical prayer of lament could make to Christian life and ministry today. First, there is the possibility of a deeper understanding and use of the Bible in Christian prayer and worship by those who find themselves in great distress. We hear much today of the biblical illiteracy that is prevalent in the churches. There are many reasons for this situation, and we do not wish to oversimplify a complex matter. Nevertheless, we suggest that one reason people approach the reading and study of the Bible only halfheartedly is that they have encountered it in a way that typically screens out experiences of negation, grief, doubt, and protest. As a result, the Bible may seem to them superficial, irrelevant, and even false. It does not readily connect with their own experience of abuse or abandonment or their longing for transformed life.

In a provocative essay, Ulrike Bail helps show the enormous spiritual power latent in the lament psalms. She argues that Psalm 55 readily lends itself to being interpreted as the voice of a woman who has been sexually abused. The psalmist laments the violation she has experienced at the hands of someone close to her and trusted by her. "But it is you, my equal, my companion, my familiar friend, with whom I kept pleasant company; we walked in the house of God with the throng. . . . My companion laid hands on a friend and violated a covenant with me" (Ps. 55:13–14, 20).[47] According to Bail, the abused woman might well wish like the psalmist to have wings like the dove and be able to fly away and escape all that she has experienced (55:6). At the end of the psalm the victim's integrity is upheld by calling upon God. "But I will trust in you" (55:23). Bail's essay demonstrates how reclaiming the lament prayers of the Bible can help provoke an honest and audacious piety rooted in the biblical witness.

Second, besides being a means of support to the afflicted, the biblical prayers of lament and protest may also serve as a source of confrontation and renewal. They may disturb the consciences of those who dwell in privileged places and move them to courageous action.

Dietrich Bonhoeffer learned this from personal experience. Bonhoeffer loved the psalms and was well aware that they contained voices of protest as well as praise. On November 9, 1938, the evening of the infamous *Kristallnacht,* when the Nazis began their terrorist attacks on the homes, synagogues, and businesses of Jews in the Third Reich, Bonhoeffer was most likely praying the psalms.[48] He and other members of the seminary where Bonhoeffer taught were accustomed to praying the psalms each morning and evening. Examining Bonhoeffer's Bible, Eberhard Bethge discovered a notation in the margin alongside Psalm 74:8–11. The verses of the psalm read:

They speak in their hearts: 'Let us plunder them!' They burn all the houses of God in the land. Our signs we do not see, and no longer does any prophet proclaim, and there is no one among us who knows how long, O God, how long shall the foe scoff and the enemy revile your name forever? Why do you turn aside your hand? Draw forth your right hand from your bosom and make an end.[49]

Alongside these verses Bonhoeffer wrote the date: "9.11.38!" Upon reading Psalm 74, Bonhoeffer recalled the cries of the Jews on a night of Nazi terror that launched the systematic destruction of the Jewish people. Bethge thinks it possible that Bonhoeffer may have translated the lament of the psalm, "O God, how long?" to mean for him personally, "O God, how long can I stand by and simply watch?" This would eventually lead to Bonhoeffer's participation in the plot against Hitler and Bonhoeffer's own execution.

Congregations need to learn to read the Bible not only through familiar eyes but also through very different eyes, and especially through the eyes of the poor and the abused. *like Lib theology*

Third, reclaiming the lament strand of biblical prayer may assist the church in recovering its relationship to the faith of the people of Israel and in this way renew its solidarity with all who suffer. The piety and theology of the church have all too often developed in opposition to that of Judaism. Even when this has not taken the virulent form of anti-Semitism, estrangement from the Jewish heritage of faith has meant a great spiritual loss to the church. The positive evaluation of this life and the good gifts of God's creation, the zeal for the ordering of all of life in accordance with the will of God, and the concern for the weak, the stranger, and the refugee are among the major contributions of the Jewish tradition to Christian faith. Moreover, the Jewish heritage is vigorously antidualistic, and Christians who have lost their Jewish moorings have always been tempted by dualistic philosophies and ideologies. We suggest that the tradition of prayer and worship that includes lament is closely associated with these emphases and constitutes another precious gem of faith that the Jewish community has shared with the church.

Finally, we suggest that serious attention to the biblical tradition of lament prayer may help heal the separation that is all too evident between theology and spirituality, and between theology and the practice of ministry. Not infrequently, books in theology are written which scarcely mention the subject of prayer. They may discuss at great length such topics as the problem of providence and evil while ignoring the ways in which the communities of Jewish and Christian faith have wrestled with the experiences of pain, suffering, and oppression in their worship and prayer. Similarly, theology and pastoral ministry have both suffered from a lack of vigorous interaction. On the one hand, theology has often seemed more concerned with providing comprehensive, systematic interpretations of Christian doctrine than with attending to those aspects of the life of faith that cannot easily be ordered within a systematic framework; on the other hand, pastoral ministry has often been content to take its guidance more from modern psychology and sociology than from the Bible and the theological tradition. Attention to the practice of biblical prayer in its fullness, we contend, may provide an important point of convergence among the theological disciplines and between all forms of theological reflection and the practice of ministry. Whether the fullness of biblical prayer, including the prayer of lament, has found adequate expression in the Christian theological tradition is the story of our next chapter.

New ways of reading the Bible — looking for boldness, honesty in prayer
Understand that our readings are informed by
     diversity of voices, literary forms
     author's cultural context, our cultural context
          ↳ lament is more meaningful to some than other
          Let your usual, comfortable readings be challenged!

Differences between lament in old, New testaments,
But Both
     acknowledge reality of evil/suffering
     voice mourning, longing for justice
     Suffering ≠ sin
     lament juxtaposed w/ praise
     God shares in lament

Reclaiming Bib Lament has contribution to make
     (1) support to afflicted
     (2) Source of confrontation + renewal
          get people to care about the suffering
     (3) renewed rel w/ Israel, Suffering people
     (4) connection between theol + ministry

CHAPTER THREE

THE PRAYER OF LAMENT
IN THE CHRISTIAN
THEOLOGICAL TRADITION

I sorrowed for my sorrow and was wasted with a twofold sadness.
—*Augustine,* Confessions

R ecalling how he reacted to the death of his mother, Augustine reports that even though he did not weep publicly, he was ashamed that he was unable to control his grief as much as he should have. So he "sorrowed for his sorrow and was wasted with a twofold sadness."

Augustine is not alone in his struggle to find a place for grief and lament in Christian life. A cautious judgment would be that the theological tradition is deeply ambivalent about expressions of lament over suffering and loss even though such laments are frequently found in scripture. Nicholas Wolterstorff, a contemporary theologian, puts the matter provocatively: to acknowledge the legitimacy and necessity of lament in Christian life and worship is to depart from the great theological tradition of the church.[1]

In this chapter we will identify several influential types of Christian theology and piety and the attitudes toward lament with which they are coupled. Given the limitations of space, we can offer only suggestive sketches rather than exhaustive treatments of the theological perspectives considered. Our primary aim is to show that while classical theologies of prayer are rich in many ways, they often show deep ambivalence in what they say about the experience of grief and loss and in particular what they make of the lament prayer. As will become evident, various interpretive strategies have been employed to mitigate the difficulties such prayer has been thought to pose. More specifically, we will note important assumptions about God and human nature present in these theologies of prayer, ask to what extent they make room for the prayer of lament, and offer a few examples of the ways in which they interpret the biblical lament psalms.

Our selective survey of the classic theological tradition intends to be both respectful and critical. We believe that we have much to learn from its understandings and practices of prayer. Yet we are also convinced that it is necessary to break with the reservations and suspicions regarding the lament prayer in the tradition.

AUGUSTINE AND THE PIETY OF DETACHMENT

As a dominant figure in the development of early Christian theology and piety, Augustine is an appropriate beginning point for our brief study of interpretations of the lament prayer in the Christian theological tradition.

According to Augustine, human beings are motivated by their desire for happiness. Whether our quest for joy and fulfillment is realized depends on the nature of the objects of our love. If what we love is unworthy or fleeting, our quest for happiness will remain unfulfilled. Augustine distinguishes between things to be used *(uti)* and things to be enjoyed *(frui)*. Worldly things are to be used rather than seen as the source of lasting joy. God alone is the proper desire of the restless human heart. Only in God do we find the abiding joy and rest that we seek. In our sinful state, however, human desire is fatally disordered. As a result, we relate to persons and things in this life as though they could provide lasting delight and indestructible happiness. Augustine's famous distinction between the earthly city and the city of God expresses in corporate terms the two different loves that drive humanity. Residents of the earthly city cling to this world and its delights while those in transit to the city of God seek fulfillment in the love of God, who alone can supply deep and lasting joy. For Augustine, the Christian life is an arduous journey from destructive attachments to things of this world to the passionate love of God alone.

Augustine's Confessions

Augustine's theology of the journey of the restless soul to God underlies his understanding of the meaning of prayer and shapes his view of the place of grief and lamentation within prayer. In the *Confessions* he gives vivid descriptions of three significant experiences of loss and grief in his life. The first is the death of a "very dear friend" about his own age that occurred when he was just beginning his teaching career in Tagaste. When his friend died, Augustine was overcome with grief and "wept most bitterly." "I simply grieved and wept, for I was miserable and had lost my joy."[2] Looking back on such episodes years later, Augustine explains the wretchedness and pains of grief that he felt as due to his being "fettered in the friendship of mortal things." Improperly attached to persons and things of this world, the soul is "torn to pieces" when it loses them. For Augustine, security is to be found only in God. "Where really," Augustine prays, "is there security save with thee? Grief languishes for things lost in which desire had taken delight, because it wills to have nothing taken from it, just as nothing can be taken from thee."[3]

A second, and the most familiar, occasion of lament described by Augustine took place when he was meditating in a garden in Milan. Exhausted from his long quest for truth and peace, he repented of his sinful life and gave free rein to his contrition. He remembered experiencing "a mighty storm, accompanied by a mighty rain of tears. That I might give way fully to my tears and lamentations, I stole away from Alypius, for it seemed to me that solitude was more appropriate for the business of weeping. I went far enough away that I could feel that even his presence was no restraint upon me."[4] It was soon after this experience of acute remorse for his past life that he heard a voice calling him to "pick it up, read it." Opening the Bible, he read Romans 13:13 and instantly received the certainty of faith he had long sought.

A third incident of grieving described in the *Confessions* occurred upon the death of his mother, Monica. Deeply moved by his loss, Augustine, now a Christian, restrained his tears and was upset that the emotion of sorrow had such power over him. When he closed his dead mother's eyes, "there flowed in a great sadness on my heart and it was passing into tears, when at the strong behest of my mind my eyes sucked back the fountain dry, and sorrow was in me like a convulsion."[5] He "sorrowed for his sorrow" and held back his tears until he was alone in his room. Augustine was obviously embarrassed that he was unable to control himself. He conjectured that some of his readers would see a sign of weakness in his weeping for his mother for "part of an hour."

These three incidents disclose Augustine's deep reservations about uncontrolled expressions of grief. Becoming Christian did not help Augustine grieve his losses. As a young man and prior to becoming a Christian, he mourned freely the death of a close friend. However, as a Christian believer he was unable to acknowledge sorrow, remorse, and lamentation except in relation to his sins. Even at the loss of a family member or friend, Augustine was convinced, the grief of the Christian should be severely restrained. Grief for reasons other than our sin and separation from God manifests an improper attachment to persons, relationships, and things of this world. When we attach ourselves to mutable, mortal, corruptible creatures, it is as if we have poured out our soul upon the sand. Thus as Wolterstorff rightly argues, in Augustinian piety, lament over loss of loved ones and delights of this world is replaced by confession of sins.[6]

Augustine on the Psalms

This judgment finds support in many of Augustine's writings, not least in his moving meditations on the psalms. Augustine not only wrote extensive commentaries on the psalms, but his *Confessions* and other writings are replete with quotations from the Psalter. As Peter Brown notes, this was a literary innovation that can only be explained by saying that Augustine found in the psalms the language he needed to give adequate expression to the profound experiences he had undergone.[7]

Two defining features of Augustine's commentaries on the psalms are their Christological reference and their construal of psalms of lament as penitential psalms. Thus the cry of Psalm 13, "How long, O God," is interpreted as a cry for knowledge of and communion with Christ. "How long wilt thou hold me back from understanding this Christ who is the Wisdom of God and the true end of the soul's every aspiration?"[8] Similarly, the cry of abandonment in Psalm 22 is understood primarily as the words of the crucified Savior on behalf of sinful humanity.[9] When Augustine prays this psalm as a Christian, "the prayer I utter is not that of [one who is] righteous . . . but of one laden with sins. He who thus prays nailed to the cross is indeed our old self who does not even know why God has forsaken him."[10] According to Augustine, the unrelieved lament of Psalm 88 also describes the sorrows of Christ. Thus when the saints repeat the difficult questions of this psalm, they have no thought of laying any blame on God. They simply seek to know the reason for their affliction. Whatever adversity Christians encounter, Augustine teaches, its purpose is that the flame of our desire for God may burst into a brighter blaze.[11]

In his meditation on Psalm 137, Augustine finds a vivid contrast between the cities of Babylon and Jerusalem. Babylon represents this world and its fleeting delights while Jerusalem represents our heart's true home. Babylon signifies "all things which here are loved, and pass away," and which when lost cause us to weep because we have been captive to them. The enemies and tormentors that are mentioned in the psalm are the devil and his minions, "who have inflicted on us the wounds of sin." The "little ones" that the psalmist beseeches God to dash against the rocks are our sinful desires in their inception, and the rock against whom they are dashed is Christ.[12]

As these passages show, a certain kind of lament is certainly legitimate in Augustine's eyes. The problem is not that sinners grieve but that they grieve for the wrong things. It is not that we lament that is wrong; it is why we lament. In Psalm 22 we are taught to implore God not with sinful words that desire a fleeting life, but with the supplications of one turned wholly toward God with the hope of possessing life everlasting.[13]

Augustinian Piety

Augustine's remarkable spiritual interpretation of the psalms has had enormous influence on later Christian prayer and piety. The piety that informs his reading of the Psalms is summarized in his comment on Psalm 27:8: "Your face, O God, do I seek." "Those who truly love will understand. [Others] might wish to live happily forever among the earthly desires and pleasures [they love]: and on that account [they] might possibly offer God adoration and prayer in the hope of obtaining a long life surrounded by everything [they enjoy]. . . . Such is not the desire of [those] who [have] asked but one thing of the Lord. But what [do they] want? To gaze upon the Lord's loveliness all the days of [their lives]."[14]

Augustine's passionate longing for the vision of God is a powerful retrieval of the biblical injunction to love God with all our heart, strength, mind, and soul. We have no reason to question the depth of Augustine's piety. What must be questioned, however, is his view that grief over worldly losses always betrays a disordered soul. As the episode after his mother's death shows, for Augustine "grief . . . seems to be so aligned with inordinate carnal affection that sorrow over any worldly loss falls under suspicion."[15] Also to be questioned is Augustine's view that suffering is always either divine punishment or a form of divine pedagogy. The distress of the innocent sufferer and the expression of anger and lament in the face of loss or injustice have no place in Augustine's interpretation of biblical laments. Whereas the author of Psalm 137 and the rabbis who commented on it knew exile as the bitter historical experience of a people's loss of freedom and homeland, Augustine construes it as an allegory of the spiritual life and the soul's yearning for the heavenly Jerusalem.[16]

Both Augustine's reflections on his own experience and his interpretation of the lament psalms betray a deep suspicion of human affections uncontrolled by reason. Backing this suspicion is Augustine's conviction that God lives in undisturbed serenity and is a stranger to emotions like grief and anger. Everlasting life in communion with God to which the Christian aspires is a life of joy untouched by the ravages of grief. To have God alone as one's delight and joy is to be beyond sorrow, for God is never wounded by any sorrow.[17] James Dittes notes that Augustine's identification of God as "incorruptible, inviolable, and immutable" is an attempt to make God "fail safe." "Augustine's way . . . [is] the way of distance. God is removed from taint and corruptibility that besets the painful human experience by being removed far above that experience."[18] Assumptions about God as distanced and inviolable go hand in hand with the piety of detachment from worldly things and relationships.

In sum, while Augustine acknowledges the appropriateness of lament in the mode of grieving for our sins, he is at least uncomfortable and even suspicious of lament for the loss of a beloved family member or intimate friend or in response to a calamity such as the exile and enslavement of a whole people. In the Augustinian piety of detachment, grief over such losses would be misdirected. As Wolterstorff explains, love for Augustine is "that mode of attachment to a thing which is such that the destruction or change of that thing would cause one grief."[19] Only God should be loved in a way that if lost would occasion grief. While recognizing that the process of detachment from the persons and things of this life is painful, Augustine nevertheless sees the proper and primary reason for grief to be human captivity to sin.

LUTHER AND THE PIETY OF THE CROSS

Although congruent in many ways with Augustine's theology, Luther's piety and theology have a very distinctive focus and intensity. The leaven at work in all of Luther's theology is his radical doctrine of justification by grace through faith alone, his theology of the cross, and his teaching regarding *Anfechtung*, or temptation. These doctrines provide the context for understanding Luther's theology of prayer and determine the particular meaning and importance he assigns to the prayer of lament.

The Psalms and Luther's Doctrine of Justification

Luther's understanding of Christian prayer is shaped by his doctrine of justification by grace through faith alone. According to Luther, prayer is rooted in the command and promise of God. God wants us to pray not simply with our words but with our whole heart, and God has promised to hear our prayers. We are to pray in faith and that means in the confidence that God will be faithful and gracious. As Luther explains, when we pray in the name of Jesus, we throw ourselves entirely on the mercy of God that has been shown to us above all in the crucified Savior.[20]

By itself, however, such a skeletal summary would be in danger of missing the fierce struggle that Luther knows to be an inescapable part of genuine prayer. Since it is the psalms that boldly record this struggle, Luther's fondness for this biblical book should occasion no surprise. The psalms were for Luther second only to the Lord's Prayer in instructing the Christian about what and how to pray. Luther says that there was no book in the Bible on which he had devoted as much labor as the Psalter.

In his reflections on the psalms Luther does not for a moment overlook the fact that they are filled with praise of God. His personal favorite was Psalm 118 ("my psalm" he calls it) in which the steadfast love of God even in the direst circumstances is affirmed. However, Luther knows the psalms are also filled with cries and laments. In his commentary on Psalm 6:3, "My soul is sorely troubled," Luther writes, "No one who has not been profoundly terrified and forsaken prays profoundly."[21] When the psalmist cries out, "God—how long?" Luther recognizes this as the voice of a soul deeply hurt by "the feeling of being forsaken and rejected by God."[22] God "gladly hears those who cry and lament" but turns away from those who feel smug and independent.[23]

Luther was convinced that the doctrine of justification by grace through faith alone is present in the psalms no less than in the writings of the apostle Paul. This conviction finds expression in the claim that for the God addressed in the psalms "weeping is preferred to working, and suffering exceeds all doing."[24] We cannot make ourselves acceptable to God by our works or by our prayers. Our weeping is our recognition of our helplessness to rescue ourselves from our sin and misery; our readiness to suffer is our acknowledgment that before God there is nothing that we can do but wait on the grace of God.

In Luther's view, those who experience the terrors of abandonment and rejection can only sigh, groan, and cry out to God. Commenting on Psalm 13:1—"O God, how long?"—Luther observes that those who have not experienced such affliction do not understand these words. To such people the words of the psalmist are like Greek and Hebrew. Such people ask: How can a pious person, a great prophet, even an apostle speak these words. Should the pious not sing: "God, we praise you," or, "Sing to God?" According to Luther, "No one understands what the psalmist says who has not experienced it."[25] Again: "For to be forsaken of God is far worse than death. Those who have tasted and experienced a little of this may ponder it, but people who are carnally secure, coarse, untried, and inexperienced know and understand nothing of it."[26]

Thus for Luther, the grace of God is the only source of consolation in our experiences of loneliness, despair, and abandonment. A theology of the cross emerges from groans and cries out of the depths. This is the point of Luther's often quoted remark, "It is by living—no, rather it is by dying and being damned that a theologian is made, not by understanding, reading, or speculating."[27]

Luther's Theology of the Cross

Luther's radical doctrine of justification by grace rather than by works of the law is one expression of his "theology of the cross." The theology of the cross is an encompassing theme in Luther and has at least three aspects: epistemological, Christological, and experiential. Epistemologically, the "theology of the cross" refers to a theology that rests on God's revelation rather than on human reason. In contrast to a theology of glory, a theology of the cross never pretends that the human situation is less desperate than it is. Rather than calling evil good and good evil, a theology of the cross "calls the thing what it actually is."[28] A theology of the cross acknowledges that we are only beggars before God. Admission of our lack of understanding of ourselves and God is the precondition of receiving true understanding from God's self-revelation. That God is revealed in the suffering and shame of the cross of Christ turns upside down all our prior understandings of God, self, and neighbor. Abandoning our own knowledge and relying on the knowledge given by God is "the way of the cross."[29]

The theology of the cross also and centrally refers to the passion and death of Christ for sinners. Christ has experienced the depths of suffering, death, and hell for us. According to Luther, the cry of Psalm 22:1, "My God, my God, why have you forsaken me?," is to be understood wholly of Christ. For our sake Christ became a sinner and a blasphemer, like one forsaken, cursed, and damned. "By this verse," Luther writes, "those are instructed who are exercised in the depths of the abyss of death and hell, and they are here furnished with an antidote against despair."[30]

For Luther, Jesus' terrible cry from the cross is the destruction of every theology of glory. As Gerhard Forde notes, "The theologian of glory always has great difficulty with that cry. In pious restraint the theologian of glory will refrain from such 'blasphemy' and flatter God by absolving Him from all blame. But such pious speech simply robs God of the right to be God. So Luther could say that there are none closer to God in this life than 'blasphemers,' who at least do God the honor of letting God be God!"[31]

The third aspect of Luther's theology of the cross is experiential. That is, it refers to the shape of Christian life lived under the cross. Believers are conformed to Christ by experiencing the cross in their lives. The process by which God justifies and renews us must necessarily include our being utterly humbled. God makes a person a sinner in order that the person might be made righteous by God. "I thank you that you have humbled me and have helped me" is Luther's daring alteration of the Hebrew text of Psalm 118:21.[32] This pattern of exaltation through humiliation is, of course, first of all true of Christ, who was forsaken of God "for a little while" before he was crowned with honor and glory (as Luther understands Psalm 8:5). But the same pattern of exaltation through humiliation also defines the justification and sanctification of sinners.

The experiential aspect of Luther's theology of the cross centers on the terrible experience of doubt and of feeling lost and abandoned by God. Such experience comes powerfully to expression in the psalms of lament. Luther calls the experience that these psalms record and that he knew all too well *Anfechtung*, variously translated as "temptation," "trial," "affliction," or "tribulation." *Anfechtung* for Luther takes many forms: it is to despair of being able to accomplish one's own salvation; it is feeling forgotten, abandoned, and rejected by God; it is doubt that the saving work of Christ is real and sufficient; it is having to endure all sorts of persecutions for the sake of the gospel despite the fact that the gospel proclaims the victory of God over the forces of sin, death, and the devil.[33]

According to Luther there is no escaping *Anfechtung* in the living of Christian life or the doing of Christian theology. When Luther identifies the three essential elements of theological study, he includes *Anfechtung*. Along with prayer *(oratio)* for the guidance of God's Spirit, and meditation *(meditatio)* on the central message of the Word, the experience of spiritual trial *(tentatio,* or *Anfechtung)* that tests one's faith in everyday life is for Luther an essential component of Christian spirituality and theology.[34] There simply is no genuine faith or theology that is not accompanied by *Anfechtung*. Indeed, the stronger faith is, the greater the trial and affliction with which it is certain to be assaulted.

Luther on Lament in Christian Life

With this background we may now ask: In what sense and to what extent does Luther permit and encourage the Christian to grieve and lament? Compared with Augustine, Luther shows a truly remarkable freedom. Whereas Augustine was embarrassed to have grieved for part of an hour when his mother died, Luther upon reading the news of his father's death took his Psalter, went to his room, and "cried so much that he could not think clearly the next day."[35] In a funeral sermon on the occasion of the death of Elector Duke John of Saxony, Luther excoriates those who want to "make sticks and stones of us by alleging that one must eliminate the creature altogether and not accept anything that is natural, even though father, mother, son, daughter [or prince] should die, one must simply go on with dry eyes and a serene heart." This says Luther is nothing other than "artificial virtue"; it is a "fabricated strength, which God did not create and also does not please God at all." "It is right and fitting, even godly, to mourn a good friend who has died." "God has not created [us] to be a stick or a stone. [God] has given [us] five senses and a heart of flesh in order that [we] may love [our] friends, be angry with [our] enemies, and lament and grieve when [our] dear friends suffer evil." Restraint from grieving is a kind of hypocrisy designed to garner praise from others who will say, "Ah, there's a man who has a firm hold on himself."[36]

Luther refuses, however, to give completely free rein to the lament that arises from the creature's experience of suffering and loss. Because Christians grieve in faith and hope, their grief must not be inordinate. To a bereaved couple who have recently lost a son, Luther writes that it is "quite inconceivable that you should not be mourning." Yet he also counsels that their mourning be moderate so that they may be comforted again.[37] To another mourner his advice is to "control your grief as much as you can." "I allow your mourning only in so far as it is not contrary to the will of God. For it is necessary to put a limit to one's sorrow and grief."[38] "If we are going to grieve," Luther writes on another occasion, "we should grieve over Christ's death. That was a real death, not only in itself, because it was so bitter, ignominious and grandiose. . . . Christ died as no one else died or ever will die. . . . Why aren't you weeping and lamenting over Christ your Lord, whose death was so much greater and more horrible than that of all [others]?"[39]

Luther elaborates on this last point in still another letter of consolation. "No such calamity can overtake any human being as once overtook the Father himself when his beloved Son was rewarded for all his miracles and benefactions by being maligned, cursed and finally subjected to the most shameful of deaths on the cross. Everyone thinks that his own cross is the heaviest and takes it to heart more than the cross of Christ—even if he had endured ten crosses. This is so because we are not so patient as God is, and consequently a smaller cross is more painful to us than Christ's cross."[40]

To these admonitions of Luther to be moderate in grief lest we lose sight of the cross of Christ, Mitchell and Anderson make the apt response that "not to grieve deeply is to grieve inadequately, distortedly." Moreover, far from separating us from the cross of Christ, "freedom to grieve intensively from the onset of loss is what makes space later for a remembrance of Christ's suffering and a reaffirmation of the loving will of God."[41]

The experience of anguish and despair that preoccupies Luther is clearly of a different order from ordinary losses. The deepest terror for Luther is the attack on faith in God's gracious promises: the awareness of the total helplessness of the sinful creature before God and the accompanying terror of utter abandonment and rejection by God. With regard to this experience, Luther is far more radical than Augustine. While both in their own way interpret lament prayers as penitential prayers, Augustine thinks within a penitential framework in which punishment and self-punishment for sins can be practiced. Luther, on the other hand, thinks exclusively of the sinner's utter dependence on the sheer and miraculous forgiveness of God.

What about times when the believer is angry with God? Luther, as usual, is remarkably candid about his own experience. He writes: "When I'm angry with God and ask . . . whether it's [God] or I who's wrong, then it's more than I can handle."[42]

Does Luther's theology of the cross lead necessarily to the conclusion that we must simply bear the suffering that comes our way whatever the cause? This is an important question for many who have been taught by church and pastor that it is the Christian's duty to remain passive and submissive in the face of suffering and abuse. Luther's instruction to the peasants who were rebelling against their rulers because of experienced injustices certainly leaves room for misuse along these lines. Luther writes to the peasants: "Suffering! suffering! Cross! cross! This and nothing else is the Christian law! . . . You have heard above that the gospel teaches Christians to endure and suffer wrong and pray to God in every need. You, however, are not willing to suffer, but like heathen, you want to force the rulers to conform to your impatient will."[43]

While acknowledging the danger in Luther's call to suffering and the ways in which it has been misused, we agree with the balanced conclusions of Mary Solberg in her study of Luther's theology within a feminist perspective. Addressing the question whether Luther's theology of the cross glorifies suffering, Solberg makes two points. On the one hand, in Luther's favor it must be said that he did not intend to glorify suffering in itself any more than liberation theologians in our time want to glorify suffering and poverty when they declare that God is to be found particularly among the poor. On the other hand, like other theologies, Luther's theology of the cross may have very different uses depending on where and with whom one is standing when one employs it. No doubt the powerful and privileged can and have misused the theology of the cross to exonerate themselves and to insist that sufferers should welcome their suffering. Properly interpreted, however, a theology of the cross continues to be a valuable resource that enables us, as Luther says, to "call the thing what it actually is." A critical theology of the cross helps bring in focus "a reality in which the privileged ignore or rename suffering too often, and bear with and protest it too seldom."[44]

CALVIN AND THE PIETY OF PATIENCE

While Calvin considered Augustine the greatest of the patristic theologians, he did not follow Augustine's practice of narrating at length his own spiritual pilgrimage. Nor did he provide details of personal experiences of grief and loss. Although Calvin's three children died in infancy, we have little record of his reaction to their loss.

Calvin's Humanity

While neither as introspective as Augustine nor as robust in describing his struggles and temptations as Luther, Calvin was not the cold, impassive, merely intellectual person his detractors have made him out to be. The death of Calvin's wife, Idelette de Bure, after only nine years of marriage, was clearly a great blow to him. After her death, Calvin wrote to a friend: "Although the death of my wife has been bitterly painful to me, yet I restrain my grief as well as I can. . . . You know well enough how tender, or rather soft, my mind is. Had I not exercised a powerful self-control, therefore, I could not have borne up so long."[45] Calvin later consoled a correspondent who had lost his wife with the words: "How deep a wound the death of your excellent wife has inflicted on you I judge from my own feelings, for I recollect how difficult it was for me seven years ago to overcome a similar sorrow."[46]

Calvin not only differed from Augustine in his reluctance to speak of his own personal experience; he and Luther both differed from Augustine in having a greater appreciation for the value and delight of this world. Along with Luther, Calvin had far less difficulty than Augustine in recognizing the naturalness of the sorrow and grief Christians, like all people, experience when losses occur. It would be inhuman, Calvin says, if anyone should remain unmoved and indifferent to their losses and sufferings. After all, Jesus wept at the death of Lazarus, and he experienced a sorrow unto death in Gethsemane.

Yet for Calvin, too, the grief of the Christian must be tempered, not because worldly goods are depreciated but because we are called to submit to the providence of God in all events. Thus the difference between Augustine and Calvin can best be described as the difference between a piety of worldly detachment and a piety of patience born of belief in the providential care of God the creator and redeemer.

The Centrality of the Psalms in Calvin's Theology of Prayer

Calvin's view of the prayer of lament must be set within the larger context of his theology of prayer. According to Calvin, prayer is the "chief exercise" of faith. In the act of prayer believers bring before God all their needs and anxieties as well as their praise and thanksgiving. Calvin clearly goes beyond Augustine here. He assures us that "we have permission and freedom granted us to lay open before [God] our infirmities, which we would be ashamed to confess before [others]."[47] Christians are not free of vexations, anxieties, and "huge torments," and their prayers should not pretend that they are. Like the psalmist, Christians know what it means to "cry to the Lord from the deep abyss."[48] Calvin formulates four rules of right prayer: that it be reverential, that it honestly recognize our need, that it begin with a plea for pardon, and that it be done in confident hope that God will hear and answer our petitions.[49]

For Calvin, as for Augustine and Luther, the primary prayer book of Christians is the book of Psalms. He speaks of the psalms as providing "an anatomy of all the parts of the soul."[50] Like a mirror, the psalms reflect every human emotion, including all griefs, sorrows, fears, doubts, hopes, cares, and perplexities.

While making room for the expression of all affections and states of mind in prayer, Calvin teaches that all such experiences must be carefully regulated. He is especially critical of "clamoring and complaining" against God.[51] As De Jong points out, "Calvin was most comfortable with a spirituality that included a wide variety of emotions expressed in moderation."[52] De Jong continues: "The most effective regulation in Calvin's estimation is to relate our joy to God's fatherly love and our grief to his possible anger with us." Centered in the Christian's participation in the cross and resurrection of Christ by the power of the Spirit, Calvin's theology of prayer attempts to hold in tension the contrary affections of joy and sorrow, faith and doubt. Calvin thinks it is fitting that "prayer arise from these two emotions, that it also contain and represent both. That is, that [we] groan under present ills and anxiously fear those to come, yet at the same time take refuge in God, not at all doubting [God] is ready to extend [a] helping hand."[53]

According to Calvin, the psalms "principally teach and train us to bear the cross . . . by doing this, we renounce the guidance of our own affections, and submit ourselves entirely to God."[54] In his commentaries on the lament psalms, Calvin shows sensitivity to what he takes to be the actual historical context in which they were composed. He does not follow Augustine's allegorical method. Instead, like Luther, Calvin finds many parallels between David's struggles and his own. Calvin especially underscores the conflicting affections that are so evident in the psalms.

Calvin's reading of Psalm 137 shows both his attention to historical context and his emphasis upon the copresence of lament and hope in the psalms. "There was danger that the Jews when cast off in such a melancholy manner should lose hold altogether of their faith and of their religion. . . . The people of the Lord might be thrown into despondency . . . by their captivity, the cruel bondage they were subjected to, and the other indignities which they had to endure. The writer of this psalm, whose name is unknown, drew up a form of lamentation, that by giving expression to their sufferings in sighs and prayers, they might keep alive the hope of that deliverance which they despaired of."[55] Remarkable here is Calvin's insight that lament is a way of keeping hope alive. Writing on Psalm 13, Calvin notes that the psalmist rises above his complaint of being neglected by God and in faith is able to apprehend God's invisible providence. As Calvin judges, David has thus beautifully united in his psalm "affections which are apparently contrary to each other." By asking not simply how long God will be hidden to him but whether this hiddenness will last "forever," the psalmist holds on to hope and gives us an example of the "exercise of patience."[56]

Calvin's exposition of Psalm 22 makes much the same point. He does not deny that both the psalmist and the Christian who read and pray this psalm voice real doubt and an acute sense of abandonment by God. But he underscores the fact that the cry of abandonment begins with the twice repeated address, "My God, my God." In Calvin's view, this shows that a "spark of faith" is present even in the believer's experience of God's apparent absence and indifference. Calvin thus both recognizes the legitimacy of lament in prayer and establishes boundaries for it. The psalmist and others in affliction are permitted to express their intense feelings of doubt and abandonment but not without limit. Grief and anger, while permissible, must not become "murmuring" against God. The cry of lament must remain within the context of submission to God's will.

Commenting on Psalm 88, Calvin is obviously disturbed by what he takes to be an excessive outcry of lament. When the psalmist cries that he is "forgotten of God and cut off from his hand," Calvin recoils. Such words, he says, are "harsh and improper," they are "ill advised," they erupt from the psalmist's "paroxysm" of grief. Overwhelmed by his sorrow, the psalmist is "stunned and stupefied." Yet even in despondency, the psalmist calls God "the God of my salvation," and in this form of address Calvin finds the presence of a spark of faith.[57]

Providence and Patience

While there are important similarities between the readings of the lament psalms by Augustine, Luther, and Calvin, the differences are also evident. Undergirding all that Calvin says about lament is his belief in God's providential care. God is the sovereign ruler of all creation, and the lives of all creatures are in God's hands.

A corollary to this belief is the call to humility and patience in face of all adversity. Since for Calvin nothing happens by chance and everything is governed by the providence of God, all adversities proceed from the divine hand. All things are governed by God's secret plan in such a way that "nothing happens except what is knowingly and willingly decreed by [God]."[58] When calamity befalls us, we must recognize that we stand under God's judgment and must submit to the will of God who governs all things. Calvin's reading of the book of Job comes to the same conclusion. As Susan Schreiner explains, Calvin sees Job in a kind of "perceptual agony." "Confronted with the disorder of history, the mind's eye squints and strains to see divine justice but cannot penetrate or transcend the present confusion which hides providence from its limited and fallen view. Calvin finds the heuristic key to the book of Job in 1 Cor. 13:12 ['Now we see in a mirror, dimly']. He repeatedly cites this verse to describe the difficulty of perceiving providence in the midst of history."[59]

Calvin describes Job as essentially in the right, but also as culpable for losing his temper and employing excessive and terrible language.[60] Calvin's insistence upon regulation and moderation in the expression of lament fits with the concern for order that pervades his theology. In Calvin's view, order pervades the world God has created, and this order is construed in hierarchical terms. As William Bouwsma notes, order meant for Calvin "the control of lower entities by higher . . . the mind should control all lower faculties . . . people should be controlled by rulers, women by men, and children by parents. God, of course, controls everything."[61] Calvin's theology of order, his wariness about immoderate expressions of grief, and his subordination of women to men are interlocked. Again quoting De Jong, for Calvin Christian prayer gathers up "a series of contrary affections that are to be controlled and channeled under the rule of God's Word."[62] Calvin thus counsels patience, avoidance of all murmuring and debating with God, and moderation in the expression of sorrow. "Gratitude of mind for the favorable outcome of things, patience in adversity, and also incredible freedom from worry about the future all necessarily follow from this knowledge [of divine providence]."[63] Thus humility, patience, and moderation are the virtues that Calvin commends to the afflicted. "All who compose themselves to this moderation will not murmur against God on account of their adversities in time past, nor lay the blame for their own wickedness upon him as did the Homeric Agamemnon, saying: 'I am not the cause but Zeus and fate.'"[64]

Calvin's theological emphasis, and the piety to which it gives rise, charts a distinctive way of dealing with experiences of grief and loss in Christian life. Whereas for Augustine we should not be so deeply attached to persons and things in this life that their loss would cause us to grieve excessively, and whereas for Luther the experiences of doubt and abandonment are inextricably bound to the proclamation of God's grace, for Calvin we should always be ready to confess our sins and manifest patience in suffering, showing moderation in expressions of sorrow because to do otherwise would be to doubt the fatherly governance of God. When adversity strikes us, God is either punishing us for our sins or purifying us for closer communion with God. Hence we must never dare to "murmur" against God. Given their distinctive emphases in theology and piety, Augustine, Luther, and Calvin make room in different ways for the prayer of lament even as they show various degrees of ambivalence and suspicion toward it.

BARTH AND THE PIETY OF GOD'S VICTORY IN CHRIST

Karl Barth must be included in any study of the ways influential Christian theologians have interpreted the lament prayers of the Bible and their place in Christian life and worship. More than any modern Protestant theologian, Barth gave serious attention to the topic of prayer and, like Anselm, stressed the indispensability of prayer in theological inquiry. Barth was in the deepest sense a biblical theologian who was concerned not so much for an abstract "system" of Christian doctrine as for faithfulness to the biblical witness in all its richness and diversity.[65]

Barth's Theology of Prayer

Barth understands prayer as centrally petition.[66] Although he recognizes that prayer has many dimensions, including adoration, thanksgiving, praise, and confession, he insists that the center of prayer is asking, requesting, petitioning God.

In prayer, Barth argues, human beings are permitted and commanded to come to God freely with their desires and requests. Prayer must not become an occasion of self-camouflage or a hiding of ourselves from God. We are not to come to God in prayer pretending to be other than who we are. Our petitions will reflect our full humanity in all our limitations and sinfulness; they will include all of our anxiety, passion, and egoism.

At the same time, Barth maintains that our petitions to God must not be arbitrary or undisciplined. Whimsical prayers or prayers directly contrary to the revealed will of God would not be genuinely Christian prayers. Prayer for Barth is a participation in the praying of Jesus Christ. Barth's theology of prayer, like the rest of his theology, is radically Christocentric. When Christians pray to God in the name of Christ, their asking is enclosed in his asking; their petition is a "repetition of his petition."[67] According to Barth, the basis of prayer is the will of God, realized in Jesus Christ, that human creatures may become in him free covenant partners of God.

For Barth, the God to whom we pray in the name of Jesus Christ is not the God depicted by what he calls the "miserable anthropomorphism" of divine immutability.[68] In contrast to Schleiermacher, whose fundamental assumption is that "there can be no relation of interaction between creature and Creator,"[69] Barth summons Christian theology to give up "the hallucination of a divine immutability which rules out the possibility that God can let [Godself] be conditioned in this or that way by [the] creature."[70] Just as the triune God lives in the eternal community of Father, Son, and Holy Spirit, so God elects to live and act in community *ad extra*. As the living God, God is free to converse with the creature and "to allow [Godself] to be determined in this relationship."[71] In sum, God wills a covenant relationship with human beings that involves "real co-operation," and the paradigmatic instance of this cooperation is the act of prayer. The invitation to pray is interpreted by Barth as an invitation to new freedom: the God of free grace chooses to be vulnerable by willing the human creature to relate to God as a free subject and active partner of God.

Unmistakable evidence of Barth's freedom from every axiom of divine immutability and impassibility is his recognition of a measure of truth in the teaching of the early Patripassians. "It is not at all the case that God has no part in the suffering of Jesus Christ even in [the] mode of being as the Father. No, there is a *particula veri* in the teaching of the early Patripassians. This is that primarily it is God the Father who suffers in the offering and sending of [the] Son, in his abasement."[72] This is an anticipation of the theme later developed by Moltmann that the experience of grief and loss belongs to the innermost being of God.

Barth's Christocentric Interpretation of Lament

Barth was one of the most prolific of modern theological expositors of scripture. In addition to commentaries on Romans, First Corinthians, and Philippians, and hundreds of sermons based on scriptural texts, Barth wrote extensively on many passages of scripture in the *Church Dogmatics*. Among these passages are the first two chapters of Genesis, numerous Old Testament narratives, the book of Job, the prologue of the Gospel of John, the Christ-Adam typology in Romans 5, the parables of Jesus, the Lord's Prayer, and the narratives of the Gospels. Unlike Augustine, Luther, and Calvin, however, Barth did not write extensively on the psalms. He does, of course, cite many individual verses of the psalms in the *Church Dogmatics,* including verses from the psalms of lament. Psalm 22:1 in particular is quoted with great frequency by Barth. On the other hand, it is surprising that Barth does not mention a psalm of lament like Psalm 137 even in his extensive treatment in *Church Dogmatics* II/2 of the relationship of church and Israel as the two forms of the one people of God.

Barth's understanding of the place and limit of lament in Christian life and prayer has its setting in the larger context of his theology of prayer outlined above. According to Barth, all lament arises basically from the recognition of human mortality and especially the threat of separation from God. Barth sees the biblical laments that are found in Lamentations, Psalms, and above all the book of Job as unsurpassed descriptions of extreme human misery. According to Barth, these various descriptions of utmost distress in which persons cry aloud to God expose the fact that humanity is powerless before the forces of death and destruction. All that human beings can do is to "cry and sob helplessly."[73] There can be no doubt that Barth sees lament as an altogether appropriate and accurate response to the human situation.

As already noted, Barth's theology is radically Christocentric. This means that he understands experiences of sorrow and loss consistently within a Christocentric horizon. A look at his exegesis of three biblical texts will demonstrate how thoroughly Christocentric his interpretation of the texts of lament is.

For a full exposition of a psalm of lament by Barth we must turn to one of his sermons.[74] Preaching on Psalm 3, Barth first reminds his congregation that the superscript of this psalm identifies it as a psalm of David written when he was fleeing for his life from his son Absalom. Recalling the sin that David had committed with Bathsheba and his plotting of the murder of Uriah, Barth emphasizes that in this psalm David surprisingly makes no confession of his sins but instead calls upon God as if God were David's best friend, who will surely support and protect him. David speaks this way, Barth says, because he looks not to himself but to God's promise, which, though dimmed by David's sins, is not taken away from him. It is because of God's fidelity that David can be so confident, joyful, and certain of victory. Although under terrible attack, David is not overcome. That is due not to David's own courage, strength, or righteousness but to the one to whom he looks, the one who is far greater than David's sins or righteousness, the one who has taken our humanity and all our sin and misery upon himself. "Beyond David and beyond us is the lordship of the sinless Son of God, who has taken upon himself the attack of hell in all its bitterness and has overcome it."[75]

According to Barth, David's trust in God is compressed in his simple cry, "O Lord!" Barth states, "My friends, as long as this 'O Lord' rushes out of the heart and mouth of a human being, everything is all right."[76] Characteristically, Barth adds that it is in the power of Jesus' trust in God that David and we are able to trust. Of what value would the prayer of David the sinner and the prayers of us sinners be if they were not taken up in Jesus' prayer on our behalf? It is not David or we who are victors and full of hope; rather, "Jesus Christ is victor. Jesus Christ is the hope. The victor and the hope also for us. For us he is yesterday, today and forever the same. And in the community of his lordship the great sinner David, and you and I, may stand as victor, as those who hope, not from our own power but from the power from on high which is given to us in him for all time and eternity."[77]

A second example of Barth's Christocentric interpretation of biblical lament is his commentary on the book of Job.[78] For Barth, Job is a witness to the grace of God and thus indirectly a witness to Jesus Christ. Job is a free human being who speaks in anguish to the free God because God is now experienced as deeply hidden. The defenders of God in the book of Job know only the "ignominious dependence and total unfreedom" of a relationship with God based on the idea that God always rewards the good and punishes the wicked. Hence they are shocked by Job's protestations of his innocence. Barth is far more critical of the friends of Job than is Calvin. Whereas Calvin thinks that the friends of Job, even if wrong in their attack on him, nevertheless say many good and proper things about God, Barth describes the speeches of the friends as being like "cut flowers." Barth sees Job and God engaged in a history of freedom in which Job freely cries out because he does not apprehend the presence of God anymore, and God in God's own distinctive freedom listens as well as speaks, and in the end declares that Job has spoken what was right.

Barth's commentary on Job is found in the last volume of the *Church Dogmatics,* and it is possible that his vigorous defense of Job's freedom to grieve and protest represents an advance on the theology of lament found in earlier volumes. In any case, Barth's exposition clearly emphasizes the legitimacy of Job's lament and questions to God, and it is worth asking whether his theology of prayer as a whole might not have to be importantly qualified if the prayer of lament and protest that he finds in the book of Job were to be given its proper due. Is not the depth of the dialogue between the God of the covenant and God's chosen covenant partner found precisely in the freedom of the covenant partner to challenge, question, and even argue with God in face of the power of evil, the inscrutability of providence, and the still unrealized promises of God?[79]

Central among Barth's references to the lament tradition of the Bible is, of course, Jesus' cry of abandonment on the cross (Mark 15:34). While acknowledging the reality of human suffering and affliction, and while emphasizing the freedom of the covenant partner to cry out honestly to the free God of the covenant, Barth is most concerned to make the point that Christians are not to invest their pain with the weight of "divine pain."[80] This he does repeatedly by calling attention to the significance of Jesus' cry of abandonment on the cross. "As God is far greater than we his creatures, so much greater is [God's] sorrow on our behalf than any sorrow which we can feel for ourselves."[81] Of Jesus' experience of forsakenness, Barth writes: "In the end [he] was absolutely alone in the world, even to the point of asking (Mk. 15:34) whether [even] God . . . , and God especially, had not forsaken [him]. He could not enter more radically than [he] did into the isolation of God in this world, or fulfil more basically [his] agreement with [God] in this respect."[82] Jesus could not see through the darkness he experienced, but simply had to traverse the darkness as though journeying through a tunnel.[83]

Thus Barth's chief emphasis in his discussion of the place of lament in Christian life is that Jesus Christ the incarnate Word of God has plumbed the depth of human misery, and hence his misery encompasses and transcends the misery of all others. "No [one] but Jesus has ever known the true breadth and depth, the true essence and darkness, of human misery. What we see and note and know and more or less painfully experience of it is only the shadow of his cross touching us."[84] Our misery can be no more than a "distant recollection" of his, our cry only a "weak echo" of his cry. "However severely we may be buffeted, there can be no question of repetitions of Golgotha. Not merely quantitatively, but qualitatively, all the content of our experience is completely transcended by Golgotha."[85]

Perhaps the most moving expression of Barth's Christocentric approach to the reality of sorrow and loss is the sermon he delivered at the funeral service for his own son Matthias, who had been killed in a mountain climbing accident a few days earlier.[86] In the sermon itself, as well as in the prayer that precedes it, Barth does not hide his, or his family's, grief and loss, but he sees their sorrow as already fundamentally overcome by the victory of Jesus over sin and death.

Barth takes as his text 1 Corinthians 13:12: "We see now in a mirror dimly, but then face to face." He chose this text because it was apparently the first biblical verse to have made a serious impression on Matthias. As we have seen, it also happens to be the text that, in Calvin's view, provides the best hermeneutical key to the book of Job. Barth tells the gathered mourners that all human life is lived on the boundary described by the words of this text: the boundary between the "now" of our partial and distorted knowledge and the "then," when we will know even as we are known. However, because of the grace of God realized in the cross and resurrection of Jesus Christ, this boundary between the "now" and the "then" is one where the light already shines in darkness, where life already rejoices in face of death, "where we doubt and nevertheless are confident, where we cry and nevertheless are joyful."[87]

Freely acknowledging his own and his family's "bitter hours and days of inner leave taking," Barth speaks of the pain of guilt feelings and the passionate wishes "to be able at least once again to take him by the hand, as he liked so much, and to be able once again to say a good word to him."[88] But for Barth such questions and wishes are helpless before the great mystery of death. He recalls the story of David's loss of his son (2 Sam. 12), and David's decision to cease fasting and crying when he received the news that his son was dead. David would have to be called a heartless father, Barth says, if Jesus Christ had not been raised from the dead. But the riddle of the suffering of the Son of God on Good Friday, whose horrors and pain cannot be compared with what we have to endure, has been solved by Easter. "Now Jesus lives and reigns and triumphs."[89] Because this is so, while death still has awful and painful power, we no longer have to respect it with questions and complaints, with crying and fasting. We are permitted to groan and cry, but in our sorrow we do not only sorrow. Even if we cannot just now ourselves rejoice, we can hear "a very different voice" rejoice even over the mountain place where Matthias died and even over the grave where he was laid. "What else can we who hear this voice do than thank our God—even through our tears—that [God] has meant and done well with our Matthias in his life and in his death?"[90]

The Dialectic of Barth's Theology of Lament

As can be seen, especially in his funeral sermon for his son, Barth's understanding of the place of lament in Christian life is highly dialectical. He recognizes the pain of grief and loss. He does not try to hide or suppress these responses to separation and death; they are natural and appropriate. Yet for him, as for the biblical witnesses, the cry of loss and abandonment is not the last or the most powerful word; it is encompassed by a stronger word of confidence and hope that is grounded in the death and resurrection of Jesus Christ. Because of what God has accomplished in Jesus Christ, all of our sorrows and losses are already fundamentally behind us.

There is a striking consistency between what Barth says in his sermons, including the funeral sermon for his son, and what he says in his reflections on lament in the *Church Dogmatics:* "When we realize the full depth of our sorrow as it is seen and borne and suffered by God . . . , any complaint of ours as to the form in which it confronts and affects us is silenced. Our lamenting comes too late and is always relatively too weak. . . . What is the use of our lamenting when the heart of our misery is that we are sinners and debtors to God, in face of whom we cannot do anything to make good? Who can complain when God has to complain, when the right to complain is [God's] right alone?"[91] In Jesus Christ, God alone bears pain and suffering to its depths. Such pain and suffering as the Son of God has borne cannot touch us as it has touched him. Thus, "in the bearing of our pain, we must be modest and unassuming, as also in our lamentation and protests against it."[92]

According to Barth, then, since Jesus has cried and suffered on our behalf, whatever pain, suffering, and injustice we might experience can no longer deeply hurt us. In the history of this person in whom God and humanity are united the cup of sorrow and affliction has been drunk to the dregs. As our representative, Jesus Christ has gone to the depths of human misery. In his cross and resurrection the grace of God has proved triumphant over all sin, suffering, and death. Confident of the victory of God's grace in Jesus Christ, Barth insists that we must observe limits in our lamentations and, like David the mourner, move forward with confidence in God's sovereign goodness. Whereas Augustine's restrictions on the lament prayer arise from his anthropology of desire according to which human longing must be freed from worldly attachments and directed to God alone; and whereas Calvin's limitations on lament flow from his doctrine of divine providence and the corresponding piety of patience and moderation in sorrow; Barth's boundaries of lament derive from his understanding of the victory of God's grace in Jesus Christ over all sin, suffering, and death.   *Luther?*

While Barth's theology of "Jesus is victor!" is unquestionably a powerful retrieval of the New Testament message, it is not without its dangers. As numerous critics of Barth have noted, one danger that attends his theology is that in his way of emphasizing the completeness of the victory already won in Christ, the very distinction that the apostle Paul makes in 1 Corinthians 13:12 between the "now" and the "then" tends to disappear. We do not think Barth loses sight of the distance between the "now" and the "then" in his funeral sermon for his son since there the dialectic of grief and joy, death and life, despair and hope, are movingly expressed. Certainly Barth's recognition of the continuing power of sin and evil in the world, and the need for prophetic indictment of injustice and violence, was abundantly displayed in his leadership in the German church struggle.

However, the danger of minimizing human misery by comparing it with the depth of the suffering of Christ and the victory of his resurrection is apparent in a little story of Barth's ministry to a woman in pain that he tells with characteristic candor and self-critical humor.

> What odd creatures we are! We talk about our anxieties, they make us miserable, yet when the great dispensation is announced and we are told not to be anxious, then it becomes evident how much we appreciate, even treasure and nurture our worries and our own self in them. I shall never forget the phone call I once received from a good old friend of mine who dished out her complaints. She was suffering from asthma and depressions and I tried to comfort her with an old nursery rhyme:
>
> The good Lord thought of me today, he gave me lots of fun,
> He watches me and blesses me: my place is in the sun.

She interrupted most violently. "No, the Lord did not think of me; no, I did not have lots of fun!" Her troubles were too dear to her heart, and she refused to get rid of them. It is, of course, also quite possible that I failed to convey to her the right word of comfort.[93]

MOLTMANN AND THE PIETY OF GOD'S SUFFERING LOVE

Jürgen Moltmann is a leader among twentieth-century theologians who have made the theme of the "suffering God" central to their theology. This theme has roots in Moltmann's own personal experience as well as in his wrestling with the biblical tradition and the doctrinal heritage of the church.

The Beginning of Moltmann's Theology

Moltmann's faith struggle began as a young German soldier caught in the middle of a firestorm in Hamburg that had been ignited by a bombing raid of the British Royal Air Force. "That night I cried out to God for the first time: 'My God, where are you?' And the question 'Why am I not dead too?' has haunted me ever since. Why are you alive? What gives your life meaning? Life is good, but to be a survivor is hard. One has to bear the weight of grief. It was probably in that night that my theology began, for I came from a secular family and knew nothing of faith."[94]

After being taken prisoner and sent to the Norton prisoner-of-war camp in Scotland, Moltmann was given a Bible and began to read it. "I read it without much comprehension, until I stumbled on the psalms of lament. . . . They were the words of my own heart and they called my soul to God. Then I came to the story of the passion, and when I read Jesus' death cry, 'My God, why have you forsaken me?' I knew with certainty: this is someone who understands you. I began to understand the assailed Christ because I felt that he understood me: this was the divine brother in distress, who takes the prisoners with him on his way to resurrection. I began to summon up the courage to live again, seized by a great hope."[95]

Moltmann's story of his own faith journey remarkably began with an encounter with the lament psalms and the great lament of Christ on the cross. His participation in this powerful tradition of biblical lament opened the way to new life and new hope for him. When his grief was given voice and when he received the promise of God who grieved with and for the victims of the war, and also for him, he was set on a course that would eventually lead to the ability to join the praise of the psalmist: "God, you have turned my mourning into dancing" (Ps. 30:11).

Critique of Divine Impassibility

A major influence on Moltmann are the writings of Dietrich Bonhoeffer, whose provocative letters from prison declared that in a world of so much tragedy, violence, and abuse of power, "only a suffering God can help." In all of his writings Moltmann vigorously contests the traditional doctrines of the immutability and impassibility of God. "You hear people saying: 'God cannot suffer.' 'God can never die.' 'God has no needs.' 'God needs no friends.' Even Christians say things like that—and thereby make of the living God a dead idol, an idol constructed from their own anxiety about life."[96] For Moltmann, love and immutability are incompatible. If God loves another, then God is vulnerable to the other. The God of the biblical witness is just such a God, a passionate God who freely becomes vulnerable to suffering out of love for the world. Moltmann draws upon the writings of Abraham Heschel and the Jewish tradition generally in support of his theology of the divine pathos.

Correlative to Moltmann's critique of the passionless God is his critique of the spirit of apathy that has increasingly come to dominate Western culture. Apathy is the attitude of indifference and hopelessness in face of suffering and evil in the world. The apathetic person or society gives up hoping and working for a new world of peace and justice and instead says nothing will ever change, things will always be the same. "If we were to live in a covenant with [the] passionate God, we would not become apathetic. Our whole life would be shaped by sympathy, by compassion. We would suffer with God's suffering in the world, and rejoice with God's rejoicing over the world. We would do both at the same time and with the highest intensity because we would love, and with the love of God we would go outside ourselves."[97]

Already in his first widely read book, *The Theology of Hope,* Moltmann attacks the spirit of apathy and resignation in the name of Christian hope inspired by the gospel of Christ's resurrection from the dead. "Those who hope in Christ can no longer put up with reality as it is, but begin to suffer under it, to contradict it. Peace with God means conflict with the world, for the goad of the promised future stabs inexorably into the flesh of every unfulfilled present."[98]

Although a theology of the cross was presupposed by Moltmann's *Theology of Hope,* some of his readers understood his emphasis on resurrection hope to be advocating a cultural gospel of optimism. A correction and deepening of Moltmann's work came with *The Crucified God,* in which he developed a powerful theology of the cross that centered on Jesus' cry of abandonment from the cross. "Basically, every Christian theology is consciously or unconsciously answering the question, 'Why hast thou forsaken me?'"[99] "The God-forsaken cry with which Christ dies on the cross [is] the criterion for all theology which claims to be Christian."[100]

Surprisingly, while Moltmann places great emphasis on the death cry of Jesus that echoes Psalm 22:1, he does not explore in depth the lament tradition in which this psalm and Jesus' use of it stands. Nevertheless, Moltmann's concentration on Psalm 22 is intense. He sees important differences between the cry of the psalmist and the cry of Jesus. "Unlike the speaker in Ps. 22, Jesus is not just making a claim upon the faithfulness of the God of Israel, as he had promised to the whole people; in a special way he is laying claim upon the faithfulness of his Father to himself."[101] At the same time, there is a deep agreement between the psalmist and Jesus. The psalm is a legal plea—the faithfulness, honor, and hence the very deity of God are at stake.

Stated provocatively: the words of Psalm 22 on the lips of Jesus mean not only "My God, why have you forsaken me?" but more daringly, "My God, why have you forsaken *yourself?*"[102]

A Trinitarian Theology of Lament

Moltmann's most original contribution is not his critique of divine impassibility in general—a theme of many theologians—but his pursuit of the question, "Is there an inner logical connection between the two special features of Christianity, faith in the crucified Jesus and in the triune God?"[103] Moltmann's answer to this question is a theology of "the infinite grief of love" developed in trinitarian terms. "To understand what happened between Jesus and his God and Father on the cross, it is necessary to talk in trinitarian terms. The Son suffers dying, the Father suffers the death of the Son. The grief of the Father here is just as important as the death of the Son."[104] According to Moltmann, the transforming Spirit of God issues from the self-giving love of the Father and the Son. Moltmann's trinitarian theology of the suffering love of God underscores the claim that loss, grief, and the feeling of abandonment are not just experiences of humanity in general or of Jesus in particular but are a defining moment of the experience of the triune God.

Moltmann contends that as God is revealed in the Gospel narrative and above all in the passion and death of Jesus Christ, the seeds of Trinity doctrine are present. The God of the Gospels is no self-enclosed individual but a Trinity of persons who indwell each other and live in mutual self-giving love. This communion of trinitarian love in which persons are identified by their mutual giving and receiving is actualized for us in the life and death of the incarnate God. By the power of the Spirit we are bound to Christ and to each other and welcomed into the communion of the triune God.

According to Moltmann, human beings develop their humanity in relation to their understandings and images of God. He calls Christians to give up ideas of Christian faith that envision God as the solitary self and the domineering father. Such images of God inevitably evoke the oedipal reaction of parricide in a desperate grasp for freedom. Christian faith rooted in a trinitarian theology of the cross calls for "the development of humanity that is capable of suffering and love in the situation of the passion of God."[105] A corollary for Christian political responsibility follows. Liberated by the gospel, Christians are called to struggle against the vicious cycles of death and violence in political and social life and to expose idolatrous systems of domination, whether political, economic, familial, cultural, or ecclesiastical.

Moltmann's retrieval of classical trinitarian doctrine and his rethinking of it in the light of a theology of the cross offers still not fully explored possibilities for the development of a theological understanding of the place of lament in Christian faith and life.

LIBERATION THEOLOGIES AND THE PIETY OF RESISTANCE

Recent liberation theologies arising out of many different contexts of suffering also offer new possibilities of understanding the meaning and importance of the lament prayer in Christian life and worship. Gustavo Gutiérrez writes on Job, James Cone on the spirituals and the blues in the African American tradition, Delores Williams on the biblical stories of Hagar, Phyllis Trible on biblical texts of terror, and Chung Hyun Kyung and other Korean women on the experience of *han* or pent-up rage in oppressed persons and communities.

Feminist and Womanist Theologies

In this section we will focus on a few feminist and womanist theologians as representative of the contributions liberation theologians are making to an understanding of suffering, loss, and grief within a Christian theological perspective. Among the principal emphases of feminist and womanist theologians has been their refusal to baptize all suffering as God's will. Instead of teaching that all suffering must be passively accepted, feminists and womanists insist that there are different sources and contexts of suffering, and it is imperative to struggle against suffering that arises from unjust and abusive patterns of life and relationship. In this context, the lament prayer can be seen as an act of resistance to evil and thus takes on a dimension often missed by many theologians past and present.

That's good stuff.

Feminist and womanist theologies privilege experiences of suffering by women in diverse contexts. In the light of these experiences the Bible is reread and the Christian theological tradition is reexamined. Elizabeth Johnson identifies four kinds of travail known to many women that require both a more differentiated way of speaking of suffering and new ways of thinking and speaking about God's participation in the pain of the world. According to Johnson, many women know from personal experience the pain that attends labor and childbirth; they know well the suffering that often accompanies struggles against injustice and domination; they are familiar with the grief that attends the injury or loss of loved ones; and they know the physical and spiritual desolation that threatens human beings afflicted by radical evil.

For Johnson, the pain that attends childbirth is an acceptable part of the process of creative love. "In a way unique to half the human race, women labor in bearing and birthing each new generation, a suffering which can be woven round with a strong sense of creative power and joy."[106] The biblical witness sometimes speaks of the birth pangs God experiences in working to bring a new people into being.

Similarly, many women are prepared to endure the suffering that accompanies the choice to act in pursuit of healing, justice, and peace. The forces of sin and evil are both strong and entrenched; they are not overcome without sustained and sometimes fierce struggle. Again, in the biblical witness the love of God is depicted not in a sentimental manner but as a love capable of righteous wrath and a legitimate anger that resists and struggles against evil.

While loss and lament are by no means restricted to women's experience, women are especially vulnerable to the grief that attends loss of loved ones by virtue of the relatively greater importance women assign to relationships. Johnson writes: "Women's relational way of being in the world typically creates in them a deep vulnerability to being rendered desolate when suffering visits those whom they love and care about."[107] "From Rachel weeping for her children to the mothers and grandmothers of the Argentinian Plaza de Mayo, we could not measure the pain of women occasioned by harm done to those they love."[108] According to the Bible, the God of Israel and the God made known in Jesus Christ is a relational God vulnerable to loss and capable of lament, not only for the elect people of Israel but for the whole suffering world.

Finally, there is the suffering that Simone Weil calls affliction, a suffering so deep and severe that it is capable of overwhelming and destroying the soul. "This is the suffering that does not come about because a woman has chosen to birth new life, or stand up for justice, or love someone. It is forced upon her by men, against her will, robbing her of everything, even life itself."[109] Johnson asks whether such experiences of suffering also offer a symbol of the suffering God. She answers that they do because "in an unspeakable way they are images of the crucified."[110]

Suffering and Divine Omnipotence

Feminist and womanist reflections on suffering point to the challenge of reshaping the doctrine of divine omnipotence. The power of God must be reconceived as different both from domination and control of others on the one hand, and from the reverse image of the helpless and powerless victim on the other. "What is needed," Johnson writes, "is to step decisively out of the androcentric system of power-over versus victimization and think in other categories about power, pain, and their deep interweaving in human experience."[111] The new shape of power that is seen both in the gospel story and in parabolic form in the diverse experiences of women is "a vitality, an empowering vigor that reaches out and awakens freedom and strength in oneself and others. It is an energy that brings forth, stirs up, and fosters life, enabling autonomy and friendship. It is a movement of spirit that builds, mends, struggles with and against, celebrates and laments. It transforms people, and bonds them with one another and to the world. Such dynamism is not the antithesis of love but is the shape of love against the forces of non-being and death. . . . Neither power-over nor powerlessness, it is akin to power-with."[112] Citing the work of Wendy Farley, Johnson speaks of the power of God as a compassion that resists tragic suffering. "Compassion is an empowering power, an efficacy, a blazing fierceness, rather than an interior emotion, and it has an efficacy for transformation."[113]

Womanist theologians, too, in partnership with feminist theologians but also showing significant differences from them, have underscored the theme of resistance to evil in their understandings of the experience of women of color and in their interpretations of the Bible. The very term "womanist"— the self-designation of women of color—refers to "audacious, courageous or willful behavior . . . Responsible. In charge. Serious."[114] In womanist history and theology special place is accorded to African American women who have struggled for the survival of their children, their communities, and themselves under the conditions of dehumanizing racist and sexist structures and behaviors.

A fundamental question for both feminist and womanist theology is whether there is an inherent conflict between their commitment to the well-being of women on the one hand and their loyalty to the Christian faith rooted in the Bible on the other. Clarice Martin has shown that at least for Maria Stewart, an African American woman of the nineteenth century, there was no such conflict. With the psalmist "Stewart exults in God's 'going down into the depths' for her and raising her up to a place of stability and safety."[115]

Feminist and Womanist Piety and the Biblical Prayer of Lament

The passion, courage, lament, indignation at injustice, resistance to evil, and confidence in God's purposes and activity that are present in feminist and womanist piety are remarkably akin to the spirit and emphases of the biblical lament tradition. Kathleen A. Farmer points out the special values of the psalms for the marginalized and the abused. She notes that psalms expressing acquiescence and nonresistance like Psalm 131 have often been presented as the only proper model of faith. As a result, the complexity and diversity of the experience of faith manifest in the psalms are obscured. "Those who speak with complete candor in the presence of God, those who articulate their doubts and their pain as well as their trust in God are all included among the faithful in the Psalms."[116]

Central to feminist and womanist piety is the theme of resistance to domination, abuse, and other evils. It is precisely this spirit of resistance that comes to powerful expression in the biblical prayer of lament. As Farmer writes: "Women who have been taught (like children) to be 'seen and not heard' in relation to faith and religion should notice that the very act of putting anger, impatience, and frustration into words often enables the speakers in the Psalms to come to a renewed sense of assurance in God's continuing care. The confessional stance of the psalmists (their willingness to articulate feelings of anger and pain as well as joy in the presence of God, their refusal to submit passively to oppressive circumstances, and their confidence in God's continuing concern for their needs) has had and continues to have a significant influence in shaping the theology, the piety, and the lives of many women."[117]

THE BLESSING AND BURDEN OF TRADITION

The great theological traditions in which Christians stand are both blessing and burden. That is apparent from the inheritance we have received from the classical theological traditions regarding the place of lament in Christian prayer. While most of us will find ourselves closer to one type of Christian theology and piety than to others, there is much that we can learn from the understanding and practice of prayer in Christian theologies and spiritualities different from our own.

Augustine reminds us that lament over sin is an important dimension of grieving in Christian life; Luther, that the experience of affliction is inescapable for those who rely on God's grace alone; Calvin, that the psalms and Christian prayer based on them hold together lament and praise in tensive balance; Barth, that the sorrow and grief of Christ encompasses all our sorrows and griefs. All of the classical Christian traditions of piety and prayer teach that Christ is our leader in prayer. A Christocentric reading of the psalms has a long and rich tradition, and this has provided a very distinctive way of interpreting many of the psalms of lament. This tradition has been especially important in guiding Christians in the interpretation and use of the imprecatory psalms.

Yet there are undeniable limitations in the classical perspectives we have reviewed. When the need for the correction and expansion of tradition is forgotten, the rich blessing of tradition is turned into a heavy burden for the life of faith. Contrary to Augustine, biblical lament includes more than lament on account of the sin of the lamenter. Again contrary to Augustine, we should not devalue our vulnerability to pain and loss because God has made us for communion, and the possibility of loss must be risked if love is to be ventured at all. Contrary to Luther and Calvin, we do not think it is wise to formulate the tensive relationship between lament and praise in terms of the control of the affections by reason or according to a principle of moderation. While agreeing with Barth and the classical Reformers that the crucified and risen Savior encompasses our sorrows and griefs, we are convinced this should not be understood in a manner that tends to minimize the reality and seriousness of creaturely afflictions this side of God's making all things new. Barth himself sometimes acknowledges this in a powerful way, as in his exposition of the drama of Job.

Theologians like Barth, Bonhoeffer, and Moltmann have led in the exploration of the meaning of the experience of suffering for God as well as for creatures. All would agree that divine suffering must not be sentimentalized. Liberation theologians in general and feminist and womanist theologians in particular have emphasized just this point: talk of the suffering God is easily misunderstood and sentimentalized if it is equated with mere passivity. Christians lament not only the abuse of power in the form of overt domination by some over others but also the less evident ways in which some people are deprived of voice, agency, and dignity.

God's new power is altogether different, life-transforming, empowering power. Despite all ambiguities and suspicions, it is, we believe, the deepest intent of the Christian theological tradition, and a central concern of Christian feminist/womanist theology, to make room in prayer and practice for passionate yearning for God's healing and reconciling power, for mourning the loss of love, for nonviolent resistance to the powers of evil, and for the celebration of signs of new life in the midst of death. Until the glory of God fills the universe, it is only in conjunction with lament and resistance that the praise of God can be truly vital and joyous. It is along this trajectory that our own theology of the prayer of lament will move. But before taking up that task, we will draw help from what recent pastoral theology has said about the meaning and value of the prayer of lament.

Summary of Augustine p 50
Luther — Grace of God only consolation.
*   Affliction accompanies all genuine faith*
Luther, Calvin, Augustine p 60
Augustine, Calvin, Barth p 66
Moltmann p 69
Women p 70

CHAPTER FOUR

THE PRAYER OF LAMENT IN RECENT PASTORAL THEOLOGY

The Rev. merely closes his eyes and trusts when he runs smack into a thorn bush. I have given up on speech with the Rev.; there is no use explaining that you have to learn where your pain is.

And what came to me were words from the Bible: "As the hart panteth after the water brooks, so panteth my soul after thee, O God. My tears have been my meat day and night, while they continually say unto me, 'Where is thy God?' I heard the phrase and all of me wanted to call out in a song, a song that doesn't have words, a song that almost doesn't have noise."

—*Jane Hamilton,* The Book of Ruth

Most ministers we have known are passionately concerned about being helpful to suffering people. They don't want suffering people to say, like the bruised and broken Ruth in Jane Hamilton's novel *The Book of Ruth,* "I have given up on speech with the Rev." They want to help people call out in a song, a song voiced to the God who gives water brooks to those parched with thirst. Ministers are concerned about lament because they frequently encounter the tears, protests, and questions of suffering people.

Theological reflection on the efforts of Christian ministers to assist people in distress is as old as the church,[1] but has taken some new turns with the emergence of the social sciences. Since the 1940s, the term "pastoral theology" has come to represent theological reflection on the caring ministries of the church, a reflection that has included serious dialogue with the social sciences.[2]

We studied several texts in pastoral care written by widely known pastoral theologians over the past forty years in order to explore two questions: What insights about the relationship between lament and hope have contemporary ministers received from pastoral care literature? What use have pastoral theologians made of the biblical lament tradition, particularly the prayer of lament?

In pursuing these questions, first we will discuss works in pastoral care that explore ministry with persons experiencing depression and grief. We find several points of consensus in this literature about the relationship between lament and hope, and several significant uses of the lament tradition. Most of these works focus on care with suffering *individuals*. Grief, for example, is presented as a universal phenomenon, and the authors explore how understanding the *dynamics* of grief can contribute to ministry that fosters movement from grief to hope.

Next we will examine some very recent works in pastoral theology that take as a point of departure the suffering that occurs in a variety of *social contexts*. In this literature, the relationship between lament and hope remains a central concern and some of these works also make explicit use of the lament tradition, particularly the lament prayer. However, in these works the focus shifts from universality to particularity, and is committed to addressing the challenges and opportunities of pastoral ministry when it takes place in socially marginalized communities.

Through the exploration of these texts we hope to trace the journey of the prayer of lament in modern and postmodern pastoral theology and to state its implications for our own constructive work.

BIBLICAL LAMENTS AND MINISTRY WITH PERSONS SUFFERING FROM DEPRESSION AND GRIEF

By far the most thorough treatments of the biblical laments in pastoral theology are to be found in texts on pastoral care and counseling with grieving persons. To a lesser extent, they are found in works on ministry with those suffering from depression.[3] In both cases the authors are convinced of a deep relationship between lament and hope.

In *The Presence of God in Pastoral Counseling*, Wayne Oates draws upon the psalms as a resource for describing the experience of what St. John of the Cross called the "dark night of the soul." Oates draws especially from Psalms 88, 109, and 139 in describing three features of this experience: the captivity of the person to what John Bunyan called the "Iron Cage of Despair"; the rage of the person at his or her enemies, which involves the feeling of abandonment and estrangement; and the felt presence of God in the darkness, even though God does not seem to hear or heed the prayers of the suffering.[4]

Oates contends that Psalm 88 describes the clinical condition of a person in a profound depression, who feels trapped in a darkness that is inescapable, abandoned by friend and lover.[5] The author of Psalm 109 rages at enemies, and in so doing is able to "break out of the trappedness" of this rage by expressing it to God directly.[6] "Psalm 139 captures the darkness itself and affirms it as part of the awesome mystery of the Presence of God."[7]

Oates goes on to describe how pastoral counseling with depressed persons necessitates an admission of the counselor's own anxieties, fears, and shortcomings; the capacity to listen and observe with prayerful, sustained, and fearless attention; the commitment to accept the sufferer with unconditional love; the ability to take bad behavior as part of the sufferer's total disturbance and not judge him or her harshly; the capacity to believe in the fundamental integrity of the sufferer; and the capacity to entrust the life of the depressed and the counselor's own life into the hands of God.[8] The art of pastoral counseling at the stage of rage involves the ability to enable persons to locate and put into words before God the precise target of their rage.[9] Pastoral counseling is "at its best in cultivating and enhancing the sense of wonder and expectancy of light as people sit in darkness."[10]

In *Pastoral Care and Counseling,* William Hulme states that the psalms are helpful because "they express the gamut of human emotions."[11] Particularly poignant is his description of how "their identification with despondency forms a bridge to hope."[12] Late in his own life and career, Hulme suffered an episode of depression so severe that he almost died in its grip. Writing about that experience, Hulme speaks of the significance of the laments for people in the throes of deep depression. Like Oates, Hulme understands Psalm 88 to be the cry of someone who is suffering from depression. But the dialogical nature of the psalm is healthy, Hulme maintains. It is a contrast to the kind of "introverted monologue" in which depressed people frequently engage. Intuitively, the psalmist believes that God understands. Amidst depression, the psalmist carries on a "lover's quarrel with God, which is a healthy antidepressant" for the sufferer.[13] Hulme cautions that the use of scripture in pastoral care and counseling with persons suffering from depression must be selective because they may read judgment even into good news. For example, suppose the minister reads texts that speak about the wonderful things God gives to those who love God, believe in God, and trust God. "The depressed person will immediately miss the good news and will instead question whether he or she really loves God, believes in God, or trusts God and will answer the question negatively. With the psalms this is much less likely to occur because conditions regarding God's favor are rarely given and the feelings that the depressed person knows all too well are expressed. It is easy then to go from the psalms into prayer."[14]

In *Shadows of the Heart,* James and Evelyn Whitehead note that much work in spirituality fails to address experiences of negativity, and their book offers a "spirituality of the negative emotions."[15] In their chapter on depression they point to the lament psalms and other lament passages, finding in these scriptures a way to "give pain a voice" and to voice that pain in the community. It is this bringing to voice in community that can bring new life.[16]

Two common convictions sounded in these works are that people are helped when they are encouraged, indeed given biblical authorization, to give voice to the full expression of their experience, and that there is a profound connection between healing and participation in the life and worship of a community of faith. It is not voicing pain in a vacuum that is healing, but voicing pain in concert with others. The psalms of lament offer a litany about depression that can be uttered in the community and shared by the community, thus reducing the pain of isolation so integral to the experience of deep depression.

As mentioned earlier, the primary locus of reference to the lament prayer in works of pastoral theology is pastoral care for the grieving. In William Arnold's *Introduction to Pastoral Care,* the author speaks of the psalms of lament as "one of the most helpful places to turn in the Bible for under-standing grief."[17] Echoing themes sounded in the literature on depression, Arnold finds help in the laments because, first, the excruciating misery of the suffering person or group is not denied but voiced, which gives contempo-rary mourners a sense of the normality and acceptability of their feelings; and second, the words are spoken to *another,* which deprivatizes the suffer-ing and ensures that the suffering is heard. In addition, Arnold speaks of the importance of remembering past mercies as a dimension of the psalms' help-fulness. There is a "rhythm" in the experience, in which voicing pain is linked to remembering God's past mercies. Memory serves as a healing resource in that writers recall God's previous helpfulness in difficult times.[18]

In *All Our Losses, All Our Griefs,* Kenneth Mitchell and Herbert Anderson are deeply appreciative of the contribution the lament tradition makes to those who grieve and those who care for the grieving. "Raging at God is a part of the Hebrew tradition," Mitchell and Anderson write. "The psalms of lament are filled with anger at God for God's absence and seeming disregard for the plight of God's people. Anger, especially as a part of grief, is not con-trary to faith or faithfulness, but an inescapable response to loss."[19] For Mitchell and Anderson, the lament psalms validate the mourner's grief and have the potential to strengthen a mourner's relationship with God by pro-moting full self-disclosure in bold trust—an act necessary for the fullness of a relationship to be realized.[20]

In a more recent essay on the grief of men,[21] Anderson regrets the "legacy of silence" about men's grief within the Christian tradition. He urges the recovery of the story and the laments of David as a gift to those who grieve. This legacy of a "a man of power who wept" is a "testimony to the possibil-ity of linking strength and vulnerability . . . It is particularly important for men to discover this resource from the heart of a strong king who wept."[22] Anderson concludes his essay with an appeal for men to learn from Jeremiah's call for mothers to teach their daughters to lament (Jer. 9:20). He urges men to teach their sons to lament.[23]

In "The Use of the Psalms in Grief Counseling," Donald Capps explores the implications of the lament psalm not only for validating the sufferer's feel-ings but also for structuring the process of grief work itself.[24] Drawing on the work of several biblical scholars, especially Walter Brueggemann and Bernhard

Anderson, Capps compares and contrasts the stage theory of Elisabeth Kübler-Ross (*On Death and Dying*) and the structure of the lament psalms.

Using the form of the lament psalm to guide the grief counseling process, Capps proposes that the process will include an implicit assumption that the conversation is addressed to God (address), the venting of negative feelings (complaint), a sense of being upheld (confession of trust), an expression of specific needs and desires (petition), an experience of support and relief from suffering (words of assurance), and the commencement of hope (vow to praise). Capps summarizes his argument: "I have wanted to show that the psalm of lament can guide this (counseling) process, helping it to move from complaint through petition to assurance and praise."[25]

The works of Eugene Peterson have frequently found their way into courses on pastoral care designed to help seminarians explore the relationship between biblical texts and pastoral ministry. Of particular importance for our study are two writings—a chapter entitled "The Pastoral Work of Pain-Sharing: Lamentations"[26] and his book *Answering God.*[27]

In "The Pastoral Work of Pain-Sharing: Lamentations," Peterson, like Capps, highlights the structural elements of lamentations that offer insight about care for the grieving. The book of Lamentations is written in the acrostic form, which "serves the needs of the anguished lament" because it ensures that grief and despair are expressed completely (grief is expressed from A to Z).

Thus the acrostic functions to give order to grief. It organizes grief, patiently going over the ground step by step, insisting on the significance of each detail of suffering. The pain is labeled—defined and objectified. Arranged in the acrostic structure the suffering no longer obsesses, no longer controls.[28]

After analyzing the way the acrostic functions to articulate suffering, Peterson describes ways that pastoral work accompanies and aids suffering people by honoring and encouraging the full expression of their pain, by offering structure, and by helping suffering individuals to discover the community of faith as a resource of support and solidarity.

In *Answering God,* Peterson's grounding conviction is that a "life of prayer forces us to deal with the reality of the world and of our own lives at a depth and with an honesty that is quite unheard of by the prayerless, and much of that reality we would certainly avoid if we could."[29] Even hate must be prayed and not suppressed, Peterson contends, for "if [hate] is not prayed we have lost an essential energy and insight in doing battle with evil."[30]

The texts by Capps and Peterson recapitulate the themes already sounded by other pastoral theologians and add yet another dimension to the body of reflection in pastoral theology on the relationship between the lament prayer and pastoral ministry. That dimension is the importance, both for the griever and for the caregiver, of providing structure for the grief experience. In the formal structure of most lament psalms, the full expression of pain is linked with opportunities for voicing specific petitions for help and offering praise. This paradoxical combination of complaint and praise contributes to the process of lamenting into hope.

COMMON CONVICTIONS IN PASTORAL THEOLOGY ABOUT LAMENT AND HOPE

In the previous section we have identified several convictions of pastoral theologians about the value of the lament prayer in times of grief and depression, and we want now to discuss these convictions in somewhat greater detail.

First, present in all the works mentioned is the conviction that bringing the particularity of one's suffering to voice is vital to healing and hope. In fact, this emphasis on the full expression of grief has been described as a "near proverbial axiom of pastoral care," and some works on grief have been critiqued for not clarifying how the full expression of suffering is related to Christian hope.[31] In this view, the value placed on bringing suffering to voice is seen as deriving mainly from modern psychology.

It is not possible to respond here in full to this criticism. While some works in pastoral theology may be vulnerable to this charge, we strongly disagree that by calling for the full expression of grief pastoral theology shows that it is simply an echo of modern psychology.

Although the emphasis on voicing suffering is now viewed as axiomatic in all literature on grief, it is important to recognize that even in Western psychology this is a rather recent development and that ambivalence about prolonged and vocal suffering has characterized the mental health field as well as the church. The psychological literature on grief both illustrates and struggles with this ambivalence.

The clinical literature on grief begins with Freud's "Mourning and Melancholia" (1917), which contrasts normal grief following the death of a loved one with pathological melancholia.[32] In Freud's understanding of human relatedness, people are driven by libidinal energy to invest in objects that can fulfill their needs and drives. When a love object dies, the task of grief is to "decathect," or detach the libido from an object no longer capable of meeting one's needs, so that one may reinvest in a new object. This process of "mourning" is very demanding because the mourner rebels against the loss and is reluctant to abandon the original attachment. But in "normal" grief the mourner will in time accept the reality of the loss. The successful outcome of grief is the relinquishing of all ties to the lost object and the gaining of freedom to reinvest in new love objects.[33]

While some of Freud's anthropological assumptions have come under sharp criticism, his views have continued to influence clinical perspectives on grieving. One problem regarding Freud's legacy is that in distinguishing between normal and pathological grief, the limits he sets on these distinctions are so narrow that most intense grief would have to be regarded as pathological.[34] While different clinicians would draw the line differently between "pathological" versus "normal" grief, it should not go unnoticed that the idea of grief as a "disease" has some roots in psychological theory.

Another problem in the psychology of grief is the length of time caregivers may assume it takes to recover from a loss. Classical psychoanalysts see lingering attachments to deceased loved ones as pathological because it is not rational to maintain attachments to the dead when they can no longer fulfill our needs. Family theorist Ester Shapiro critiques the mental health field for enduring assumptions about how quickly people are able to recover from serious losses, arguing that it takes much longer than most clinicians have postulated; in fact, it may take a lifetime to fully come to terms with some losses.[35]

Finally, some ideas about "healthy" versus "unhealthy" grief found in the social science literature betray a deep cultural bias. Shapiro criticizes Freud's understanding of human relationality and argues that it thrives in a particular cultural milieu: "The vision of human relatedness and grief perpetrated by this theory, namely, that human beings view each other as interchangeable objects of need gratification, persists in part because this egoistic point of view strikes a resonant chord in our individualistic, self-referential culture."[36]

One of Shapiro's agendas is to counteract the prejudices she has found in the mental health field regarding cultural groups who are not Euro–North American, noting that it is not uncommon for mental health practitioners to describe the grief behaviors of members of these groups as pathological.

Thus, while there is common agreement on the normalcy and necessity of the intense emotions related to substantial loss, there is no unanimity about the depth and duration of lament, either among clinicians or pastoral theologians. We note, however, a trend toward more openness to the intensity, complexity, and longevity of the process of recovering from traumatic losses.

The grief literature in pastoral theology reflects this shift in consciousness. Pastoral theologies of grief have needed to attend both to diverse attitudes about grief shaped by different pieties and to an expanding clinical and research literature on grief. To greater or lesser extents, they employ psychological theories that demonstrate how the intensity and complexity of grief is a normal and inevitable dimension of being human. They reflect the conviction, supported by more than thirty years of research scholarship on grief, that "the single most important factor [in a person's recovery from grief] is the individual's free and full expression of his or her grief feelings."[37] At the same time, these writings seek to justify theologically the conviction that the experience of grief, with all its complex emotions, provides an opportunity for deepening rather than alienating one's relationship with God.

Mitchell and Anderson are explicit about their core psychological and theological assumptions and the rationale for utilizing the lament tradition in care for the grieving. A fundamental premise that grounds Mitchell and Anderson's work is that grief is not a disease, but an inseparable component of love.[38] The thesis they argue is that "the genesis of grief lies in the inevitability of both attachment and separation for the sustenance and development of human life."[39] They briefly describe three different psychologists' work on attachment and separation—Margaret Mahler, Melanie Klein, and John Bowlby, all of whom studied infant development. Each theorist's work on attachment and separation is nuanced in a distinct way, and Mitchell and Anderson contend that each theory offers a helpful perspective on the experience of loss.

Mitchell and Anderson use all these theories to support their thesis that deep grieving is not a sign of pathology, immaturity, or inadequacy of faith. Rather, the capacity to grieve deeply is a mark of psychological maturity, rooted in processes that are essential for human life and development. The inability to mourn diminishes life.

The authors argue their thesis on theological as well as psychological grounds. In fact, it is their theological stance that fuels their critique of Freud and their search for other understandings of the experience of loss. Christianity, they profess, "continues to be the most materialistic of all religions," despite its expressions of otherworldly pieties.[40] They draw from Luther's insistence that there is nothing "disgraceful or unfaithful about natural affection," while acknowledging and critiquing Luther's insistence that grief should be "moderate."[41] Luther believed grief should be "moderate" because "excessive grieving leaves no room for consolation; and uncontrolled sorrow may lead the believer to lose sight of the cross in comparison to which all our crosses are light or as nothing."[42] Mitchell and Anderson note that Luther sees a truth at this point, but draws an erroneous conclusion.

> [Luther] understands that if we grieve deeply, we shall for the moment not be able to see God's suffering in Christ. The problem with Luther's admonition is that not to grieve deeply is to grieve inadequately, distortedly. Premature consolation is pointless when people are filled with sorrow. To quell the grieving is not to stop the storm but merely to build a wall so that we do not see the storm or its effects. Freedom to grieve intensively from the onset of loss is what makes space later for a remembrance of Christ's suffering and a reaffirmation of the loving will of God that seemed so strange when the pains of grief were acute.[43]

Turning the tables on traditional theological restrictions on grief, Mitchell and Anderson contend that it is actually a sign of "unfaith" when people are unable to deeply mourn because "the capacity to love and be loved is a remaining mark of the 'image of God,' distorted by sin as it may be."[44] In the words of Colin Murray Parkes, grief is the "cost of commitment."[45]

It is within this framework that the laments are understood to facilitate hope. The laments validate the embodied experience of grievers,[46] giving expression to the variety of bodily sensations and complex web of feelings associated with grief. They present an image of a God who prefers "opening oneself unashamedly" in relationship to God rather than keeping polite distance, and they convey the sense that others have traveled the road of terror and rage, thereby mitigating some of the isolation of grief.[47] Understanding, validation, and the assurance of presence amidst the flood and chaos of grief's powerful emotions are pastoral activities that promote hope.

A second conviction of pastoral theologians, not always explicitly stated, is that the biblical laments offer a form or structure for expressing acute suffering that facilitates the turn to hope. Since the pioneering work of Elisabeth Kübler-Ross on the grief process of dying people there have been variations on the theme that the experience of grief has some familiar movements or "stages" through which sufferers pass.[48]

The idea that grief has "stages" has been both helpful and problematic to grievers. On the one hand, some find the emphasis on stages helpful because they find validation for the varied and volatile emotions they are experiencing, an intimation of order amidst the chaos of grief, and a glimpse of hope that in time there will be relief for their suffering. On the other hand, others find that "stage" theories of grief do not account for the particularity of their grief or the enduring quality of grief, and lead would-be comforters to generalize and categorize their experience in ways that seem dismissive or overly clinical. Ann Weems, a contemporary psalmist, reports the many times even her friends brought her "books with ten steps to overcome grief as though healing comes in paperback" and told her she must "grieve correctly."[49]

Accompanying suffering people is a delicate art, and there are serious pitfalls to generalizing about experiences of suffering. Likewise there is also a danger in seeing suffering as completely formless and chaotic because sufferers struggle desperately to find meaning in their affliction and some framework for naming and understanding their experiences. We agree with Capps that the lament psalms provide a basis not only for understanding the dynamics of grief but also for the process of counseling the grieving.

As noted earlier, Capps's work builds on Brueggemann's exploration of how the form of the biblical lament psalm may be compared and contrasted with the Kübler-Ross schema for describing the stages of grief that dying persons experience.[50] Capps's major contention is that the lament psalms, far more than Kübler-Ross's stage theory, provide a way for pastors to help the grieving give "form" to their experience. In undertaking that task, he especially urges pastors to deepen their understanding of the complaint stage and take seriously the last three stages of the lament psalm because they reflect the "transforming intervention of God." He emphasizes, however, that "this intervention gains its entry through the complaint stage, so the importance of this stage can hardly be exaggerated."[51]

Capps's description of how pastoral counseling with the grieving might trace the movement of the lament psalms may be briefly summarized:

Address to God. For the counselor, counseling the grieving begins with the understanding, usually implicit rather than explicit, that the words of the sufferer and the conversation between the sufferer and the counselor are addressed to God.[52]

Complaint. The laments, Capps argues, can sensitize us to the "range and depth" of complaints in the grief process. Complaints arise out of the "welter of feelings" occasioned by grief, some of which are circumstantial (for example, that a death could have been avoided). "But the deeper and more intense complaints of the grieving are not circumstantial, but relational."[53] Many lament psalms focus on relational complaints; for example, "Whom may I trust in this time of suffering and loss?"[54]

This question of trust, which underlies many relational complaints, may be addressed to other people ("Why won't you try to understand what I am going through?"), the deceased ("Why do you condemn me, even in death?"), to God ("Where were you the night my child was murdered?"), or to oneself ("Why can't I accept what has happened and move on with my life?"). The role of the counselor is to be "really accepting" of the sufferer's negative feelings.[55] Without the capacity to hear and accept the depth of these negative feelings, the counselor undermines the ability of sufferers to trust that there is someone who can possibly understand and accept them; that help and comfort are possible.

Confession of Trust. "The pastoral conversation can itself provide a context in which trust is not only discussed but actually experienced," not usually in "grandiose terms" as the answer to one's complaints or end to one's suffering, but as a "simple confidence that one will be able to cope."[56] The griever who finds adequate grounds for trust in others, self, and God will be able, like the psalmist, to make a confession of trust. This is a moment of "turning the corner," the "nevertheless" that often "follows the catharsis of negative feeling."[57]

Petition. Capps suggests that the bereaved often petition God to intervene in "a hesitant though hopeful way." However, often this petitioning is not heard or supported by pastors because they are either too intent on helping the bereaved move toward acceptance or because they interpret petitions as attempts to "bargain" with God. Capps emphasizes that petitions are important in the grief process, arguing that petitioning helps mourners "do something" about their complaints.[58]

In verbalizing these petitions, the counselee gives clearer focus to the sense of trust that was beginning to emerge in the preceding stage but was as yet unfocused. Now the counselee is beginning to place trust and confidence in those things which, if realized, will bring this grief experience to a good resolution (e.g., overcoming loneliness, understanding the meaning of the loss for his or her future, having strength to meet the demands of life, and so forth). The pastor's role here is to help the counselee clarify the petitions, to gain a clearer sense of what the petitions are.[59]

Words of Assurance. Two pastoral initiatives characterize this stage of the grief counseling process. One is the assurance, through words or attitude, that the petitions of the sufferer are shared and that the pastor and others will offer active and committed support. The second is the assurance that God hears the petitions of the sufferer.

Vow to Praise. The counselor fosters a spirit of praise not by communicating that it is the sufferer's Christian obligation, but by assisting in clarifying what, in the grief experience, invites or warrants praise to God. As in the psalms of lament, praise is not general and abstract, but quite specific. Whenever the sufferer begins to sense, in clear and concrete ways, that his or her petitions are being received and new spiritual energies are being made available, the task of the counselor is to encourage praise. "The spirit of praise is vitally important to the resolution of grief, because it reinforces the hope that was rekindled in clarifying one's petitions and checks the drift toward apathy that typically follows the release of those petitions."[60]

Interestingly, Capps contends that the lament psalm "reflects the sense in which grief counseling involves a nondirective [counseling] method."[61] Like the psalms of lament, grief counseling is not "rigid or forced." The varied length of the laments reflects the different pace at which mourners process their anguish; sometimes the "process is relatively brief, other times it is long and torturous."[62] Because the process is understood primarily to reflect the sufferer's experience with the healing power of God, the pastor's role is not to direct the healing process. Rather, the "pastor's role is primarily to remove barriers that are impeding a spiritual process."[63]

Capps's linking of a nondirective or client-centered counseling approach with the structure of the lament prayer makes for a fascinating psychological and theological coalition. Implicit in the nondirective method is the assumption that human beings have a great capacity for healing, growth, and hope if they are offered a hospitable climate. This hospitable climate requires of the counselor an attitude of unconditional positive regard, a confidence in the person's capacity to move toward growth and wholeness, and the capacity to convey warmth and genuineness. It is indeed more about "removing barriers [that impede] a spiritual process" than directing the process. On the other hand, as Capps also contends, it is essential for pastors to help the grieving give "form" to their experience.[64]

Capps doesn't completely reconcile the differences between these two different approaches to counseling the grieving (being "nondirective" and "helping give form"). He simply insists that the lament psalm was not a rigid form and was augmented by new variations as a consequence of new circumstances. By pointing to the relationship between order and freedom in the process by which a mourner moves through sorrow toward new life and hope, Capps implicitly recognizes the important role of the community of faith in the healing process.

A third common conviction of the pastoral theologians we have cited is that community is indispensable to healing. Hope is born and nurtured in community. "One of the strategies of pastoral work is to enter private grief and make a shared event of it. . . . Response to suffering is a function of the congregation," writes Eugene Peterson.[65] For Peterson, as for virtually all pastoral theologians, Christian community is presupposed as the context for pastoral care and counseling, although it is often the case, as Hulme notes, that the "congregation . . . is the most unused, undeveloped, and unorganized of all the unique resources of the pastoral counselor."[66]

Peterson is particularly eloquent about the role the community plays with those who lament. When the community joins a suffering person or family in lamenting, there is " 'consensual validation' that the suffering means something. The community votes with its tears that there is suffering that is worth weeping over." Community participation counters "the threat of dehumanization to which all pain exposes us," sanctions the expression of emotion, and places the suffering before God in common prayer.[67]

According to Peterson, using the "set forms of communal lament" in times of suffering enables people to enter the "invisible company of those who have had similar . . . sufferings."[68] On some occasions, Peterson speaks of communal lament in a very general way, as weeping with those who weep. At other times, he speaks of communal lament in a quite specific way, as bringing individual grief "into the sanctuary where it becomes part of the common grief, is placed at the foot of the cross and subjected to the powers of salvation."[69]

While Peterson does not thoroughly explore the place of ritual in enabling and structuring communal lament, Elaine Ramshaw gives considerable attention to this topic. Ramshaw advocates worship that can hold "loss and hope together in the church's ritual embrace."[70] Criticizing worship services that are unrelentingly positive in tone, Ramshaw argues for services that can "allow symbolic room" for a wide range of feelings, including mourning and protest. Ritual meets deep human needs—that is, the need to experience the bonds of community, the need to experience order and structure amidst the chaos of suffering, the need for public reaffirmation of meaning when meaning has collapsed, the need for ways to express ambivalent feelings that can be communally sanctioned, and the need to encounter mystery.[71]

We believe Ramshaw's view of the importance of ritual takes us a step beyond Capps's analysis of the importance of the structure of the lament prayer in providing order to the grief experience. We would contend that it is not only the form of the lament prayer itself but the embodied presence of a community of believers open to such prayer that helps give form to experiences of loss and grief and thereby resists utter disorder and chaos. We are not saying that pastoral counselors cannot provide any structuring help—quite the contrary—but that sustained efforts to cope with suffering require the presence and companionship of community, however small that community might be. The grace of God enables hope, and hope is mediated in and through community.

LAMENT AND HOPE IN THE FACE OF VIOLENCE AND SYSTEMIC EVIL

Having briefly reviewed literature in pastoral theology whose primary focus is the grieving individual, we now turn to recent literature in pastoral theology that focuses on the suffering and hope of persons and communities with marginal social power. We will especially attend to ways in which ministries of care are shaped by the authors' grappling with the experience of cultural difference and the dynamics of social power that configure communal and individual relationships.

In very distinctive ways, the works of James Poling, Denise Ackermann, Larry Graham, Theresa Snorton, and Christie Neuger take social context and struggle into account in their reflection on the experience of suffering and abuse. All are concerned about the empowerment of marginalized people. But more than this, they contend that the experiences of marginalized people critique dominant psychological and theological understandings about suffering, help, and hope. The aim of this critique is the transformation of both church and culture. An important affirmation in modern pastoral theology is that theology and ministry are mutually related. In these recent works we see another theme rising to prominence: personal and social transformation are mutually related as well. We are aware, of course, that the works included in this section do not exhaust the efforts of contemporary pastoral theologians to deal with the interface of personal and social transformation in pastoral theology and pastoral care. We also acknowledge that we are not dealing with any of these works in their fullness. Still, we hope that our discussion is true to the purpose and spirit of each author's work.

In recent decades, pastoral theology has addressed the reality of violence in human life. Often hidden from view in the life of many congregations and largely missing in the writings of earlier work in pastoral theology, the subjects of domestic and sexual abuse, racial violence and hate crimes, the lasting damage inflicted by war and exile, and the debilitating effects of social marginalization and poverty now claim the attention of many contemporary pastoral theologians. It is not that the situations themselves are new, of course. But they are now being *named and voiced* with passion and urgency by those pastoral theologians who have personally experienced these evils and by those whose lives and work have been transformed by encounters with those who have.

Drawing on the work of Wendy Farley, pastoral theologian Nancy Ramsay makes a distinction between "radical suffering" and the suffering that arises from our own sin or the unavoidable sufferings of finite human existence (such as illness, failure, and the eventual death of loved ones). "Radical suffering such as child sexual abuse describes the painful reality of suffering that is not only undeserved and unanticipated but arises from intentional violation and harm at the hands of another."[72]

How does someone survive an experience of radical suffering and evil? How is hope nourished in situations that by their very nature rob persons of trust and hope? How can people flourish in situations where injustice, the undermining of self-respect, and physical and/or psychological violence are part of everyday life? How can care be offered in ways that address not only the anguish of the victim of radical suffering but the social context that permits and may even support the violence? These are the kinds of questions that much contemporary pastoral theology is trying to address, not only in the realm of theory but in concrete strategies for pastoral care and counseling as well. They are unavoidable questions for pastoral theology in any treatment of the relationship between lament and hope.

We will look at three pastoral theologians' efforts to take up such questions with persons and communities struggling with different faces of violence: James Poling's work on issues of sexual and domestic violence; Denise Ackermann's study of the conditions that make for healing after the violence of apartheid in South Africa; and Larry Graham's study of the suffering and the "persistent hopefulness" of those who face social isolation and marginalization because of their sexual orientation.

Sexual Violence

James Poling's writings about the suffering that results from sexual violence began in 1991 with the publication of *The Abuse of Power: A Theological Problem*. The theological problem with which Poling struggles throughout this book is the radical evil of sexual violence against women and children. Experiences of such violence raise fundamental questions about selfhood, the human community, and God. In later works Poling has continued to explore the reality of evil and the ways in which evil is resisted in human communities.[73]

In his essay "Resisting Violence in the Name of Jesus,"[74] Poling briefly presents some of the themes he takes up in greater depth in his larger works. This essay centers on the psalms and prayers written by women who have survived various forms of violence. An explicit agenda of Poling's work is bringing to the attention of both seminary and church the voices of survivors. He utilizes a hermeneutical principle of much liberation theology, that those with the least power can reveal the most about the nature of good and unmask the abuse of power. "Those who are in positions of power need to hear the voices of those who suffer from abuse or deprivations just as surely as those who suffer cry out to be heard. Only through this kind of conversation can humanity be restored to both oppressed and oppressor."[75]

Thus Poling understands the psalms, stories, and poetry of survivors to be a primary source for theological reflection, a witness from which the whole body of the church can learn and to which the church needs to be accountable. Understanding these psalms, stories, and poems as a religious witness through which God's voice might be heard by the whole people of God, Poling urges the church to allow these voices to call into question harmful legacies of traditional Christian doctrine, especially damaging images of God and Jesus. The psalms and poetry of survivors

> follow the great tradition of biblical psalms and New Testament stories in their honesty and ability to trust God with all of their feelings. They bring their experiences with evil and violence and call their enemies to accountability just like the psalmist. I present these psalms and stories in order to provide a window into the faith of persons who have been abused by the family and by the church. I present these psalms and stories because of the new religious witness that God is giving in our generation. Their raw suffering and hope reveals the power and love of God who cannot be controlled by the official theologies and practices of the churches.[76]

It is striking how the witness of the survivors studied by Poling so closely resembles the biblical psalms in their bold questioning of God, their graphic description of pain, and the hope that is manifested in their petitions for God's help. For example, the following psalm by Karen Doudt begins with the cry of abandonment voiced in Psalm 22:1. For survivors of child sexual abuse, it is basic trust in the goodness and reliability of those on whom one depends for existence itself that is compromised and often shattered by abuse. In Doudt's psalm, this sense of forsakenness is coupled with profound petitions for God's help. As in the biblical psalms of lament, this asking is itself a gesture of hope. Included in the petitions is the plea that God will melt Karen's defenses against trusting others— that communion with God and others will be possible and that she will "find the things that make for peace." The restoration sought is restoration of the damaged self, to be sure, but the psalm also points toward the restoration of community, which is only made possible through the restoration of the capacity to trust.

My God, my God
Why have you forsaken me?
My body cries out.
My hands are in knots
My neck is pained with tension
My chest is tight, breathing is labored
My stomach groans with unrest
My mouth is dry
My eyes will not close with sleep
My ears ring
My mind is pregnant with unrest
My legs are curled, the muscles crying with tightness
My heart beats on while pain abounds
Oh God, my God
Where are you now?
My spirit longs for thee
for the peace that comes with rest
for the peace that comes on the footsteps of truth
for the peace that comes with the healing of brokenness
for the peace that comes with the release of the
painèd soul from bondage
for the peace that creeps in when I can share the
depths of my pain with trusted ones.
Oh God, my God
release the wells of my eyes
break down the remaining walls of my defense
destroy the fear that enfolds my being
awaken the courage to continue to reach out, to unfold
Grant me patience, Lord, to endure
—the time required for healing
—the pain of the width and depth of my emotion
—the pain of aloneness
—the search for truth and understanding
—the search for meaning
O God. I feel like the abandoned child, hardening
myself to survive because I feel so alone. I cry out
again—please enfold me in your arms and wrap me with
care. Melt my defenses. Help me to surrender to
complete trust in significant others so my story can
be told and I can find the things that make for peace.
I pray that through this death I may find life.[77]

Without detailed discussion of the relationship between survivor psalms, stories, and poems and the biblical laments and New Testament stories, Poling briefly names three important points of connection. First, honest feelings about experiences of violation are entrusted to God. Second, enemies are called to accountability. Third, Jesus is discovered to be one who understands what it means to suffer the wounds of violence and oppression because he himself was wounded and scarred; he both suffers in solidarity with others who are scarred by violence and his spirit accompanies and empowers them in their resistance to violence.[78]

Poling does not use the term "laments" to describe the survivor literatures he shares, but it is clear that he sees in these writings something that has also long fascinated readers about the biblical laments: they evidence at once both the depth of radical suffering and the resiliency of human hope. If we take these works seriously, they can challenge familiar and inadequate understandings of self, world, and God and point to new understandings. According to Poling, the task for the church is to hear those voices and to attend to the ways that God and Jesus are imaged from the perspectives of survivors. To identify with those voices and images and to join in solidarity with all who resist violence in the name of Jesus is the way we recognize and participate in God's love and power at work in the world.[79]

Racial Violence

In the work of white South African pastoral theologian Denise Ackermann, we find the recurrence of two convictions that we have just identified in Poling's writings. The first is the conviction that fully hearing the testimonies of survivors of violence stands at the beginning of the transformation of religious and civic consciousness. Ackermann's essay "On Hearing and Lamenting: Faith and Truth-Telling"[80] begins with the pain and disorientation of hearing the laments of survivors, when to hear them means that one's known world of the past is exposed as full of "lies, dissimulations, misconceptions, ignorance, apathy [and] heads buried in tons of sand."[81]

The second conviction is that once the lament has been heard, the Christian's responsibility is to lament as well. Ackermann explores the role of lament in the lives of young white South Africans who must wrestle with the legacy of apartheid, which encompasses not only those who were its obvious victims but also those whose lack of awareness and lack of moral courage allowed the evils of apartheid to go unquestioned and unresisted.

> Through the work of the Truth and Reconciliation Commission, the consciousness of many . . . young Afrikaners is now being flooded with stories of suffering, of torture, of alienation and of grief. Profound questions about what it means to have faith, about human

suffering, shame and guilt, about the nature of God, surface in a time of awakening. "What can I do now?" many may wonder. Is reconciliation possible? I am concerned that whites in this country not miss out on a crucial step in the process to reconciliation. This concern prompts me to suggest that we need to *lament* the injustice and the pain of the past before we can hope for meaningful reconciliation.[82]

Three sources help ground Ackermann's insistence that lament is the appropriate faith response for white South Africans. The first is a secular group called the Black Sash, a white women's organization for human rights that persistently opposed Afrikaner nationalism and apartheid in the long years that apartheid was the law of the land. The women of the Black Sash protested in various ways, but their "most visible and most reviled public activity was to stand silently in public places with black sashes across their chests, overtly lamenting injustice."[83] When these public "stands" were forbidden by the Riotous Assemblies Act, the women continued to stand—not in a group, but ten meters apart. Nelson Mandela once said that the women of the Black Sash were "the conscience of the white nation."[84]

The witness of the "secular" Black Sash group prompted Ackermann to ask as a Christian what happened to lament as a public act in the practice of Christian faith. She is deeply concerned to discover a Christian spirituality that is "awake" rather than numb to forces of injustice, that will, in the words of Adrienne Rich, try "for memory and connectedness against amnesia and nostalgia" rather than "dull the imagination by starving it or feeding it with junk food."[85] Ackermann writes:

> By choosing not to know, by knowing a little and saying, "What's the use of protesting anyway?" and, in Dorothee Sölle's words, by "screaming too softly," we deliberately choose powerlessness and apathy. The dominant whites and those who supported them in the old regime, were hardly without power. . . . Yet they lacked moral and spiritual power, that reciprocal and collective energy which engages us personally and communally with God and with one another in such a way that power becomes synonymous with the vitality of living fully and freely.[86]

Is there a correlation between the lack of corporate lament in the Christian church and increased susceptibility to amnesia and nostalgia? The experience of the absence of lament in Christian prayer, worship, and public life led Ackermann into the work of biblical scholars on the lament tradition in both the Hebrew Scriptures and the New Testament. She found in the biblical witness substantial evidence of the practice and value of lament. For Ackermann, the witness of the Black Sash and the witness of the Bible through its many lament texts are supporting evidence that public lament has much to contribute to both individual and social transformation. Ackermann also draws on Dorothee Sölle's book *Suffering* to describe how lament facilitates healing by helping suffering people move from a condition of muteness to the "language of lament." In finding common language, the isolation of suffering is broken by an experience of solidarity that is essential if change is to occur. Lament is not an end in itself. The goal of lament is healing. "The call to lament is an appeal to all, both to the victims and to the repentant perpetrators of suffering, to engage in public acts of mourning which will enable true reconciliation and healing to take place."[87]

There is deep personal suffering involved for those who face their complicity (however unintentional and unwitting) in the web of evil and injustice that privileges some, sacrifices others, and ultimately damages everyone involved. Ackermann contends that public lament offers a bridge to healing, by providing a way to articulate the many faces of that suffering in public, communal ways. She accents the *public* role of lament and its role in shaping social consciousness. But there is a deep interconnection between the opportunity for public lament and the breaking of the seductive hold that amnesia and nostalgia have on individuals caught in powerful social systems.

Internalized Violence

Larry Graham is still another pastoral theologian who is exploring the relationship between suffering and hope within marginalized communities. In his book *Discovering Images of God: Narratives of Care among Lesbians and Gays*, Graham tries to help bridge the abyss that divides heterosexuals from gays and lesbians.[88] His thesis is that examining the lives of lesbians and gay men, especially through a variety of caregiving situations, discloses their capacity for "creative, deep, and loving communion with God, self, neighbor, and the natural order."[89] It is this kind of capacity for communion, which Graham calls "relational justice," that reveals what it means to be created in the image of God.

For the purposes of our project, we will focus on one aspect of the suffering of gay men and lesbians that we find particularly significant for a discussion of lament and hope. When one is different from what is considered to be the norm, part of the suffering that one experiences is the belief, taught and learned in social interactions, that one is not just different but "bad," "sick," or "crazy." This negative labeling of oneself because one does not fit in has been explored by many theorists as the experience of internalized oppression.[90] It is a common struggle in the lives of lesbians and gay men to deal with a world in which anything other than a heterosexual orientation is presumed to be unnatural (abnormal) and wrong. There are very real and dangerous risks even in telling oneself the truth about one's orientation, let alone others. Thus the power of isolation and negativity is so strong that many lesbians' and gay men's laments and struggles may never even come to self-expression, let alone public expression. The risks are too frightening.

Graham, however, hears in the stories of lesbians and gay men many occasions in which silence has been broken, truth-telling has happened, and new power for life and relationships has been released. Out of experiences of isolation and negativity have come "compelling examples of communal solidarity, theological affirmation, and liturgical recognition."[91] One is the response to the AIDS crisis.

> On repeated occasions it became clear to me how much the AIDS crisis has generated communal solidarity and sensitivity to ultimate values in the gay and lesbian community. . . . The imminence of death for many has mobilized a courage to come out of the closet, to identify publicly as lesbian or gay, and to minister with one another as well as challenge the larger society.[92]

Unlike Ackermann, Graham does not explicitly include the theme of lament in his book.[93] Nevertheless, the aim of his study is to assist readers in listening to the witness of a marginalized community that speaks not only of their suffering but also of their experiences of gracious healing and resilient hope. Earlier we underscored the role of community in providing support in the midst of suffering and helping to nourish hope. In Graham's interviews we learn that sometimes it is a powerful experience of shared grief and anger that brings community into being where little public solidarity existed before. Sometimes lament *forms* community.

LAMENT AND HOPE IN PASTORAL CARE AS AN ART OF EMPOWERMENT

Pastoral theologians have long recognized that the experience of any kind of suffering makes people terribly vulnerable. Suffering involves feelings of powerlessness because the event that has occasioned the suffering is beyond the sufferer's control and the feelings evoked by the event are often experienced as out of the sufferer's control as well. Thus when suffering people seek help, especially in a professional context (such as pastoral counseling or therapy), one of the features already at play in the relationship is the kind of "inequality" that comes when one is dependent on another for care and help at a vulnerable time. This inequality is exacerbated when there are additional inequalities of social status and power and when it becomes clear that the minister does not really comprehend the social and cultural world of the sufferer.

Pastoral theologians have also long asserted that pastoral care and counseling should strengthen and empower people. But since the beginning of the modern pastoral care movement that assertion has been linked to the assumption that the way to "help people help themselves" is through a process of helping them to gain understanding of their inner conflicts. Seward Hiltner, who strongly articulated this view,[94] recognized that there is a danger in this "inward" focus; a danger in viewing people's inability to adjust to their circumstances as a sign that there is something wrong with the individual. According to Hiltner:

> If individual difficulties are always and only symptoms that some-thing is wrong in the individual, if nothing more than the mores of a particular society are available to suggest what the proper adaptation should be, then the counseling enterprise—wittingly or not—becomes if not a tool of the state at least a mere reinforcer of the low-est common denominator of the cultural patterns of a society.[95]

This awareness, however, did not play a significant role in the pastoral counseling methodology Hiltner advocated. Nor did he consider in his methodology how differences in culture or social status affect the pastoral counseling relationship itself.

Space does not permit an extended discussion of how deeply personal and social transformation have been separated in theological education and Christian ministry. Suffice it to say, more than a few seminary students and pastors have inherited the dualistic notion that one behaves one way in offer-ing pastoral care (that is, warm, accepting, and "pastoral") and quite another way in the pulpit or at a community meeting (that is, forthright, confron-tive, and "prophetic"); and that pastoral care focuses on the internal forces that injure and constrain life while social action ministry engages the exter-nal, sociocultural forces.

In North America, Archie Smith's landmark book *The Relational Self: Ethics and Therapy from a Black Church Perspective*[96] was one of the first texts in pastoral theology to examine the dynamic relationship between personal and social transformation, and to do so from a particular sociocultural per-spective, that of the black church. Other texts quickly followed, with increas-ing attention paid to examining the principles of *empowering* care with per-sons whose voices have been left out of both dominant psychological and theological interpretive frameworks. It is an important goal of the more recent literature in pastoral theology to determine how pastoral counseling can avoid pastoral versus prophetic dualism and be concerned simultane-ously for both personal and social transformation.

This concern for the mutual relationship of personal and social transfor-mation in both theoretical construction and ministry practice is present to some degree in the works we have already considered. However, for fuller

development of the implications of this mutual relationship for actual practices of pastoral care and counseling, we turn to two additional works.

The Importance of Cultural Context

In her essay "The Legacy of the African-American Matriarch: New Perspectives for Pastoral Care,"[97] Theresa Snorton contends that an understanding
of the social and historical experience of African American women is necessary for understanding both the suffering and strength of African American
women and for offering pastoral care that is helpful and empowering.

Although Snorton describes four cultural images of African American
womanhood (mammy, matriarch, Jezebel, and welfare mother), it is the
image of the matriarch that is the centerpiece of her own constructive work.
The cultural image, or stereotype, of the matriarch has often been used to
describe those African American women "whose experience has required
them to be 'strong, persevering, and determined.'"[98] Building on the work of
Alice Walker and Jacquelyn Grant, Snorton reframes this cultural stereotype
to the self-consciously chosen image of the "womanist," whose strength and
faith, inherited from the tradition of her elders, have enabled her own survival and the survival of her family and people. The womanist is both exalted
and condemned for her strength. She does not find many safe spaces that
allow her both to express the emotional costs of her struggle and to affirm
her great spiritual strength.

Before making her proposals for pastoral care, Snorton describes the coping style of the womanist, a style fashioned by historical and social exigen-
cies. Since one of the ways the womanist copes with suffering is her faith in
a God who will eventually intervene on behalf of the oppressed and in the
meantime will be present in the midst of her suffering, giving in to grief can
be experienced as a potential denial of faith (and therefore the rejection of a
trusted way of coping as well).[99] Another aspect of the womanist's coping
style is "sparing others" and seeing any expression of one's own personal pain
and needs as self-indulgence. Snorton illustrates these aspects of the womanist's coping style by quoting Bridgett Davis's testimony about how she
coped with multiple grief experiences:

> It seemed a betrayal of faith, of a belief in God to totally surrender
> myself to grief. . . . I fought myself not to break down. I wouldn't cry. I
> wouldn't talk about it. I wouldn't give in. . . . I didn't want to lose con-
> trol. My primary incentive was to spare my mother the heartbreak. . . .
> She had been so strong throughout these tragedies, even though I
> know she feels a deep pain that those of us around her can't compre-
> hend or save her from. To breakdown and give my mother someone
> else to worry about was a selfish indulgence I didn't think I deserved.[100]

Still another important aspect for the womanist's coping style is the value placed on her own spiritual strength by black culture, particularly the African American church.[101] The woman who can manifest unswerving strength and trust in God is given tremendous authority and honor by her community. In times of deep personal crisis she may respond by giving testimony that "God will not place on you any more than you can bear," rather than voice her suffering or struggle.[102]

Through her supervising of hospital chaplains and her teaching, Snorton has had multiple opportunities to reflect with pastoral caregivers on their encounters with African American women. She notes the frequency with which Euro-American pastoral caregivers incline toward one of two responses to the womanist who, amid illness or tragedy, responds with a strong witness of God's providential care. Some admire the womanist and sometimes even put themselves in a position of receiving help from her. Snorton cites chaplains who say of their ministry encounters with African American women, "Her faith is so strong," or "I don't know what I could possibly offer her as a chaplain," or "She ministered to me as much as I did to her."[103] These responses, which may feel to the caregiver as validations of the womanist's strength, run the risk of sacrificing the intimacy of empowering pastoral care for the safe distance of admiration or of giving the subtle message that the only acceptable role for the African American woman to play is that of a caregiver (which may be related to the cultural stereotype of the black woman as "'mammy,' who even in her moments of need continued to give and to care for others").[104]

Another response of Euro-Americans is to see an African American woman's spiritual testimony, when spoken with a lack of visible vulnerability, as evidence of "denial."[105] In the first response, the pastoral role is abdicated because it is perceived as not needed because of the womanist's strength. In the second response, her behavior is negatively labeled and perceived as weakness.

> The pastoral care provider should be sure not to label the womanist's coping style as "denial." The womanist is all too aware of her precarious existence. She neither denies nor minimizes her troubles. She reinterprets them. What this means is that at a very basic human level, the womanist experiences the same emotions as anyone else. Culturally, she has learned to ascribe a different value to those feelings which move her too closely to her pain, too closely to despair and hopelessness. Bell hooks subscribes to the notion that the sociopolitical status imposed on the African-American woman leads to her "addiction to being tough."[106]

How does the pastoral caregiver navigate between the dangers of these opposing responses, one which elevates the African American woman beyond the need for care and the other which negatively labels her behavior as a denial of suffering and of the need for support and care? Snorton urges pastoral caregivers to understand that pastoral care with African American women is "typically informed by the same conceptual understandings that inform pastoral care to Euro-American women" and needs to proceed instead on the basis of careful attention to the historical experience and real needs of African American women.[107]

What is especially instructive for our exploration of the relationship of lament and hope is the way Snorton encourages pastoral caregivers to offer "safe space . . . for the womanist to express her deeper feelings without having to give up her strength." She is not to be prodded to become so vulnerable that she cannot continue emotional and spiritual responsibility for her loved ones.[108] At the same time, she is to be encouraged to reclaim aspects of the Christian tradition that help the womanist share her vulnerability without undermining her strength.[109] Although Snorton does not turn explicitly to the lament tradition of the Hebrew Scriptures, she does claim the gospel witness to the affective responses of Jesus to his own suffering as central to the womanist's response to her suffering.

When the critical voice says, "Be strong. Thou shalt not cry," the womanist is aided in recalling that Jesus cried. This image will be more meaningful for the womanist than the notion of her "need" or "right" to cry. In addition, for the womanist who is striving to be "Christlike" in a crisis, her own definition of such a virtue can be expanded to include human emotions.[110]

Snorton's work reminds us not only that helping people name and voice their suffering and hope always takes place in a cultural context, but that in situations of cultural difference we may seriously misread people's behaviors. Moreover, her portrayal of the struggle of the womanist leaves us with a crucial issue for pastoral care. Snorton observes that vulnerability is highly valued in the discipline of pastoral care.[111] How is vulnerability recognized, tended, and empowered in those contexts where showing vulnerability is extremely risky? Snorton approaches this issue from a particular social-historical perspective and leaves us with some road markers in caring for the womanist. She also leaves us with a question that has deep relevance for other social situations as well, reminding us that wherever vulnerability is encouraged or discouraged, we must be keenly aware of the social arena of the sufferer's struggle to survive and flourish, as well as the position of the caregiver within that arena.

A Methodology for Empowerment

In moving from the work of Theresa Snorton to that of Christie Neuger, we recall how Snorton resists allowing the categories created by Euro-Americans to define the experience of African American women or to determine the appropriate process of pastoral care. In creating strategies for care with womanists,

Snorton claims the experiences of African American women as primary data for theological reflection and pastoral response. She attends to the perspective of those whose voices have not played a role in articulating the definitions for what health and wholeness mean and how the healing process should proceed.

In "Pastoral Counseling as an Art of Personal Political Activism," Neuger names this methodological choice as "privileging the unheard or left-out voices";[112] that is, suspending or bracketing the categories created by those who have spoken for all people on the basis of their own cultural experience, so as to fully attend to those whose experiences do not easily fit the categories of the dominants—or whose experiences are labeled as different or deviant from the norm.

Neuger's essay focuses specifically on the process or methodology of a feminist pastoral counseling process. Although she recognizes that feminism has not always embraced an analysis of and struggle against multiple sources of oppression, she defines contemporary feminism as "a political and cultural enterprise built out of a commitment to the experience of those who are disadvantaged in the cultural power arrangements. It is very personal in that it is built out of the hearing and privileging of those disadvantaged and normally ignored perspectives, and it is always political."[113] According to Neuger, pastoral counseling can only claim to be feminist insofar as its goal is not just personal transformation but the transformation of the culture—including the church—as a part of the counseling process.[114]

How does all this work in the actual practice of pastoral counseling? We cite one case of pastoral counseling used by Neuger to shed light on what it means to see suffering as both personal and political and to respond in ways that address this interrelationship.

Margaret, a thirty-year-old African American woman, came to pastoral counseling having attempted suicide three times. She felt out of control of her life and unable to understand why she was having so much trouble. She lived in an all-white neighborhood, was married to a police officer, and had a twelve-year-old daughter and a six-year-old son. She wanted the pastoral counselor to keep her from being so unhappy.[115]

> Margaret had over one hundred unpaid parking tickets. . . . She worked for a collection agency in an unpleasant work environment, and she was in so much debt that most of her salary was garnished to pay her bills before she even saw it. . . . her children went to white schools where they felt uneasy and isolated. Her twelve-year-old daughter, especially, was engaging in risky behavior in order to find a way to belong. Margaret was worried, depressed, hopeless, and she saw herself as a failure.[116]

It will make a tremendous difference in the care offered to Margaret how the pastoral counselor sees the sources of her deep personal suffering. In the kind of pastoral work Neuger describes, the counselor brings to the labor of counseling an awareness of the complex dimensions of power and power-lessness in Margaret's life.

Margaret's self-diagnosis is that she is a failure, unable to "stop being so unhappy" in an all-white social environment or at home with a husband who is often angry with her. If she could just marshal the resources to be less unhappy, she could gain control of her life. Much contemporary pastoral care and counseling would accept that framework, and the caregiver would try to help find ways to help Margaret make a better adjustment to her world.

Neuger, pointing to the reversal that often occurs in Jesus' parables, in which the realities accepted by the dominant culture are turned upside down,[117] locates the "pathology" not in Margaret's inability to be happy in a culture that daily hurts her, but in the power of the culture to make her see herself through the deeply internalized lenses of racism, sexism, and classism.

This awareness of the power of the "pathology" or harmfulness of the culture in which Margaret struggles for survival is not imposed on Margaret as another "diagnosis" that comes from outside, by an external authority, to replace her own self-understanding. The process of counseling begins with deep listening to Margaret's experience, encouraging her to name the "lay-ers" of her own life experience, and working to clarify both the difficulties posed by her environment and the choices she has made in relation to those difficulties. Of that process, Neuger writes:

> As we worked to clarify the layers of her life situation, it became help-ful to frame her depression as resistance to living in a toxic environ-ment. The parking tickets and unpaid bills took very little reframing in order to see them as attempts to express what little power she experi-enced herself as having. When we began to understand her symptoms of depression and suicide through the lenses of racism, sexism, and . classism, Margaret's options began to expand. She began to attend a Black church in another neighborhood and intentionally to develop a supportive group of friends there. She also got her children involved in the youth choirs, where they had the experience of being with other kids who shared some dimensions of their experience that the children in their schools did not. Margaret began to see her current experiences in light of her history of abuse (incest and racial threats) and to under-stand the nature of her healthy resistance to systems of oppression. Her need then became to find ways to resist that did not do harm to her.[118]

In creating strategies for "resisting" in ways that help Margaret rather than harm her, building ongoing networks of support and solidarity are crucial. If "pathology" is seen as an individual phenomenon, then counseling is about getting adjusted and sent back into the culture. But if the culture itself is seen as deeply broken and damaging, then the struggle to engage in healthy resistance and to make life-giving choices for self and others will be a lifelong task. The pastoral counseling described with Margaret eventually embraced her husband and involved the whole family in building community.

The case described by Neuger is a *different* situation from that of the grieving person who is faced with an acute crisis of loss that needs to be absorbed and worked through in order that healing may occur. Pastoral care-givers do well to be concerned about encouraging depressed people *only* to vent their feelings of sorrow and hopelessness; that process, *in and of itself,* will not help the depressed person even though it is a part of the journey. Somehow *resistance* to the trappedness, a liberative reframing of the narrative is needed. The reframing must help persons in pain recognize and marshal their resources, must help them exercise responsibility and choice, and must help them reach out for the long-haul support and community that extends beyond the pastoral counseling relationship.

In making her case that this reframing is both personal and political, Neuger draws on several theological sources, but not on the prayer of lament. Can the lament prayer be a resource for this process, helping the sufferer to recognize and mobilize resistance to bondage, exercise responsibility, and seek community? If so, how and under what circumstances?

THE PRAYER OF LAMENT AND PASTORAL THEOLOGY

In concluding this chapter, we circle back to recall three central convictions we found in the literature on grief and depression in pastoral theology that specifically encourage the use of the lament prayer in pastoral care. First, we found the conviction that bringing one's experience of suffering to voice is (1) vital to healing and hope; that it is an act of faith to trust God with the honest rendering of our experience, with all the tumult that might involve, rather than to deny or avoid the truth. Second, among works in pastoral theology that use the biblical laments we found the conviction that some sense of formfulness or flexible structure is also important for suffering people; that (2) freedom of expression is enhanced rather than stifled when there are boundaries that help give shape and form to that expression. Third, we found the conviction that lamenting into hope requires community, not only because (3) the community can validate and help give form to the experience of suffering, but also because hope itself is grounded in the experience of relationship.

While the purposes and theoretical tasks of the two groups of writings we have explored are different, there is significant continuity. We can perhaps best name that continuity with the word "testimony." Pastoral theology, in its earlier and its more recent forms, attends to the testimony of sufferers and to the question of the meaning of pastoral care in response to such testimony. By "testimony" we mean the unique witness of sufferers whose experience calls in question the "basic presuppositions, metaphors, and rules" of modern rational discourse.[119]

Earlier pastoral theology attended to the testimony of individual sufferers. That work has enduring value. It is doubtful that any of the more recent authors of pastoral theology would deny the importance of such themes as the freedom to express sorrow fully, the value of form or structure in the grief process, and the indispensability of community in the emergence of hope.

The difference we have underscored—and it is a marked difference—is that more recent work in pastoral theology has shifted attention from a single focus on the plight of suffering individuals to a bifocal study of particular persons in particular communities of suffering. It is not only personal but communal testimony that demands the attention of pastoral theologians, and more attention is being devoted to the experiences of marginalized groups. The aim of pastoral ministry in the light of the biblical witness and the historic Christian faith becomes not simply the refiguring of personal worlds but also the reimagining and transformation of social worlds.

The innovations we find in recent pastoral theology for an understanding of the prayer of lament could be summarized as follows. First, the focus is not so much on the experience of suffering as a generic category but on hearing the particular challenges that voices of suffering in oppressed communities bring to theology and the work of ministry.

Second, pastoral theology and pastoral ministry are called to attend to the frightening realities of violence, hidden patterns of abuse, and deeply ingrained hatreds. The testimonies of survivors of holocaust, domestic abuse, racial hatred, and other experiences of radical evil are deeply disturbing and have often been hidden in ministry and theological reflection on ministry. The testimonies of the marginalized and the abused have become the new context for pondering the meaning and use of the prayer of lament.

Third, pastoral theology and pastoral ministry are discovering the inseparability of the pastoral and the political. The hope of renewal and reformation of life, as in the biblical witness, widens to communal and even global scope.

Fourth, more recent pastoral theology refuses to shrink from the task of asking how the testimonies of suffering challenge, correct, and enrich the caregiver's understandings of self, the world, and God. It emphasizes that those who minister to the needy and the suffering must be clear about their own faith and social location as well as the faith and location of the persons and communities to whom ministry is offered.

What might a pastoral theology of the prayer of lament offer to ministry in a time characterized by the testimonies of sufferers and survivors, and what would that theology look like? To these questions, and to our own constructive work, we now turn.

CHAPTER FIVE

TOWARD A PASTORAL THEOLOGY OF THE PRAYER OF LAMENT

Will I find you in the dark?
—*Nicholas Wolterstorff,* Lament for a Son

A few years ago there was a newspaper account of a terrible car accident involving a large family. Both parents and three children survived, but five children were killed. According to the report, the parents found comfort in the belief that this tragedy was the will of God, that they and their surviving children would be sustained by God's love, that their deceased children were in heaven, and that they would someday understand the meaning of their suffering. They saw no need to question the ways of God and emphasized instead their desire to praise God despite what had happened. Reporters gave a detailed account of these statements, along with testimonies of several people who spoke of being inspired by the strong faith of these parents.

It is easy to understand the admiration many have for persons who, like these parents, appear to have an unshakable set of beliefs on which to rely in times of crisis. Their witness is comforting to many because it doesn't challenge friends and supporters with the chaos of uninterpreted, raw pain, and it seems to hold out the hope that, for people of faith, there are no storms that cannot be weathered. For many Christians, unquestioning submission to the will of God in times of personal tragedy is what is expected of believers and is viewed as demonstration of a robust faith.

It is certainly not the purpose of this chapter to suggest that pastoral ministry with this family should set out to discredit their faith stance. No responsible pastoral work with persons struggling to survive a tragedy proceeds by stripping away whatever theological resources people may have to cope with pain. The processes of healing and meaning-making in times of crisis are complex and involve ongoing theological, cultural, and psychological tasks. For these bereaved parents, ways of comprehending and coping with such deep and multiple losses may well undergo significant change with the passing of time.

In all occasions of pastoral ministry it is important to attend not only to what people affirm but also to how their faith functions, what it enables persons to understand and bear, what its "fruits" are. How much of these parents' response is deep, authentic trust, how much a desperate coping strategy, how much the voice of shock and dissociation from the full impact of the losses, are questions that cannot be answered in a quick judgment on the basis of one's own theological, cultural, or psychological presuppositions. A caring pastor would no doubt see her first task as that of listening to and companioning this family over a lengthy stretch of time.

Nevertheless, the understanding of the ways of God that these parents expressed soon after their terrible accident does not ring true for many Christians. During times of loss and tragedy, our relationship with God may be so profoundly troubled that our earlier beliefs, never seriously questioned, may be exposed as "a house of cards."[1] It is the experience of this kind of severe disruption in one's relationship to God, especially with regard to how that relationship is expressed in prayer, that is the concern of this chapter.

Just such an experience of disruption is recorded by theologian Nicholas Wolterstorff in his book *Lament for a Son,* a theological meditation on the loss of his young son in a mountain-climbing accident. How, Wolterstorff asks, do we talk to God in the presence of a pain so overwhelming that it shatters familiar theological frameworks and modes of prayer? And of God, he asks the question that began this chapter, "Will I find you in the dark?"

> Faith endures; but my address to God is uncomfortably, perplexingly altered. It's off-target, qualified. I want to ask for Eric back. But I can't. So I aim around the Bull's-eye. I want to ask that God protect the members of my family. But I asked that for Eric. . . .
> I must explore the Lament as a mode of my address to God.[2]

In company with Wolterstorff and other seekers we take up the task of exploring the prayer of lament as "a mode of address to God," believing that such prayers of pain and protest arise not from faithlessness but from faith under duress. We are convinced that faith does endure for those who cry out to God in outrage and sorrow, but it may be thoroughly reshaped and reformed in the crucible of suffering.

In our effort to weave an integral pastoral theology of the prayer of lament, we will draw from the strands of our earlier studies of the biblical lament tradition, its reception in classical Christian theology, and its use in modern pastoral theology. We will contend that inclusion of the prayer of lament in all aspects of Christian life and ministry (alongside our prayers of praise, thanksgiving, intercession, and confession) can help to support the life of faith in several ways: offering a needed language of pain; confirming the value of embodied life; granting permission to grieve and protest; challenging inadequate understandings of God and preparing the way for new understandings; strengthening our self-understanding as responsible agents; purifying anger and the desire for vengeance; increasing solidarity with others who suffer; and revitalizing praise and hope.

OFFERING A LANGUAGE OF PAIN

Acknowledging the reality of terrible suffering, negation, and evil is never easy. That is true whether the suffering is one's own, one's family or community, or that of strangers. The weight of suffering and evil may be so great that it renders people helpless and speechless. One of the cruelties of suffering is that it is often "language shattering."[3]

Since the capacity to name and to speak is a distinctive mark of human life, being without voice only compounds the anguish of the sufferer. Human beings have a vocabulary and a discourse for virtually every experience. There are languages of politics, economics, sports, the arts, and many other forms of cultural activity. The computer programmer can explain the workings of a computer in exquisite detail; the investment counselor has a special discourse to speak about the intricacies of the economic system; the poet has a rich language to speak about the joys of friendship, beauty, and love. Intense pain, however, borders on the inexpressible, and our resources to speak of it are sparse.

This is true first of all for the afflicted person or community. When unexpected suffering strikes, and especially when it persists, the sufferer literally does not know how to express what is happening except to groan or cry or scream. Acute suffering creates an abyss of speechlessness for the person in pain. This loss of voice is also shared by those who try to accompany persons in distress and offer whatever help and comfort they can. The frustration of lacking the power of speech in the face of suffering is well known to pastors and other caregivers. They often literally do not know what to say to the sufferer or how to pray appropriately with her.

If we ask why people are robbed of speech when they experience acute pain, the answer lies in part in the limitations and vulnerability of embodied life. Physical pain has the power to destroy language. When the body is tormented with pain, a person may lose the capacity to concentrate her attention and coordinate her breathing and voice-producing organs in ways necessary to speak clearly and coherently. She may be able only to sigh and groan. In her study of the experience of pain, Elaine Scarry writes that "physical pain does not simply resist language but actively destroys it, bringing about an immediate reversion to a state anterior to language, to the sounds and cries a human being makes before language is learned."[4]

But in addition to the relentless demands of raw physical pain upon a person's concentration and energy, there are other factors that assault the sufferer's capacity to speak. The sufferer may feel ashamed of her brokenness and helplessness and may consider herself unworthy of the attention of others. Acute suffering attacks a person's self-respect. Moreover, the sufferer may feel profoundly isolated because both friends and strangers are made uncomfortable by her cries and may subtly signal that their desire is that she suffer in silence. Then, too, there is the awful fatigue of pain that eventually wears us out. Accompanying all this is the feeling of hopelessness that grows with persistent suffering and leads the sufferer to think: Since nothing will ever change, what difference does it make what I do or say? Thus are sufferers often pressured by internal and external forces to follow the ways of withdrawal, resignation, and finally silence as the only acceptable responses to the experiences of suffering.

Survivors of abuse, torture, and the terrors of death camps testify to the veil of silence that falls over the eruption of massive evil and suffering. The flames of Auschwitz, writes Elie Wiesel, drive speech to silence.[5] Wiesel's writings bear witness to the almost unbearable burden of speaking of the horrors of the Holocaust. The same is true of other people's histories of experienced brutality such as that of Native Americans and African slaves in America. It is far easier to suppress the memory of such events or to entomb them in silence than to bring them to memory and speech with all the pain this entails.

What is true of the communal experience of suffering is true also of the suffering of the individual. Karen's story, told in James Poling's *The Abuse of Power: A Theological Problem,* reveals the plight of a child who was abused at the age of four by her churchgoing father and then later in life by a clergyperson.[6] She did not allow herself to recall these events because they were so painful. Family, society, and church were co-conspirators in suppressing the truth of her life. As Karen's psalm, quoted in the previous chapter, indicates, her healing process began only when the horrible memory she carried silently was allowed to surface and the anger that it generated was given voice. Many survivors of abuse testify similarly: that acknowledging and speaking the truth to oneself, to others, and to God is enormously difficult and yet is crucial to recovery.

As is clear from Karen's story, some experiences may be so painful that they are kept secret for long periods of time as a survival strategy.[7] There are memories too abysmal to recall unless someone shares their burden. Those who are facing severe traumas in their lives need the support of people who will hear and share their stories of suffering. They need a community in which lament is honored and given voice. We believe that one of the important ministries of Christian congregations is to provide a place and a language to give voice to suffering. The prayer of lament provides an irreplaceable language of pain.

Rightly understood and practiced, all prayer is a transcending form of discourse. In prayer we name present reality in its brokenness as well as its beauty, and we reach out toward the transforming reality of God. By its very nature, then, prayer resists easy acceptance or accommodation to present conditions. As J. B. Metz writes, the language of prayer is "the only language capable of expressing many situations and experiences in our lives."[8] Understanding prayer in this way is especially apt if lament is included as one of its important elements. The prayer of lament and protest provides a language of suffering missing in the language of the everyday as well as in the technical jargon of science. Lament is an indispensable vehicle to articulate the pain and outrage that would otherwise remain voiceless. Neither the banal discourse of a consumer society nor the one-sidedly affirmative "official Christian language of prayer"[9] offers a form of speech that might give voice to the language-shattering experience of suffering.

It is precisely such a discourse of pain that we find in the biblical psalms of lament. In these prayers we encounter a language for all who are gravely sick or dying, or who have been abused and abandoned. As Patrick Miller writes, "giving voice and language to the experience of suffering is what happens in the form and words particularly of the psalms of lament or complaint. . . . There in the psalms the mute voice of pain receives speech and a mode of prayer, a way to ask for help when the ordinary modes and structures of human life cannot provide that any more."[10] In situations where all language has been shattered by suffering, the prayer of lament becomes a speech-enabling gift of God.

Pastoral care, worship, and all other aspects of Christian ministry must be informed not only by the need of the human spirit for a language fit to celebrate God's grace; they must also be sensitive to the need that suffering people have for a language of pain. When people dare to give voice in their prayers to their suffering and grief, they stand in the Old Testament tradition of lament and they pray alongside the Christ of Gethsemane and Golgotha. The prayer of lament is the language of the painful incongruity between lived experience and the promises of God. Without it we would be left speechless and hopeless in the midst of affliction.

CONFIRMING THE VALUE OF EMBODIED LIFE

The prayer of lament is closely linked to the reality and vulnerability of embodied life. Biblical prayers and cries of lament are accompanied by bodily actions—the tearing of garments, the wearing of sackcloth and ashes, the sounds of wailing and sighing. The psalms are graphic in their inclusion of the body's responses to pain and peril. They speak unabashedly of bones being "out of joint," of mouths being "dried up like a potsherd," and tongues that "stick to [one's] jaws" (Ps. 22); of eyes that "waste away because of grief"

(Ps. 6), of praying with "head bowed on [one's] bosom," of being "bowed down and in mourning" (Ps. 35).

As these prayers remind us, we lament with our whole selves. The experience of loss is felt by the whole person and that means also in our bodies. C. S. Lewis begins *A Grief Observed* with a description of what is happening in his body: "No one ever told me that grief felt so much like fear. I am not afraid, but the sensation is like being afraid. The same fluttering in the stomach, the same restlessness, the yawning. I keep on swallowing."[11]

Much work has been done on the physiological dimensions of grief. Mitchell and Anderson offer this list of bodily responses to grief:

> The whole of one's being grieves a loss. It should not be surprising that people report that their bones ache, their hearts throb, and their bowels are in ferment. These same symptoms are recorded in the thirtieth chapter of The Book of Job: "By night pain pierces my very bones, and there is ceaseless throbbing in my veins" (Job 30:17 NEV). Two phenomena often associated with acute grief are physical pain in one's limbs and sleep disturbance. The sleep disturbance is so common that one could almost call it universal; the limb pain is less common but still frequent. The pain, which is not actually in the bones but the muscles, is apparently the result of muscular tension associated with repressed feelings.[12]

The lament prayers and the feelings associated with them serve to remind us that we are embodied creatures, that our bodies and the bodies of others need attention and care. Biblical prayers do not confine the cry for help to the rescue of the soul. The petition for forgiveness is not sharply separated from petitions for bodily renewal and wholeness. Dualisms that tear soul from body and humanity from nature are alien to the biblical tradition, and they have played havoc with the life and worship of the church over the centuries.

A faith that confesses that God has created this material world and called it good, that honors and blesses the deep bonds and relationships that embodied existence supports, and that dares to speak of God's own embodiment in Jesus Christ places enormous value on life in the body.

It is a striking fact that the Gospel narratives underscore the embodied presence of God's grace in the life and ministry of Jesus: the austere physical conditions of his birth; his healing of the sick, often by touching them or being touched by them; his sharing of meals with disciples and outcasts; his physical as well as spiritual agony on the cross; and his bodily resurrection from the dead. Elaine Scarry notes that the single most captivating artistic representation of Christ for many people is the *Pietà*, the crucified Jesus lying in his mother's lap. In this image there is a conflation of the infancy and crucifixion narratives of Scripture, stories which accent the reality and urgency of bodily claims and needs.[13] The *Pietà*, we suggest, might be aptly described as a sculptured lament prayer.

The urgent need of a spirituality that affirms the value of the body is evident not only in harmful attitudes toward our own bodies or the bodies of our neighbors but also in destructive attitudes toward our natural environment. To a far greater extent than in previous ages of the church, the prayer of lament for despised and damaged bodies today must also include concern for the body of nature, ravaged by greed, exploitation, and reckless abuse. Our concern for the welfare of persons and communities must also embrace the needs of the world that surrounds and nurtures us.[14] As the apostle Paul says, the whole creation is groaning like a woman in labor, waiting for its release from bondage and longing for the appearance of the children of God (Rom. 8:19 ff.). This groaning of the creation makes a moral and theological claim upon all who pray to God the Creator in the name of the Word made flesh.

It is always the loss or diminishment of embodied life that is mourned in the prayer of lament. The prayer of lament and protest will belong to Christian spirituality as long as embodied life is cherished and its loss mourned. Conversely, the eclipse of the lament prayer in the life of the community of faith is a warning signal of a decline of commitment to the flourishing of all life created by God. Bonhoeffer captured the spirit of biblical prayer when he wrote: "Only one who cries out for the Jews may sing Gregorian chants."[15] Gregorian chants and hymns of exultation have their rightful place in the prayer and worship of the church, but until all creation is renewed and all broken bodies healed true praise will never be divorced from lament.

GRANTING PERMISSION TO GRIEVE AND PROTEST

If the community of faith has need for a language of suffering as well as a language of praise, there is also a need for permission to express grief and protest in face of suffering. Do Christians have permission to lament? At first this may seem a strange question since at least one form of lament is built into most worship services in the common confession of sin. In spite of their frequent and familiar lament for sin, however, many Christians wonder whether lament over suffering, abuse, or injustice is appropriate or permissible, especially as a form of prayer.

Who gives or withholds permission to lament within a community of faith? As already noted, the sufferer may withhold permission from herself to lament and protest out of a sense of shame or fear or hopelessness. But the permission to lament is also granted or withheld to a considerable degree by external factors, and in particular by the pastor, the congregation, the liturgy, the Bible, and the doctrines that regulate our faith and life.

Permission to lament is implicitly granted or withheld by a pastor in the way she relates to people who have been unjustly treated or who are in some other situation of distress. Pastors who are obviously uncomfortable when members of their congregation respond to experiences of suffering with complaint or anger give the unmistakable message that lament is inappropriate for a person of strong faith.

Permission to lament is also indirectly granted or withheld by the members of a congregation. A congregation may hasten to help and support or may isolate and withdraw from sufferers in their midst. These very different ways of responding to those who may be journeying through the valley of the shadow of discouragement, loneliness, illness, abuse, or death will do much to legitimize or delegitimize cries of pain and protest.

Granting or withholding permission to lament is further determined by what happens in the worship and liturgy of a congregation. Congregations and their leaders who insist that the worship service in all of its parts be "upbeat," even in the case of funeral or memorial services, declare thereby their unwillingness to permit full and honest expressions of loss, sorrow, and anger in the face of suffering and death.

Still another major factor in the granting or withholding of permission to lament is the way in which the Bible is read and used by a community of faith. In an earlier chapter we stated the case for seeing the prayer of lament as a strong strand of the prayer tradition of both Old and New Testaments, and we will not repeat what was said there. We need only underscore the primacy of the scriptural witness within the Christian community in giving direction and form to Christian life and piety.

We recall vividly an occasion on which one of the lament psalms—Psalm 88—was read in a seminary chapel by the colleague of an anguished professor mourning a son who had committed suicide.

Your wrath has swept over me;
your dread assaults destroy me.
They surround me like a flood all day long;
from all sides they close in on me.
You have caused friend and neighbor to shun me;
my companions are in darkness. (Ps. 88:16–18)

This is only one of many passages of Scripture that might be cited as granting permission to the community of faith to express feelings and thoughts that might otherwise be repressed. Whether the experience be that of abandonment by friends and even by God (Psalm 22), the ravages of illness and old age (Psalm 38), the sense of defeat and discouragement (Psalm 69), the suffering of abuse and other injustices (Psalm 55), the biblical witnesses are far freer and far more daring in their address to God in difficult circumstances than are many Christian congregations today.

Perhaps the most important factor in determining whether permission to lament is either given or withheld is our understanding of God. An understanding of God that implies that we must submit without question to whatever happens obviously constrains free expression of lament and outrage. On the other hand, belief in God emboldened by biblical interlocutors of God like Job and centered on the Christ who wept for his friend Lazarus, lamented over the city of Jerusalem, and cried out in agony on the cross liberates people for honest lament. In the final analysis, for the community of faith it is the living God attested by the biblical witnesses who grants the decisive permission to lament.

In speaking of the permission-granting value of the prayer of lament in Christian life and worship, we must be careful not to turn a permission into a mandate. There are important psychological, cultural, and theological differences among people that should not be overlooked. Pastoral theology and care must attend to context. As noted in the previous chapter, Theresa Snorton argues that the great strength and courage shown by African American women in the face of overwhelming odds, and the expectations that such strength of character has created, poses special challenges to the pastoral caregiver. While African American women have developed various survival strategies in their struggles, showing vulnerability and openly lamenting have not been typical responses. As Theresa Snorton notes in the essay cited earlier, "vulnerability is extremely risky for the womanist who outside the pastoral care moment must continue to contend with sexism, racism, and classism."[16] This cautious attitude toward public lament on the part of many women of color cannot be accounted for by speaking of denial or excessive pride. It has to do instead with the womanist's commitment to her community and with the special responsibilities she has within this community.

When we take such contextual factors into account, we will recognize that *permission* to lament is not to be equated with the *mandate* to lament. With this understanding we are prepared to appreciate Snorton's comment that it is helpful for the African American woman to know that Jesus, too, wept. The image of the lamenting Christ who embodies vulnerability in strength will be more meaningful to the womanist than being told of her "need" or "right" to lament. It is in the company of Jesus that there is safe and restorative authorization to lament.

PREPARING THE WAY FOR NEW UNDERSTANDINGS OF GOD

A crucial benefit of opening the practice of prayer to include complaint and protest against terrible loss and injustice is that our familiar understandings of God may be challenged and deepened. What does it mean for our understanding of God that believers are invited by the biblical witnesses and by Jesus' own action to engage in prayer in a manner that includes honest lamentations, hard questions, and angry protests?

To begin with, it means that we must acknowledge that there is much about God and God's purposes that we do not comprehend. Prayers of lament honestly acknowledge that we may now experience God as hidden, absent, or silent. In such prayer God is not experienced as familiar, predictable, or comforting but as shatteringly different and "other."[17] In such times faith is shaken to the foundations. While it is usually effortless to praise God for "all things bright and beautiful," it is terribly difficult to praise God when our eyes behold not the reign of goodness and justice but the loss of the beloved, the suffering of the innocent, and the triumph of injustice.

Such is the experience that lies behind the question to God asked by Wolterstorff in his lament prayer quoted at the beginning of this chapter: "Will I find you in the dark?" This is a question that never has a quick or easy answer. If the biblical tradition assuringly points to the presence of God even in the depths of Sheol (Ps. 139:7–12), it also holds before us the awful experience of abandonment at Golgotha (Mark 15:34). That God is to be found in the dark as well as in the light is never a matter of course. The life of faith involves real struggle. Just for that reason, it becomes clear why lament is by no means faithless prayer but instead the prayer of "a bruised faith, a longing faith, a faith emptied of nearness."[18] The prayer of lament gives voice to those struggling to find God in the darkness, in the "detours, labyrinths, even radical interruptions"[19] of communal history and personal life. This experience of God's hiddenness must not be quickly dismissed with ready-made formulas about the love of God. As David Tracy writes, "It is self-destructively sentimental for Christians to allow their understanding of the God who is Love to be separated from the Hidden God."[20] A sense of the absence or hiddenness of God is expressed in many biblical passages and is voiced by many survivors of the horrors of the twentieth century and by much of its literature and art. In the prayer of lament, we would argue, there is honest acknowledgment of this experience of the radical hiddenness of God.

If the prayer of lament enables us to give honest expression to the experience of the hiddenness of God, it is also paradoxically a form of resistance to all ideas about God as immutable and unaffected by what happens in the world. Nothing is more destructive of the spiritual life and the discipline of prayer than the fear that God does not care, is indifferent, is not deeply affected by what happens to God's creatures. Unfortunately, the theological tradition is itself partly responsible for eroding the vitality of the spiritual life by ascribing attributes to God such as immutability and impassibility that seem to render prayer useless and meaningless. Scholastic theologies

(handwritten margin note: OK) Don't agree with this.)

were inclined to describe God as so exalted, absolute, and self-contained as to be incapable of being moved by another. Those who cry out of the depths, however, fight against the ideas of divine immutability and divine apathy. For what reason would one lament or protest to God if one believed that God cannot be affected or touched by such prayer? If God is believed to be heartless, why should and how can people open their hearts to God? Measured by scripture, the idea of God as immutable and impassible is only, in the words of Karl Barth, a "miserable anthropomorphism."[21] We do not honor God by ascribing to deity what A. N. Whitehead labeled "metaphysical compliments." Far from being a lifeless metaphysical absolute who is unaffected by the creation, the God of the biblical witness is "vulnerable" to prayer.[22] The passionate prayers of lament and protest assume that God can be affected, that God is vulnerable to the cries and questions of the afflicted.

Indeed, contrary to axioms of divine immutability and impassibility, the biblical witnesses understand God's perfection to include the freedom to share the suffering of the creation. In response to the objection of some theologians that God's perfection entails only God's acting to relieve the suffering of creatures but excludes any experience of suffering by God, Elizabeth Johnson writes:

> The notion of love as simply willing the good of others prescinds from the reciprocity entailed in mature relations. . . . As actually lived, and paradigmatically so in the light of women's experience, love includes an openness to the ones loved, a vulnerability to their experience, a solidarity with their well-being, so that one rejoices with their joys and grieves with their sorrows. This is not a dispensable aspect of love but belongs to love's very essence.[23]

Perhaps the deepest challenge and correction that the lament prayer offers to our inherited understandings of God has to do with our deeply ingrained assumptions about the power of God. God's omnipotence has sometimes been construed as God's total control and domination of all events. In reaction to a doctrine of divine power as totalitarian control, Harold Kushner in a widely read book describes God's power as necessarily limited.[24] Since God is not the cause of everything, Kushner argues, God is not responsible when "bad things happen to good people." God has created a world of free creatures and cannot manipulate events in the world without destroying that freedom. Being good but not omnipotent, God is doing, so to speak, the best possible under the circumstances. Indeed, Kushner interprets the speeches of Yahweh to Job as saying in effect: "If you think being God is easy, why don't you try it sometime?"

According to Kushner, then, while it would make sense to be angry with the *situation* in which "bad things happen," it would be senseless to be angry with

God. Even if Kushner's alternative interpretation of the power of God may offer a kind of consolation to some people, it is questionable whether the countless Rachels of history would take much comfort in the knowledge that God is simply helpless. Are Rachel's cry and other lament prayers of the Bible taken seriously in Kushner's view? Has he not tailored them to fit his own doctrine of God?

Speaking on behalf of victims of the Holocaust and the survivors of child abuse, David Blumenthal describes God's power in a way that is diametrically opposed to Kushner. Blumenthal argues that in the light of historical experience as well as the evidence of many passages of Scripture, God is in fact "abusive, but not always." Hence, according to Blumenthal, lament is not only appropriate but necessary. God is not only to be loved but raged against, for while often benevolent, God is also sometimes abusive. We might wish the state of affairs were different and that God were not abusive at times, but we must take God as God is. Blumenthal concludes: "We will try to accept God—the bad along with the good—and we will speak our lament. We will mourn the bad, and we will regret that things were, and are, not different than they are. . . . These steps alone will enable us to have faith in God in a post-holocaust, abuse-sensitive world."[25] If Kushner's view sentimentalizes God's power, Blumenthal's view comes close to demonizing it. Can an abusive God be worshiped, and if God is abusive, is a theological foundation for ethics any longer posssible?[26]

Wanting to remain in deeper continuity with the biblical lament tradition than does either Kushner or Blumenthal, we think two things must be said about divine power, and their relationship is highly paradoxical. The first is that those who lament and protest call upon God to exercise redeeming power to overcome the evil and suffering that is being experienced. They trust that God has the power to save them even as they ask why God has not yet so acted. What would the prayer of lament mean if the one who prayed did not believe that God had the power to rescue and redeem?

The second thing that needs to be said about divine power from the standpoint of the prayer of lament is that if God can be affected by prayer, then the power of God is different from absolute, unilateral power. The biblical witness as a whole, and the lament prayer within it, demand a radical rethinking of the meaning of power in general and of the way God exercises power in particular. Brueggemann speaks of the prayer of lament as, in a sense, redistributing the power relationship between God and petitioner so that "the petitionary party is taken seriously and the God who is addressed is newly engaged in the crisis in a way that puts God at risk."[27]

The lament prayer is thus full of tension and paradox. On the one hand, it signals the breakdown of previous ideas about God that have foundered on the harsh facts of experience, with the result that God seems utterly hidden and frightening. On the other hand, it expresses a trust in the goodness of God so profound that it continues to cry out for God in the agony of God's apparent absence and silence and looks for redemption in the midst of God's terrible hiddenness.[28] Paul Ricoeur rightly speaks of "the enigma of a lament that remains . . . caught up within an invocation."[29]

In the light of the Christian gospel, we say what most needs to be said about the identity of God in relation to the prayer of lament when we say that it is prayer in the company of the one who cried in abandonment from the cross. Christians confess that God's boundless compassion is both deeply hidden and most fully revealed in the cross of Christ. The cross definitively marks the mystery of the costly love of God that embraces sinners, the alienated, the abused, and the abandoned.

The mystery of divine love also finds powerful expression in the classical Christian doctrine of the Trinity. The deep grammar of this doctrine points to the mystery of shared love as the very essence of God. Unfortunately, the model of relationships that has guided traditional interpretations of this doctrine has been hierarchical, and the exclusive imagery of Father, Son, and Spirit in which it has been cast has seemed to point to an essential divine maleness. Such an understanding of the doctrine, far from advancing a redefinition of divine power in terms of mutual self-giving love and openness to others, only reinforces oppressive views of power and order in human life and relationship. We agree with Elizabeth Johnson that our practice of prayer and liturgy, as well as our theology, "need a strong dose of explicitly female imagery to break the unconscious sway that male trinitarian imagery holds over the imaginations of even the most sophisticated thinkers."[30]

Recent reinterpretations of trinitarian doctrine have attempted to retrieve its meaning as a summary of the gospel of God's costly love. To affirm that God is triune is to declare that God is a living and dynamic reality, that God's being is in relationship, that God lives in the communion of three equal and mutually indwelling persons, that in the words of Catherine LaCugna, "the mystery of God is revealed in Christ and the Spirit as the mystery of love, the mystery of persons in communion who embrace death, sin, and all forms of alienation for the sake of life."[31] Properly understood, Trinity doctrine affirms that the eternal life of God, extended to us in the love of the Creator and the gracious missions of Christ and the Spirit, is freely open to experiences of negation, grief, loss, and abandonment for the sake of our healing and reconciliation to God and others in new community.[32]

To understand the doctrine of the Trinity this way is to require a radical reconception of divine power. The creative and redemptive power of the triune God is different from our standard models of power; it is neither totalitarian power nor what we call powerlessness but rather the empowering power of mutual self-giving love and shared life. The tripersonal mystery of divine love is the foundation and "ultimate paradigm of personal and social life."[33]

The task of interpreting both the doctrine of the cross of Christ and the doctrine of the Trinity as affirmations of the costly love of God on the one hand and of the radical hiddenness of God on the other drives theological language to its extreme limits. Yet this way of speaking is required both by the biblical witness and by the realities of human experience. The love of God is a mystery beyond our capacity to comprehend, and the mystery of God is none other than the freedom of the divine love. Making room for the prayer of lament alongside the prayers of praise and thanksgiving respects the hiddenness of the gracious God. That God's love is mysterious and God's mystery ultimately loving is the deep truth attested by Christians in countless different ways: in Julian of Norwich's vision of the motherhood of the crucified Christ, in Luther's doctrine of God as one who kills in order to make alive; in Barth's description of the history of Jesus Christ as "Servant Lord and Lordly Servant"; in Moltmann's portrayal of the infinite pathos and joy of the triune God; in Johnson's theology of the incomprehensible compassion of She who is; in Gutiérrez's meditations on the mystery and grace of the God to whom Job and Job's many sisters and brothers pray in anguish and in hope.

STRENGTHENING OUR SELF-UNDERSTANDING AS RESPONSIBLE AGENTS

Still another benefit of recovering the prayer of lament and protest is that it strengthens our self-understanding as responsible agents. This thesis may seem counterintuitive at first. More plausible on the surface is the charge that those who lament or complain to God about the condition in which they find themselves are simply evading their own personal responsibility. Since everyone is a sinner, the argument goes, no one is really innocent, and there is no basis for complaint regardless of what suffering one experiences. Confession of sin is a mark of taking responsibility; lament, it is implied, fosters irresponsibility.

This argument has particular force in churches that emphasize the radical nature of human sinfulness and the need of all people to receive the free grace of God. We have no desire to deny the truth that we are all sinners in need of God's forgiveness. But that is not to say that we deserve whatever evil may befall us. As pointed out in an earlier chapter, such an assumption was sharply repudiated by the psalmists, by Job, and by other Old Testament writings, as well as by Jesus who rejected a simplistic connection between sin and suffering.

The question of the relationship of the prayer of lament and personal responsibility, however, may be raised in a very different guise. One serious misunderstanding that may arise from speaking of the suffering of God is that suffering becomes a virtue in itself, or God is reduced to powerlessness, and believers are called to emulate this condition in their own lives. As Johnson notes, this misunderstanding has been particularly harmful to women in their struggle for full humanity. "In the long run the antidote to an impassible, omnipotent God is neither the reverse image of a victimized, helpless one nor silence on the whole subject. What is needed is to step decisively out of the androcentric system of power-over versus victimization and think in other categories about power, pain, and their deep interweaving in human experience."[34]

One way of stepping out of "the androcentric system of power-over" is to grasp the intimate bond between prayer and responsibility present in the prayer of lament. There are at least two aspects of this connection between lament and new awareness of responsibility.

One is that if we are permitted and encouraged to bring not only our praise and thanks to God but also our laments, questions, and protests, we are thereby given a special assurance that God honors us in the fullness of our humanity and wants to relate to us as responsible subjects. In prayer we are not only servants of God and children of God; we are also partners and co-workers with God. This is daring language, but it cannot be avoided if the fully personal relationship that God intends to have with us is to be honored. We do not need to try to hide any dimension of our life, however messy and terrifying, from God. We do not have to suppress our doubts, anger, outrage, or experiences of disappointment. We do not have to withhold our protest that things are not right. The freedom to pray in this way is a bedrock of human dignity and responsibility before God and others.

Prayer helps to form us as responsible persons. We become persons and discover our identity and responsibility in relationship with others. This is true above all in our relationship with God. Moreover, only relationships that permit us to assert ourselves without fear of shame or punishment, that give us room to take initiative as well as being recipients of the initiative of others, provide the contexts for moral and spiritual growth. The God who hears prayer—including questioning and contentious prayer—is the God who empowers human freedom and responsibility. In genuine prayer we do not become less human but more fully human as we speak and act in response to God's invitation to become partners and co-workers with God in the mending of creation. In sum, prayer that is bold enough to question and to argue is person-forming and person-empowering.

In an article entitled "The Sin of Servanthood," Jacquelyn Grant contends that terms like "servant" and "servanthood" often used to describe Christian life are frequently unhelpful and even damaging to women of color in a society that has relentlessly relegated them to servant status.[35] Such words have to be redeemed from their cultural captivity if they are to be rightly used and properly understood in a Christian context. Grant argues that a more liberat-

andro centric?

ing understanding of Christian life is to be found in the notion of discipleship. Consistent with Grant's approach, we would claim that the lament prayer helps to liberate the idea of God from identification with tyrannical deity and helps to liberate the meaning of being human from mere passivity and servitude. The God who honors the complaint of those unjustly treated and values argumentation over unquestioning submission is the God who has created and redeemed us to be free and responsible subjects.

A second way in which the prayer of lament fortifies human responsibility is that it counters the drift into apathy that threatens people who feel powerless. What J. B. Metz writes of all prayer is especially apt, we think, of the prayer of lament: "Prayer is an assault on the prevailing apathy with which we consistently and increasingly protect ourselves against hurt and disappointment until we finally reach the stage where nothing can touch us any more."[36] If we were to pray cautiously, guardedly, elegantly, passionlessly, passively, our prayer would be not only useless but harmful. Prayer of this sort sickens the soul because it only contributes to a spirit of hopelessness and resignation in face of evil. It makes us less than the subjects, less than the agents that God has created and called us to be.

Far from undercutting human responsibility, the prayer of lament activates "dangerous memories," to use the phrase of J. B. Metz.[37] The story of the passion of Jesus Christ is, of course, the central "dangerous memory" of the Christian community. Every time we remember the passion and death of Jesus, especially in the context of partaking of the bread and wine in the eucharistic meal, we encounter the power of God's renewing promise and grace. For the memory of his passion, while singular and irreplaceable, also exposes and sets under judgment the countless occasions of injustice and brutality in human history. "The cross of Christ . . . reveals the suffering of all God's preferred ones—the forgotten, the oppressed, and the marginalized of all history."[38]

Building on the work of Metz, a number of theologians have explored the importance of "dangerous memory" in the struggle of individuals and communities against defeatism and negative self-images. Remembering actual occasions of resistance to evil encourages continued resistance. Memories of suffering and acts of resistance are "dangerous" because they threaten to expose forgotten or suppressed truths. Since such dangerous memory questions the present order of the world, all tyrants do everything they can to suppress or eradicate it.

We have been contending that the prayer of lament strengthens rather than diminishes the sense of selfhood and agency of the one who laments. It is equally true that when Christians hear the cries and prayers of others for help, they know that a moral claim is laid upon them. The lament prayer prompts all—victim, perpetrator, and onlooker—to a new awareness of responsibility. It is too easy to ask God to feed the hungry, or protect the weak, or end racial discrimination, and then let the matter go at that. In the wake of *Kristallnacht*, we recall, Bonhoeffer read the psalmist's prayer, "How long, O God," as also a question he had to ask himself: "How long, O God, will I remain silent in the midst of this monstrous treatment of the Jews?" In different ways, the voicing of the lament prayer challenges abused, abuser, and bystander alike to a new and deeper sense of responsibility before God. Whether lament or praise, confession or intercession, all prayer presupposes "the readiness to assume responsibility."[39]

PURIFYING ANGER AND THE DESIRE FOR VENGEANCE

In our prayers we can and sometimes do build barriers between ourselves and others. Still more disturbing, our prayers can fuel hatred and can conspire to bring God into our plans of violent retaliation on our enemies. As we noted earlier, some of the lament psalms of the Old Testament and the cry for vengeance in the book of Revelation raise acute moral and theological concerns. Referring to the prayers of vengeance in Revelation, A. Yarbro Collins states: "One must ask whether prayers (and their equivalent) for the destruction or impoverishment of one's enemies should ever be encouraged. Justice may seem to call for them at times, but there is also the very real danger of becoming like the oppressor in one's opposition."[40]

Collins's concern is legitimate. Prayer can indeed be a way of exacerbating the hostilities and separations between people. It can be manipulated by zealots and generals to give moral and theological sanction to violence in response to violence. Used in this way, prayer becomes an instrument not of reconciliation and peace but of perpetuating the vicious circle of violence that poisons human relationships and human history. If we call for the freedom to lament and protest in prayer, are we advocating a spirit of divisiveness and hostility? Are we encouraging self-preoccupation, dwelling on wounds, and promoting an "us-versus-them" mentality? If we rage before God because of experiences of abuse and injustice, do we not implicitly call down the wrath of God on those who have injured us? Is not intercession rather than protest the true form of Christian prayer?

These questions are complex but unavoidable. One important issue is whether anger, counted in medieval Christian thought as one of the seven deadly sins, is ever morally legitimate. As Carroll Saussy and Barbara J. Clarke have argued, anger can be both destructive and constructive.[41] There are persons for whom the expression of rage is a regular response to the pain and turmoil of their lives (for example, batterers). There are also those who repress their anger at being abused and become self-destructive or misdirect their anger at innocent people.

Much of the current literature about anger suggests that repressed anger has much more destructive potential than anger that is openly acknowledged. This is especially true for those who have experienced the helplessness of victimization. Expressing anger and the desire for vengeance serve as "an alternative to living in the realm of inner deadness caused by the victimization."[42] Counselors with survivors of abuse testify that it is not possible to move toward forgiveness before acknowledging the reality and power of our anger. Of course, the expression of anger is not the end of the healing process, but can be an essential part of it if such expression occurs in contexts that help people not only to vent negative feelings but to explore them and make choices about how to live with them.

Anger can be constructive as well as destructive. The prophets and Jesus expressed anger at injustice and the disregard of God's purposes for life. The Bible does not say, "Never be angry," but instead, "Be angry, but do not sin" (Eph. 4:25). The moral quality of anger depends upon the reason for our anger. Anger is critically important in those situations where suffering could have been averted; where change is desperately needed. There is something terribly tragic about a theology and practice of care which encourages people to share their sorrow and yet does not help them protest and resist the sources of that sorrow in situations where protest is deeply needed.

The congregation that stands with people as they bury their slaughtered children stops short of its calling if it does not protest the violence that diminishes and destroys the lives of children. The community that mourns those who die at a hazardous railroad crossing and does not fight to get the needed safety equipment installed so that others may not suffer similarly is missing a critical dimension of life together. In addition to being sensitive to the groanings of hurt and abused people, Christian communities need to encourage struggle against conditions that cause suffering that could be prevented. We believe the cross symbolizes not only the "yes" of solidarity with sufferers but also a resounding "no" to senseless suffering.

But our reflection on the rage often present in prayers of lament must press beyond recognition of the psychological value of catharsis and the legitimacy of prophetic outrage against evil. We must also acknowledge that it is essential to bring one's rage to God so that it may be transformed. As Miroslav Volf writes, "By placing unattended rage before God we place both our unjust enemy and our own vengeful self face to face with a God who loves and does justice."[43] When we pray to God, who is present in the crucified One, we are constrained to recognize that our enemy is also one for whom Christ died even as we are also sinners who have not always acted justly toward others. Bringing our rage to God and relinquishing it to God is entirely different from the way of repression or the way of exacerbating the thirst for vengeance.[44]

One of the most problematic aspects of many of the biblical prayers of lament is their language of "enemies" and the deep hostility that is expressed against them. There are several points to make about such language. The first is that the enemies spoken of in biblical prayers of lament are not merely personal enemies but enemies of God and of God's purposes. It would be completely naive and misguided to want to cleanse biblical prayers of all reference to enemies as if there were no enemies of God, no persons and groups who set themselves against the purposes of God for the whole creation. Since such an assumption is not only false but dangerous, it is more faithful to the biblical witness as a whole to understand the language of enemies as referring to all that opposes the peace, justice, and reconciliation that God intends for the world rather than removing such language because it seems so offensive.

A second point is that almost without exception the psalmist prays that God will justly repay the enemies rather than asking for the personal power to act out of vengeance. It is one thing to leave judgment to God and quite another to take judgment into one's own hands. As Bonhoeffer stated in his sermon on a psalm of vengeance (Psalm 58), given in July 1937 in the midst of Nazi persecutions and imprisonments: "Whoever entrusts revenge to God dismisses any thought of ever taking revenge himself. Whoever does take revenge himself still does not know whom he is up against and still wants to take charge of the cause by himself."[46] Bringing our rage to God may, as Denise Hopkins suggests, even prevent a hateful action, "especially if it is offered up in the context of worship within the community of faith."[47]

And third, while as Christians we are called to love our enemies, this is not the same as pretending that we have no enemies, no one who has not injured us in some manner. As Christians, we are called to forgive our enemies. But when heinous crimes like genocide, "ethnic cleansing," child abuse, and mayhem are experienced, is forgiveness of enemies really possible? The answer to this question depends on whether we think forgiveness is a simple matter and something that is within our strength to do. If there is a power of victims to forgive those who have wronged them deeply, it is a power that comes from God and not themselves. As John Patton states, forgiveness is something we discover before it is something we do.[48] As recipients of God's gift of forgiveness to us, we are called and empowered to forgive others. Our resentment, hatred, and desire for vengeance thus need to be brought to God, need to be prayed away. The will to retaliation and the impulse to return violence for violence need to be purified in the fire of God's righteous love.[49]

Earlier we spoke of the dangerous memories of injustice and of struggles against it. Such memories can be dangerous in more than one way. They can be dangerous to defenders of systems of injustice and violence, but they can also be dangerous to those who retain these memories. By reminding us of injustices of the past, memory keeps bitterness and hatred alive. Can there be real forgiveness without forgetting? Should we then simply forget? But would not forgetting mean glossing over the evil that has been done?

This profound spiritual dilemma brings the central importance of the dangerous memory of the crucified Jesus into view. Christians are not counseled simply to forget past evils and let bygones be bygones. Rather they are summoned to set all these memories of evil in relationship to the event of the cross of Christ. The injustice and evil are remembered and named. Yet the vicious circle of violence is broken here. Forgiveness is far from easy; it is something to be discovered at the foot of the cross, where God offers forgiveness to all and renders judgment on all. As Miroslav Volf puts the matter with disarming honesty, we may not be able to forgive our enemy, but as Christians we know that we should.[50]

The prayer of lament is not to be exploited to fuel and perpetuate feelings of hostility and desire for revenge. Nor are the wounds of those unjustly treated to be ignored or minimized by calling their pain inconsequential in comparison with the sufferings of Jesus. Rather, the prayer of honest lament and protest is to be set within the narrative of the passion of the triune God. In Christ we are enabled to remember in a way that recognizes evil for what it is, that commits us to struggle against all injustice, and that nevertheless frees us from the vicious circle of violence and revenge.

PROMOTING SOLIDARITY WITH ALL WHO SUFFER

A further benefit of recovering the prayer of lament is that it often provides those who pray an opportunity to discover their solidarity with others who also suffer and long for salvation.

As we stated in the previous section, prayer does not always bond us with others. We must be very candid about that. Jesus told the parable of the Pharisee who, in his prayer, compared himself self-righteously with his fellow prayer: "I thank you, God, that I am not like other people: thieves, rogues, adulterers, or even like this tax collector" (Luke 18:11).

Although we have not heard many prayers that begin with such obvious self-congratulation as the Pharisee's prayer does, we have heard and participated in many prayers (in churches and around dinner tables) which thank God for our having things other people do not, or that express gratitude for escaping the tragedies that have befallen others. In the short story "Crazy Mary Katherine," Martin Bell describes the visit of two church representatives to the home of Mary Katherine to collect her pledge for the church's stewardship campaign. They essentially tell her that she should give out of gratitude that she is not like other people who are hungry, poor, or the victims of terrible tragedy. Mary Katherine, however, has just returned home from a short stay in a psychiatric hospital, where she has witnessed enormous tragedy and misery. She is no longer able to give thanks that she is not like those "others," because she has lived a life in common with them. The foundation of her own piety has been changed.[51]

The book of Job offers support for the claim that being honest before God about one's own experience of abuse, injustice, and abandonment, far from turning one in on oneself, or leading to a spirit of vengeance, may well occasion spiritual growth and increased sensitivity to others. In his commentary on Job, Gustavo Gutiérrez makes the point that Job rejects an abstract way of relating to God that characterizes the three defenders of God in the story. Job will have nothing to do with any way of speaking about or to God "that does not take account of concrete situations, of the sufferings and hopes of human beings."[52] As a result of the tenacity that keeps Job close to the realities of his own experience rather than giving in to the dogmas of the theologians around him, he is actually in a far better position to attend compassionately to the sufferings and needs of others. Because Job "sees more deeply into his own experience and refines his thinking," he comes to the realization "that he is not the only one to experience the pain of unjust suffering."[53] In chapter 24 of the drama, Job gives "the most radical and cruel description of the wretchedness of the poor that is to be found in the Bible."[54] Attending to his own misery does not isolate Job from fellow sufferers; instead it makes him acutely sensitive to their plight.

Job's experience in this regard is echoed in the moving reflections of Nicholas Wolterstorff on the loss of his twenty-three-year-old son in a mountain-climbing accident.

> Each person's suffering has its own quality. No outsider can ever fully enter it. Yet more of suffering is now accessible to me. I still don't fully know what it's like to be one of those mothers one sees in poverty posters, soup tin in hand, bloated child alongside, utterly dependent for her very existence on the largesse of others. I still don't fully know what it's like to be a member of a people whose whole national existence is under attack, Armenian or Jew or Palestinian. Yet I now know more of it.[55]

Wolterstorff recognizes that suffering both bonds and differentiates us. Even when people experience a common tragedy (war, exile, plane crash, fire, flood), each person's, each family's suffering has its own character. At the same time, we may become deeply aware of a common vulnerability and anguish—a sense of shared *humanity*—that helps us place our suffering in a larger context and experience a new sense of connection with other suffering human beings amidst our own pain.

According to the Gospel narratives, Jesus' personal anguish in prayer in the Garden of Gethsemane did not make him self-preoccupied or bitter. Rather, it was the preparation for the prayer on the cross where he not only cried out in abandonment but also asked for the forgiveness of those who

crucified him (Luke 23:34), offered assurance to one of the criminals crucified by his side (Luke 23:43), and persevered to the end, even when he may
have doubted the efficacy of his mission. Similarly, Paul's reflections on his
own sufferings made him sensitive to the groanings of the whole creation.
The Spirit of God, who is at work in our prayers and who enables us to
groan when our pain is too deep for words (Rom. 8:26), bonds us with all
suffering creatures. In the tradition of the psalmists, and of Jeremiah, Jesus,
and Paul, the prayer of lament and pain does not end with self-absorption,
but with a journey to the depths of our pain to the point where it is shared,
opening us to new solidarity with the whole creation that groans for the
coming "freedom of the glory of the children of God" (Rom. 8:21).

REVITALIZING PRAISE AND HOPE

Lament is often thought to be the very antithesis of hope and praise, and the
assumption of their incompatibility may help explain why the voices of
lament are often met with fear and exclusion both inside and outside the
church. Surely the primary purpose of human life from a Christian perspective is doxology: to praise, glorify, and serve God.[56] As the first question of
the Westminster Shorter Catechism states: the chief end of human life is to
glorify and enjoy God forever. If joy, praise, and hope are so basic to
Christian life and worship, how can there be room for bold and honest
lament and protest in prayer?

Paradoxical as it may seem, genuine hope cannot be separated from the
experience of suffering, and authentic joy and praise cannot be divorced
from the permission to lament and protest. Just as we come to know the true
meaning of hope only through the experience of suffering, so we can praise
God with a full and joyful heart only if we are free to grieve and lament the
real pain and injustices of our world. As Walter Brueggemann insists: only
grief permits newness; only lament makes way for praise.[57]

As studies of the psalms of lament have shown, their literary structure
itself offers a way to move with authenticity from honest naming of the evil
that oppresses to new hope and praise of God, who alone can rescue from
bondage and destruction. A movement of transformation is recorded in
many lament psalms, a movement from the depths of grief and anger to fresh
hope in and praise of God. This movement is neither automatic nor direct
and orderly. It tracks a fierce struggle for faith in God that has its ups and
downs and that may last a lifetime. "A quick reading of all one hundred fifty
psalms in order takes one on a roller coaster ride of emotion, from joy to
despair, to anger, to thanksgiving, and back again."[58] Though the way of the
lament prayer is circuitous and uncertain, the testimony of many of the
psalms is that pain can be transmuted into praise. How this transformation
occurs is never explained; there is, nevertheless, the witness that it happens.

What is most important to emphasize here is that the doxology that accompanies biblical laments does not come cheaply. The hallelujahs are never "hollow."[59] According to Brueggemann, "The doxological act of self-abandonment, done completely without grudge, is the culmination of the process in which there has been testing, risk, and now resolution."[60]

The connection between freedom to lament and genuine hope can be further clarified by distinguishing Christian hope from resignation, presumption, and illusion. Resignation is accepting the way things are without complaint or resistance. It is, in effect, saying, "This is the way things are. They will never be different. I must simply accept the way the world is with all of its suffering and injustice." Lament refuses to make this concession. It is therefore on the side of hope, which fights the spirit of resignation. By refusing to concede that the present state of affairs is the last word, and by recalling the mighty acts of God in the past, those who lament prepare the way for new hope and new praise.

In the words of Samuel Balentine: "It is the very nature of lamentation to resist resignation and to press for change. Where there is lament, there is life, and even in the midst of suffering, this life will be vital and expectant. When the lament ceases to function and all questions are silenced, then what is, is accepted as what will be, in religion, in society, in the political and economic structures of life."[61]

Hope and praise are also different from presumption. The presumptive attitude is that we have in our possession and control all the resources necessary to bring about the desired change. The future is entirely of our making, and it is ours to shape as we will. If hope rejects the spirit of resignation, it also refuses to follow the way of presumption. Genuine hope presupposes another in whom one hopes and a community with whom one hopes. William Lynch describes hope as the sense that there is a way out, and hopelessness as the sense that there is no way out, no exit.[62] The prayer of lament, at least as it is expressed in the biblical tradition, presupposes that there is a way out, but that this way out lies in the first place in the hands of God. Hope in God differs radically from presumption, and praise of God is totally different from an attitude that evil is no longer a threat and does not have to be resisted.

Hope also differs from illusion. Illusion lives on unreality. It no longer has an interest in recognizing the need for change or of asking what resources there may be to bring about this change. It abandons the world to hopelessness and indifference and lives instead in a world of fantasies and fictions. As we noted in chapter 3, the essence of a theology of glory according to Luther is that it calls the bad good and the good bad. A theology of the cross, by contrast, "calls the thing what it actually is."

The importance of being honest with oneself, with others, and with God about the awesome power of evil is emphasized by Cecil Williams, pastor of

Glide United Methodist Church in San Francisco, in his book *No Hiding Place*. Williams graphically describes Glide's effort to address the staggering problem of crack addiction in its community. As he struggled to develop an effective ministry in this situation, Williams came to the realization that no one was facing the truth: that African American urban communities are in danger of a form of genocide. Without clear recognition of what is actually going on in one's life and one's community, there can be no help and no hope of recovery.

> *Recognition* is the first act in the drama of recovery. Each of us must recognize the cunning characteristics of addiction, admit our true feelings, and face whatever pain we've tried to hide through our addictions. No secret is too terrible, no memory is too horrible, no rejection is too harsh. With courage, and in the company of others, we can tell the truth. . . . We don't need drugs when we come to recognize ourselves and are honest with one another.[63]

What Williams helped his congregation see is that there can be no help or hope apart from telling the truth and calling things by their right names. While illusions may resemble hope, they are in fact mere counterfeits of hope. As Andrew D. Lester states, "People who hope do not need to dodge the facts or obscure the objective data. Hope does not function as an opiate that causes people to deny reality. In fact, hope provides the courage to face whatever chaos and trauma life throws at us. Hope does not try to avoid the pain of finite existence nor is it naive about suffering."[64]

Rightly understood, the act of lament, far from being the antithesis of hope and praise, is their necessary companion in a world full of suffering and injustice. Those who lament dare to name the brokenness of reality rather than denying it; they refuse to pretend that it is other than it is; they want nothing to do with empty consolations. At the same time, they refuse to resign themselves to the given. Like Rachel mourning for her children who are no more, they refuse to be consoled apart from the transformation, not only of their own lives but of a world in pain.

If those who dare to lament in their prayers refuse both the false comforts of illusion and the empty consolations of resignation, they also distinguish themselves from arrogant and presumptuous attitudes because they look not to themselves but beyond themselves for redemption. The bond between honest lament and genuine praise is simply and beautifully expressed in the lines of an African American spiritual:

Nobody knows the trouble I've seen,
Nobody knows but Jesus;

Nobody knows the trouble I've seen,
Glory, Hallelujah.

Contending that "lamentation is an indispensable expression of doxology," Catherine LaCugna sees the prayer of lament as "a form of praise in which God is rightfully held accountable to God's promises: to comfort the widow, heal the afflicted." She argues that "the true atheist would be not the one who does not believe in God but the one who cannot bring to God his or her suffering, doubt, and anguish, in the expectation that God will respond."[65] LaCugna sees an analogue of the place of lamentation in relationship with God in intimate human relationships. When partners grow distant because one or both feel the other has reneged on the promise that binds them together, expression of lament is "a call back to fidelity." The wounded partner places the present difficulty within their history as lovers "just as lamentation reactivates our relationship with God and enables us to resituate ourselves within, not outside, the history of that relationship."[66]

To summarize: contrary to the notion that lament and hope, protest and praise are incompatible pairs, the fact is that genuine hope and authentic praise do not exist in a vacuum; they presuppose a spiritual struggle. Without this struggle, there is no recognition of the real bondage and alienation of present reality, no honest naming of the experience of abandonment, no genuine cry for deliverance, and no openness for new acts of God's grace. The apathy and numbness that threaten hope and stifle praise in the face of massive oppression and chronic suffering are challenged by the passion of the prayer of lament.

Having outlined our pastoral theology of the prayer of lament, the task of our final chapter will be to offer some sketches of the embodiment of the prayer of lament in the practices of Christian life and pastoral ministry.

What are the functions + fruits of faith? A psych/couns oriented question.
Sometimes grief disrupts our usual relationship to God. How do you express that in prayer? Faith reformed in suffering + lament. So faith doesn't disappear in such contexts — it's changed
How including lament prayers helps Christian life:
  Offers language to pain
  confirms value of embodied life
  permission to protest/grieve
  stretches understanding of God
  strengthens understanding of self as responsible
  purifies anger, desire for vengence
  solidarity w/ others who suffer
  revitalise hope + praise — vs illusion presumption resignation

So this is why the prayer of lament is theologically important in their view

CHAPTER SIX

THE PRAYER OF LAMENT AND THE PRACTICE OF MINISTRY

Ministers might better think of themselves as pastoral midwives.
—*Margaret L. Hammer,* Giving Birth

I n the preceding chapters we have traced the prayer of lament in the biblical tradition, explored its reception in classical Christian theology, and described its use in the writings of twentieth-century pastoral theologians. We have also ventured an outline of our own pastoral theology of the prayer of lament. In this chapter we ask where and how the prayer of lament is concretely embodied in Christian life and pastoral ministry. Our intent is to be suggestive rather than definitive.

According to Scripture, giving birth to new life is a valuable image of God's creative and redemptive work (John 3:3). Christian ministry, therefore, is appropriately viewed as assisting in this process in which God brings forth new life. More precisely, pastoral ministry is aptly described as a kind of midwifery, offering assistance and care to those who are struggling for renewed faith in God in the midst of suffering and grief.[1]

The image of the midwife has had a long history in Western philosophy and theology. Socrates spoke of his dialectical method of drawing out ideas from his students as midwifery. Through skillful questioning he claimed to be able to bring forth latent knowledge of concepts like justice and wisdom among those who were thought to be utterly ignorant. Sigmund Freud, too, spoke of his method of therapy as a kind of midwifery.[2]

Long before Socrates and Freud, biblical writers honored the role of the midwife. According to the book of Exodus, two Hebrew midwives by the names of Shiphrah and Puah were charged by Pharaoh to kill all the Hebrew boys at whose birth they assisted. By defying the royal order and saving the lives of the infants, Shiphrah and Puah were celebrated by the biblical witness as partners in God's life-giving activity on behalf of the people of Israel in bondage (Exod. 1:15–21).

There are several reasons why midwifery, especially of the sort represented by Shiphrah and Puah, is an apt image of pastoral ministry. In the first place, the midwife is present at the birth of new life but is not herself the primary agent through whom the new life appears. She assists in the birthing process rather than being the source of life or the one through whom new life arrives. Second, the midwife is well aware that there is struggle, risk, and danger in the birthing process and does not pretend otherwise. Nevertheless, she is present to offer what help she can. Finally, the midwife seeks to be obedient to God's work of bringing forth new life and hope, especially for the vulnerable. Unable to finally control the outcome of her labor, or the labor of those she assists, she strives to be faithful where uncertainty and disappointment are present alongside grace and promise.

It is in this sense that we speak of ministers as midwives of the prayer of lament. Our point is not that ministers should impose prayers of lament on situations where such prayers are not in some way already present in the lives of those who suffer. Rather, we contend that where mute pain reaches for sound and cries of protest search for words, ministers can best assist the sufferer by interpreting these cries as a testimony of faith under trial and as inarticulate prayer. In continuity with the biblical lament tradition, the ministry of the church assumes that the passionate prayer of lament can be a way that hope is reborn.

If pastors are to serve as midwives of the prayer of lament and protest in Christian life and ministry and in this way serve the cause of healing and hope, they will need the courage and imagination to discern the rudimentary presence of the prayer of lament and the appropriateness of its explicit use in the practices of ministry in concrete and varied contexts.

Christian life and ministry, we think, are best understood as practices or as sets of practices. Just as Christian life is not simply saying yes to a list of doctrines or church teachings, so Christian ministry is not simply following a set of "how-to" rules. By describing Christian life and ministry as practices, we simply mean that being Christian is embodied in a number of regular activities. There are particular habits and practices that shape the character of Christian communities and their members over a period of time, giving a distinctive identity, direction, and meaning to their life of faith.[3]

Speaking and hearing the Word of God, celebrating the sacraments, singing hymns, and addressing God in prayer are practices of Christian life and ministry. So too are caring for others, especially those who are poor, sick, or otherwise vulnerable; offering forgiveness to those who have injured us as well as accepting forgiveness from those we have injured; and working for justice and peace in all relationships of life.

In this chapter we will explore concrete embodiments of the prayer of lament in several important practices of Christian ministry: corporate worship, pastoral care, the struggle for justice and reconciliation in the public arena, and the cultivation of theological reflection in congregations.

THE PRACTICE OF WORSHIP

Worship is the central activity of a Christian congregation, and worship is primarily doxology. Can Christian worship also make room for lamentation? Can the prayer of lament be part of Christian worship in a way that strengthens hope and promotes resistance to the forces of death?

When Lydia Villanueva began her pastoral ministry at St. Mary's Hope Lutheran Church a few years ago, she quickly became immersed in the joys and sorrows of life in Humboldt Park, a predominantly Hispanic community in Chicago's northwest side.[4] A lovely, well-maintained park, bright banners across the main boulevard running through the neighborhood, and the music and conversation that often flows from house to house, testify that energy and pride are present in the community. An affirmation of hope is enshrined in the very name of the church. The weekly communion services feature joyous liturgies and contemporary music, accompanied by a skilled pianist and often a drummer and guitarist. It is common practice to gather after the worship service for food and conversation in the church fellowship hall.

At the same time, many Humboldt Park residents struggle with pressures of economic and social survival. Older family members miss their native homes in Central America, Mexico, and Puerto Rico, while their children attempt to make their way in large urban schools. The street on which St. Mary's Hope is located divides the territories of two rival gangs. Members of the church are accustomed to the sound of gunshots, and families and neighbors of the congregations have lost loved ones to gang and drug violence. Particularly devastating are the deaths of children and teenagers. In Humboldt Park, and countless communities elsewhere, many people survive by adopting a way of life that comes close to adjusting to the violence, becoming almost numb to it, even when it creeps up to their very doorsteps.

Survival strategies in difficult circumstances involve both benefits and costs. Villanueva was concerned about the church's practice, established before she arrived, of renting out the church hall for neighborhood gatherings and parties. On the one hand, the practice was intended to be an act of hospitality as well as a way to provide much-needed income. On the other hand, alcohol use, and at times alcohol abuse, occurred at these parties, and occasional fights erupted. These parties, coupled with an increasing awareness of the deaths of neighborhood children and teens from drugs and violence, troubled her deeply. One day, in a Hebrew translation practicum she attended, the group worked on a passage from Amos, and Villanueva was moved to action by the passage they translated:

> Alas for those who . . . put far the evil day, and bring near a reign of violence. Alas for those who lie on beds of ivory and lounge on their couches and eat lambs from the flock and cows from the stock, who

sing idle songs to the sound of the harp, and like David improvise on instruments of music, and who drink wine from bowls, and anoint themselves with the finest oil, but are not grieved over the ruin of Joseph. (Amos 6:1a, 4–6)

Villanueva describes that practicum as a kind of epiphany experience. She recalls hearing the teacher translate "the ruin" that Israel does not grieve for as "the sons" or "the children." The image of people partying coupled with the lack of visible grief and protest over the children being destroyed was so powerful that she felt it was literally a vision that she was called to preach. The following Sunday she lifted up that image and called her congregation to a new accountability for the use of the church hall as a first step in a larger accountability for the lives of children in the community. What surprised her was the congregation's response to her sermon. "I thought the people were going to be judgmental, but no, they just began to cry. . . . I realized in that moment that they were running from the pain; how they were hiding the pain; how they were not doing anything. And I told them: 'I hope we can stop this and begin to look at the pain and the suffering, and to look at what's happening to our own children, and to our own Puerto Rican community.'"[5]

Following the grief response of that day, Villanueva began to plan another service, a service for All Saints' Day, that would create a place for people to grieve and reflect about what was happening in their community. She describes the process of building this service as a "conversation with God" that eventually led to a new experiment in liturgy at St. Mary's Hope.

The pastor informed her congregation in advance that there would be a special time in the All Saints' Day service set aside for *Un Memorial,* a memorial for those who had died, especially children who had died and were continuing to die as a result of violence in Humboldt Park and other neighborhoods. The overall order of service was familiar to the congregation, with the usual opening service of gathering, confession, and praise; the proclamation of the Word through Scripture readings and sermon; and the response to the Word through the offering and the prayers of the people. The service ended with the celebration of communion. *Un Memorial* was placed after the prayers of the people and before the communion liturgy.

Un Memorial begins with a litany on the Beatitudes, adapted by Villanueva, focusing on Jesus' promises to those who hunger and mourn and who struggle to show mercy and peace. To the promises of Jesus the people respond: "So be it! Thank you Lord, our King. We draw near to you with the sadness that is in our heart and with the burdens that weigh us down."

Un Memorial proceeds with five ritual activities that involve tangible symbols and physical action on the part of the participants. The first activity invites remembrance of departed loved ones, with the assurance that "the darkness of sorrow and death is not able to erase from our lives the ones whom we loved passionately." A unison prayer for God's comfort and hope accompanies the lighting of the candles.

The second activity involves the distribution of flowers and, if the participants choose, the sharing of names of lost loved ones. After the naming, the flowers are gathered into a vase and placed on the communion table.

A third activity centers on the "bitter tears that choke us," symbolized with salt water. Participants dip a finger in the salt water and taste it, and then they pray a unison prayer of lament that brings together excerpts from several psalms of lament and other biblical passages. Included in the prayer are laments for the children killed daily because of violence, including in the St. Mary's Hope neighborhood.

The fourth activity moves from a cry of pain and protest to a prayer for God's help in recovering from loss and sorrow and includes the treasuring of the memory of loved ones. The symbol used in this part of the ritual is honey, representing the moments of sweetness loved ones brought to the lives of their survivors. Everyone is invited to dip their fingers into the honey and taste it. A unison prayer that concludes this activity is from Psalm 121: "Where will my help come from? My help comes from God."

The final ritual activity in *Un Memorial* looks to the future. The God who forgives sins, heals infirmities, frees life from the grave, fills with love and tenderness, and rejuvenates the weary like an eagle (Ps. 103:1–5) is blessed, and the participants are signed with consecrated oil. After the blessing and sharing of the peace, a festive communion service begins.

The first time this special service was held, the pastor went to the fellowship hall afterward and saw people sitting together, quietly telling stories—especially persons who had lost loved ones in sudden and tragic circumstances. She sat down and simply listened to stories of her parishioners that she had never heard before. The All Saints' service has become a tradition at St. Mary's Hope. Its aim remains the same—to provide a place for lament within the structure of congregational worship, so that people might experience solidarity in their suffering and inspiration to be agents of God's hope.

There are many ways that the prayer of lament can be used in the worship life of a congregation. Obviously, the way just described for embodying the lament tradition is only one, and it would not fit the worship practices of every congregation. Nevertheless, there are at least two important insights for the practice of lament in congregational worship suggested by the St. Mary's Hope experience that are pertinent to other Christian worship traditions.

First, it is clear from the St. Mary's Hope All Saints' Day service that any inclusion of the lament prayer in worship must take account of the deep interplay between communal context, Christian tradition, and the faith experiences of the congregation and the worship leaders. The design of liturgy must never be arbitrary or casual. It must develop within a rich dialogue between the texts of the Christian tradition and the life contexts of the community and its individual members. If the familiar pattern of Lutheran liturgy, with its regular practice of Holy Communion, was important to the St. Mary's Hope congregation and its pastor, so also was their Hispanic cultural heritage. Consequently, the pastor attempted to offer a worship experience that remained faithful to the classical pattern of Christian worship while also incorporating cultural symbols like white flowers that would have special meaning to members of the congregation, most of whom are Puerto Rican. Taking up the familiar and introducing new meaning in ancient practices can deepen, even transform the worship experience.

Also important in the construction of the St. Mary's Hope liturgy was the pastor's own personal discipline of prayer, her study of the Bible, and her immersion in the life of her community. This engendered a creative spiritual ferment from which she drew images and ideas for worship. At its best, worship leadership is never perfunctory or routine but deeply spiritual work. No "how-to" approach to embodying lament in worship can capture or domesticate the process of transformative encounter present when the cry of pain and protest, found in the lament tradition, intersects with the particular social context of a community and the spiritual lives of its members and leaders.

The pastor's own discipline of prayer and Bible study were important factors in the development of the St. Mary's Hope liturgy. An encounter with the prophet's lament over the ruin of Joseph roused her to action. Through her own experience she had come to believe, in the words of Walter Brueggemann, that Christians must "practice grief against denial."[6] Contrary to her religious upbringing, which discouraged any questioning of authority, this pastor had learned that her own life with God could only flourish when she could, as the old hymn says, "carry everything to God in prayer,"[7] including protest and anger at entrenched injustice and violence.

Second, it is clear from the St. Mary's Hope All Saints' Day service that the lament prayers and narratives of the people are properly set within the framework of the narrative of the gospel of Jesus Christ and his passion, death, and resurrection. The wounds that have been suffered are not absolutized and thereby allowed to have the final say about one's identity and one's future. The prayers of the people of God, their laments, thanksgivings, petitions, and praise are appropriately gathered into the eucharistic celebration and become part of the Great Prayer of remembrance and hope that focuses on Jesus Christ and that embraces the whole groaning creation.

In his worship resource *Liturgies of Lament*, J. Frank Henderson discusses several principles for creating liturgies of lament and identifies a variety of shapes that lament liturgies can take.[8] The St. Mary's Hope All Saints' Day service, taken as a whole, is shaped like a psalm of lament, with the opening

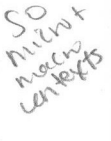

of the service conveying the address to God; the movements of *Un Memorial* conveying complaint, confession of trust, petitions for help, and words of assurance; and the eucharistic service conveying the vow to praise. Other shapes that liturgies of lament can take are liturgies of the Word, evening prayer, procession, and penitential services.[9]

It is not always the case that lament "shapes" a worship service in the way it does in the St. Mary's Hope service. Sometimes it functions simply as one element in a traditional service, serving a specific and limited use—providing a way to focus the prayer of the people (for example, a special litany for the grieving), being one of the hymns sung by the congregation or choir, or providing the subject matter for a sermon or homily. Thus the lament prayer can be introduced in quiet and simple ways in regular Sunday worship as well as in "occasional services" (for example, funerals, healing services, etc.) of the church.

Homiletical reflection on the meaning of lamentation might take many different forms: a teaching sermon about the lament psalms; an effort to connect the lamenting psalmist's circumstances and present-day circumstances in people's lives (for example, connecting the lament of Psalm 55 and the experience of victims of domestic violence); or a dialogical sermon that gives ample space for the articulation of hard questions and deep feelings in the face of personal loss or communal calamity. As noted in an earlier chapter, there are certain lament texts, such as those which contain themes of vengeance and hatred of enemies, that require homiletical interpretation and guidance in the light of the gospel of God's forgiveness and the call of Christ to love even our enemies.

It should be emphasized that it is not the use of texts, hymns, or sermons alone that can make room for the lament tradition in the worshiping congregation. We recall the ministry of a friend, who made it a weekly habit to walk into the midst of his congregation to hear the prayer requests of the people. One Sunday a woman raised her hand. He stood beside her to hear her request. As she began to speak, she was overcome with emotion and could not continue. The pastor said gently, "Take your time," and patiently waited until she could resume speaking. His ability to receive tears without undue anxiety, his way of communicating that expressions of pain when loss is experienced are normal rather than unusual or problematic, helped make hospitable space for lament and laughter to coexist in the prayer life of the congregation.

THE PRACTICE OF PASTORAL CARE

We will offer some thoughts on the potential role of the prayer of lament in the concrete practice of pastoral care by focusing on the following two episodes of ministry. (Names and all identifying information have been altered.)

Susan was seventeen years old when her pastor made sexual advances to her. She felt a deep attachment to the pastor and blamed herself for the romantic relationship that gradually developed between them because, as she later put it, she really "wanted him to love her." She continued to be active in the church, even when she went away to college and the relationship ended. Ten years after the beginning of Susan's romantic relationship with her pastor, she contemplated entering the ministry but began to be overwhelmed with feelings of rage and confusion. For the first time, she grasped the magnitude of the betrayal of trust on the part of her former pastor. While she continued to harbor feelings of guilt for her own part in the relationship, she was now primarily struggling with her anger. She knew she needed help but was unsure where to turn. She joined a Bible study group that was helpful to her in many ways, especially because people shared stories from their own lives in relation to the topic being discussed. One evening, during a conversation about guilt and forgiveness, Susan could not hold back angry tears as her Bible study partners spoke of the importance of forgiveness. Susan recounted the story of her relationship with her former pastor and her anger both about his behavior and about the counsel she had frequently received to forgive the pastor and let it go at that. Some members of the Bible study were completely silent about her story; others asked her several factual questions about what had happened, leaving her feeling not believed; others emphasized the importance of forgiveness; some recommended further counseling. Feeling misunderstood and humiliated, Susan stopped attending the meetings of the group and wondered whether she should simply give up on the church.

Philip, an ordained deacon, was frustrated by his attempts to offer emotional and spiritual support to George and Sally, a middle-aged couple whose sixteen-year-old daughter, Jenna, had been killed in an automobile accident. He joined the pastor and many other members of the congregation in offering support through many means, from providing them food and childcare for their small children to making phone calls and visits. George and Sally expressed deep gratitude for the support, but bewildered Philip and some other members of the church by behaving stoically in the face of the tragedy. The parents repeatedly stated they were confident that what happened was part of God's plan and insisted on an "upbeat" memorial service with the understanding that Jenna was a fun-loving person and would have wanted it that way. Months after the service, they still answered questions about how they were doing by speaking of Jenna's death as God's will to be accepted. While some church members praised the family for how well they were coping in the face of tragedy and saw them as a fine example of faith, Philip worried that this interpretation of God's activity amounted to a denial of their suffering.

The juxtaposition of these two stories exposes some of the complexities of including the prayer of lament in pastoral care. While we have explored many aspects of our thesis that the prayer of lament is an important resource for suffering people, the actual practice of pastoral care, as well as other ministry practices, reminds us that ministry is an art rather than a technique.[10] How is the prayer of lament embodied in the ministry of pastoral care, amidst the varying circumstances church leaders encounter in congregations?

A proper response to this question must begin with the emphasis that pastoral care, like all the ministry practices discussed in this chapter, is offered within and is sensitive to the communal contexts in which people of faith live and struggle. Pastoral care cannot be rightly understood if it is limited to what happens between caregivers and individuals (see chap. 4). As the preceding section on worship makes clear, pastoral care is part and parcel of the total life and practices of the community of faith. Susan was clearly seeking a community that would provide sanctuary for her cry of pain and protest. Her experience reminds us that congregations often need help in creating hospitable space for the prayer of lament. In our exploration of the prayer of lament and the practice of worship, we saw how the worship life of a congregation can make room for cries of sorrow and protest. Susan's story reminds us that small groups within congregations (for example, recovery groups of all kinds, lay pastoral care groups, Bible study groups) have the *potential* to provide opportunities for exploring and practicing how the church can be a sanctuary for the prayer of lament, although they can also function to stifle such prayers. We recall Brueggemann's suggestion that the lament psalms may have been used not in the temple worship but in small communities analogous to "house churches," in which rituals of rehabilitation were practiced.[11] Philip's story reminds us that even when the hospitable space is there, not every sufferer is able to immediately take advantage of it. Lament is risky—both for the sufferer and for the community.

Taken together, the stories of Susan and Philip remind us that sufferers have different expectations about Christian communities. Not every gift sought is given in Christian community, and not every gift offered by the community can be received by an individual at any given point in time. In the following paragraphs we will attempt to trace the movement involved in the utterance of the prayer of lament: from silence, to tentative efforts to articulate the cry, and then to its full expression. We will also attend to the role of ministers in accompanying and facilitating this movement.

Silence and Screams: The Cry of Lament Begins in the Body
We have said that the prayer of lament confirms the value of embodied life (chap. 5). Psalms of lament and other lament passages, such as those from

the book of Job, speak graphically of bowels in tumult, of pain in the limbs, of weeping, of sleeplessness, of pain and protest that is known first, and perhaps most deeply, in the body.

In *The Poet's Gift*, Donald Capps speaks of pastoral conversation as an "embodied language"—never concerned with just words alone but with "the language of the body."[12] Drawing on the poetry of Denise Levertov, Capps shows how the body is a source and a means of understanding for pastoral caregivers.

At times, the beginning of speech, amidst unspeakable suffering, is simply to be able to say, "It hurts *here*"—in the heart, the stomach, the head, the limbs. Sometimes there is no speech for a long time to express the particularity of the wound. In Susan's case, wounds were carried for years before they found expression. Before words, there are emotions and memories, carried and felt in the body.

In the case of George and Sally, it would be easy for the pastor to overlook the body in attending solely to the words being spoken. The bodies of grieving persons have their own speech. Attending to the tightened jaw, the clenched fist, the slumped shoulders, the sighing, the trembling hand, the tone of voice is as important as listening to the words that someone utters.

Lamentation as prayer teaches us that all our senses are called into service in attending to others in pain. It also teaches us that the physical sensations and aches are a good place to start when praying with suffering people, especially when speech is taxing or seems impossible. Facilitating lament begins with attentiveness to the messages of the body.

Bearing Witness: Lament as Tentative Speech

The turn from silence to speech occurs with the desire to describe what has happened, or perhaps simply with the hope that it might be possible to describe what has happened.[13] Lament may begin very tentatively, so tentatively it may go unrecognized by those who care for the suffering. It is made all the more tentative when Christians believe that lament is an unfaithful act.

Susan's experience with her Bible study group was all the more painful because it took so much effort to risk speaking up. It was her first effort to make public what had been so privately shameful and confusing. She wanted to give voice to her frustration about how the Bible study members' statements about guilt and forgiveness were missing an important truth—that anger cannot simply be ignored, that there is such a thing as cheap forgiveness. Her confidence was not yet strong enough to utter fully her testimony of pain and protest without feeling judged and rejected. In various ways, people may test out the *possibility* that they might be heard and in that hearing their testimony might be refined and strengthened.

We know of no other way to provide sanctuary for the "tentative speech" of lament than for church leaders to learn and teach what it means to listen with understanding and compassion. The discipline and commitment required for that kind of listening may have to begin with a few people in the congregation who have the desire to learn. But such a group, if effectively educated and supported in their practice of such a ministry, may become a leavening influence on the congregation as a whole, much like the "house churches" that practiced rituals of rehabilitation that Brueggemann believes may have first sheltered the laments of Israel.

In contrast to Susan, George and Sally had the resource of a theological framework that provided meaning and orientation in the pain of their daughter's death. Just as certain psalms (the "psalms of orientation") assert the control and providence of God, George and Sally's belief in such providence lent a certain point of orientation amidst their suffering. The psalms of lament, by contrast, are "psalms of disorientation," providing a window into the breakdown of a previously unquestioned theological framework (see chap. 2). According to the book of Job, the effort of his friends to account for his suffering within their own theological frameworks was not only rejected by Job but by God as well. A framework of meaning that is imposed upon the vulnerable is hardly a gesture of care.

With that said, it is important to recognize that the quest for meaning is an ongoing life challenge, and that rigidly held interpretative frameworks have the potential to shut out new life and threaten chaos. Ester Shapiro asserts that in the face of tragedy families face two challenges simultaneously (see chap. 4). The first is to reestablish stability in circumstances that have shattered a family's equilibrium. The second is actively to grieve a loss and to explore its meaning for personal and family development throughout the rest of the life cycle. While initially families may cling fiercely to whatever equilibrium is possible to maintain, even if it comes at the sacrifice of family growth and development, each new development in the course of the family life cycle presents new opportunities for revisiting the modus operandi of family life.

Although Shapiro does not spell out the pastoral opportunities, the reminder that such "revisiting" is possible is tremendously important for pastoral ministry. Individuals, families, and congregations whose allegiance is to the living Word of God rather than to any fixed theological framework may discover new possibilities of meaning amidst the tragedies of life and new possibilities of understanding and relating to God. The use of the psalms and prayers of disorientation in worship, Bible study, and congregational support groups provides images of how pain may be borne and expressed in a faithful life. The goal of pastoral care, we would underscore, is to *reform and expand* the life of Christian piety, not hastily to disparage one form and insist on its replacement with another.

The Cry Fully Uttered: Lament as Testimony of Hope

When lament comes fully to speech, it offers a testimony to realities that ordinary rational discourse overlooks or conceals.[14] The prayer of lament portrays human life at its most naked and desperate, exposing a reality so often hidden from view. The inclusion of these prayers in the Bible and in Christian spirituality offers the hope that God witnesses a reality that others cannot or will not acknowledge, and that the shrieks, raised fists, and anguished questions of the suffering will be embraced rather than condemned by God.

In the waning months of a lifelong battle with cystic fibrosis, Bill Williams wrote about the long and arduous wrestling with God that accompanied his struggle for life and breath. The last paragraphs in his book, written not long before his death, include these words: "The day I became free to wail without punishment was the day the word grace came to mean something real to me; and it was only after digesting that word that I came to the point where I could say, quite simply and truly, 'Do you know I love you?' and have it be the beginning, middle and end of a prayer."[15]

Telling the truth is at the heart of the lament prayer. It speaks the truth that the sufferer has experienced even though it may provoke opposition from the guardians of rationality and orthodoxy. The pleading, the bargaining, the desperation, the wild attempts to get the attention of God, to influence the powers of heaven, do not portray perfection. Just the opposite is the case. The prayer of lament portrays human life at its most desperate and vulnerable. The inclusion of these prayers in the Bible and in Christian spirituality communicates that human beings are still loved by God, even in their most desperate and self-serving moments.

The prayer of lament did not fully come to speech in either of the two ministry situations described above. Susan was on the verge of voicing her anger to God and the church but was not given support to do so. George and Sally were not ready to employ a form of prayer that they likely would have seen as a denial of their faith, even though some members of their congregation would have supported them had they chosen to pray in this way.

Caregivers may sometimes find themselves targets of bitterness and anger. In these circumstances they may be helped by visualizing the angry questions that are often directed at them as being addressed ultimately to God. Whether or not the cries of pain and protest are identified as prayer by the afflicted, when suffering is experienced in the presence of God, the prayer of lament is in process of formation. The caregiver's role is to hear and help bring this prayer to voice. By being aware that the cries and groans of the Spirit are indeed a form of prayer (Rom. 8:26), the caregiver can relate to the afflicted without fear or judgment.

One of the things risked in voicing the prayer of lament is the security of our theological frameworks. In each of the stories told above there are colliding pieties, to use the term we employed in chapter 3. Pastoral care takes place in congregations where different understandings of faithfulness may be present, understandings that are also shaped by the cultural contexts in which Christians live. This is true for church leaders as well as members of congregations. As a lay pastoral leader, Philip viewed George and Sally's response to Jenna's death through the interpretive category of "denial," a term he probably learned through his pastoral care education about grief. His belief that George, Sally, and some other members of the congregation were engaged in denial troubled him, but he didn't know what to do with his sense of unease because he was fearful of undermining an important source of strength for them both. Susan's familiar piety was crumbling and a new one was struggling to be born, a piety which could take in the whole of her experience—anguish and rage, as well as trust and hope. She sought help in giving birth to new faith understandings and, in so doing, implicitly asked other people in the congregation to expand their own understandings of God.

The prayer of lament is a vivid reminder that persons can survive the disintegration of their previously unquestioned theological frameworks. What endures beyond the collapse of the frameworks is the relationship with the living God, a relationship strong enough for the telling of truth, whatever that truth exposes about our weakness and strength, our capacities for manipulating and being manipulated, our faith and our faithlessness, our suspicion and our trust. It is the deepening of that relationship with the living God that is the goal of pastoral care, and it is to that end that the prayer of lament has its place in Christian life and ministry.

THE PRACTICE OF JUSTICE AND RECONCILIATION

Christian witness and ministry have both a vertical and a horizontal dimension. The good news is that in Jesus Christ we are reconciled with God and called to live in reconciliation with each other. The gospel has to do both with God's justification of the ungodly and with God's will for justice and peace in all relationships of life. What place does the prayer of lament have in the ministry of justice and reconciliation?

For one response to this question, we turn to the life and witness of Fannie Lou Hamer. The civil rights movement of the 1960s in the United States is one of the great struggles for social justice in our century. The story of Fannie Lou Hamer epitomizes this struggle and shows the importance of faith and prayer, including prayer as lamentation, for many who participated in this struggle.[16]

Hamer grew up as one of twenty children in a sharecropper's family on a cotton plantation near Rueville, Mississippi. From the age of six, she knew the grind of labor in the cotton fields that lasted every day from before dawn till darkness. She was steeped in the faith and spirituality of the black church, especially through its hymns and spirituals. Hamer would sing her prayers to God as she worked through the rows of cotton:

O Lord, they said you'd answer prayer,
O Lord, we sure do need you now,
O Lord, you know just how I feel.

In August 1962, Hamer attended a service in Rueville led by civil rights workers from the Southern Christian Leadership Conference and the Student Nonviolent Coordinating Committee. The speakers at this service were James Bevel and James Forman. They urged their hearers to stand up for justice by taking part in a voter registration movement. Their message made profound sense to Hamer. It is no exaggeration to say that she experienced their call as a summons from Jesus. She volunteered to take part in this new movement for justice in reliance on God's word of promise.

Within a few weeks, Hamer traveled with seventeen other people to the Sunflower County seat of Indianola to register to vote. They were on a dangerous mission, and people were afraid. As was so often to be the case on such missions, Hamer encouraged her companions with her songs of faith:

Have a little talk with Jesus
Tell him all about our troubles,
Hear our feeble cry,
Answer by and by,
Feel the little prayer wheel turning,
Feel a fire burning,
Just a little talk with Jesus makes it right.

The terrible costs of participating in the voter registration movement were soon evident. Hamer was evicted from her home, received many death threats by phone and by mail, was kept under surveillance by both the Ku Klux Klan and the FBI, and became the target of drive-by shootings. Early the following summer, Hamer and some friends were arrested and jailed in Winona, Mississippi, on their way home from a voter registration workshop in Charleston, South Carolina. Over a period of three days they were brutally beaten and tortured. As a result of her beating, Hamer sustained permanent damage to a kidney and an eye. Although charges were brought against the attackers, they were eventually acquitted by an all-white jury.

Hamer's experience of torture increased her anger at the unjust treatment of African Americans and strengthened her resolve to continue the struggle for freedom. She became a legendary leader in the civil rights movement. In the late summer of 1964, she was a key figure in the unsuccessful efforts of the Mississippi Freedom Democratic Party to be recognized at the national Democratic Convention in Atlantic City. Hamer's testimony before the Credentials Committee of the convention received national televised coverage. She was uncompromising in her stand for the rights of the poor people of Mississippi. She refused to bend to pressures from Democratic Party leaders, including the President, whose guiding principle in dealing with the claims of the Mississippi Freedom Democratic Party delegates was political expediency rather than justice. As Hamer later noted, one of the things she learned through these events was that racism was not something confined to Mississippi, but was America's problem.[17]

Hamer was proud of her black heritage. At the same time, she welcomed into the voter registration movement everyone who was sincerely concerned for the rights of the weak and the poor. Of the mostly white summer volunteers who put themselves in harm's way, Hamer said that if she had to choose between the church and the community constituted by these young people, she would choose the latter.[18]

The powerful testimony of Fannie Lou Hamer and her courageous and costly leadership role in the voter registration movement cannot be fully understood apart from her faith and her spiritual life. In many meetings of the movement she sang hymns and spirituals that her mother taught her or that were learned in black church services. Her prayer to God was simple and honest, most often expressed in songs and spirituals that contained both hope and lament. It did not hide the unjust realities of her life or discount the significance of life here and now in favor of the next life. A person practiced in speaking to God with honesty and in freedom is unlikely to close her eyes to injustice and poverty in her own life and in her community and nation.

Charles Marsh emphasizes that while Hamer's strong evangelical faith motivated her social protest, she did not hold to that faith because it was socially useful. Faith for her was "infinitely more than the utility it offered."[19] She believed that what she was doing only made sense finally within the context of the gospel story. Hamer did not reduce the gospel to a secular ideology, but extended the gospel into the public arena. Although the meetings of the voter registration movement, with their calls to struggle for justice, were energizing, what must never be forgotten is that for Hamer and many others in the movement, "'these meetings were *church*, and for some who had grown disillusioned with Christian otherworldliness, they were better than church.' Only in church could one apprehend with such intensity both the theological expression of society's wrongs and the hope for decisive change; only there were the memories of the people and the promises of the future secured by trust in God."[20]

Hamer's faith was centered on Jesus. For her, as for countless black Christian women before and after her, "Jesus was the central frame of reference."[21] Jacquelyn Grant explains what Jesus meant for suffering black Christian women like Hamer. Jesus was "the divine co-sufferer" who empowered believers in their struggles against oppression. Jesus was God incarnate, who knew and shared the sufferings and humiliations experienced daily by black women.

It was primarily through their prayer and their song tradition that black women remained connected with Jesus. In their prayers the women conversed with the Savior who had walked the sorrowful road to Calvary and who now companioned with them on their difficult journey. In their songs of faith black women were free to lament, "Nobody knows the trouble I see . . . nobody knows but Jesus."[22]

To say that the love of Jesus was the foundation of the faith of Fannie Lou Hamer is not to say that she reveled in a passive and sentimental version of love. As Grant says, the love of Jesus for them was a "tough, active love."[23] It was a love that poured itself out for life, justice, and freedom. According to Grant, "Fannie Lou Hamer articulates, perhaps better than anyone else, Black women's understanding of Jesus in relation to freedom. . . . Freedom is the central message of Jesus Christ and the gospel, and is concisely summarized in Luke 4:18. Based upon her reading of this text, Hamer's consistent challenge to the American public was that to be a follower of Jesus Christ was to be committed to the struggle for freedom."[24]

Hamer's faith does not fit the usual definitions of liberal or conservative. For Hamer, Christ was both the miraculous, resurrected Christ and the gritty, revolutionary Christ. These two images of Christ were not contradictory for Hamer, but in their unity were the very source of her confidence and strength. As Charles Marsh writes: "Fannie Lou Hamer gave voice to a distinctive Christian discourse, evangelical in the most vigorous sense of the term, a robust and disciplined love of Jesus of Nazareth, of the whole scandalous story of his life, death, and resurrection."[25] Her retelling of the good news was "full of subversive undercurrents and iconoclastic impulses."[26]

The cry that was voiced by Fannie Lou Hamer was never only a personal cry but one that both spoke for and was shared by her sisters and brothers. She belonged to a community of suffering. As her work and witness within the civil rights movement makes clear, Hamer never saw herself as a heroic, solitary freedom fighter. She drew strength from a community of suffering and hope, a community that embodied and exemplified, at least to some extent, the just relations and mutual respect that the members were struggling for in the larger society.

For Hamer, prayer was of vital importance, but it was not to be divorced from action. She did not equate prayer with passivity. Prayer increased rather than diminished a sense of responsibility for the cause of justice. As she said, "You can pray until you faint, but if you're not going to get up and do something, God is not gonna put it in your lap."[27] She would not have understood a view of prayer that interpreted it as mere resignation and passivity. Prayer not only enabled people to survive under oppression, it empowered people to do those things that could be done to help change the oppressive situation.

While there was plenty of anger in Hamer, it never hardened into a blinding desire for revenge. Neither in her prayer nor in her public speeches did she suppress her anger and indignation. At the same time, she recognized that, although her anger and that of the young people she mentored could be terribly destructive, it could also be made to serve creative purposes. She refused to mimic the behavior of the oppressors. Vicki Crawford says of Hamer: "Her deep faith and understanding of human injustice instructed others, especially angry youth, of the need to use anger and indignation in creative ways that would be empowering rather than debilitating. . . . When she told her story, she would say, 'But you have to love, for they know not what they do. And you had better get this anger out of you. And organize your people.'"[28]

We cannot say for sure that Hamer's singing was a way of "praying out her anger" and leaving it with God. We do know that she harnessed her indignation over personal injury and social injustice to serve creative and redemptive ends. We do know that she was a Christian woman for whom honest prayer and the struggle for justice went hand in hand.

Kay Mills concludes her biography of Hamer with these words: "Mrs. Hamer resisted being beaten down, literally and figuratively, by a political system that refused to give poor people like her, white or black, a voice in running their lives."[29] Her spirit of resistance is etched in the epitaph on her gravestone: "I am sick and tired of being sick and tired." This was a familiar rallying cry that Hamer used in many of her speeches. There is reason, however, to think of it as far more than an emotional outburst or a political slogan. It can also be understood as a prayer, a prayer of hope in God, a cry like that of Rachel refusing to be comforted; a resolve, by God's grace, to continue the struggle for truth, justice, and reconciliation—whatever the costs.

As the witness of Fannie Lou Hamer shows, Christian life and service are inseparable from the practice of justice and reconciliation. For Hamer that connection was grounded in the ministry of Jesus, who not only proclaimed good news to the poor, release to the captives, recovery of sight to the blind, and liberty to the oppressed, but who also taught and embodied the suffering, nonviolent love of God in a violent world.

The story of Hamer reminds us that the ministry of the church will always give special attention to the cries of the abused and the oppressed. A ministry that is sensitive to these cries often meets with intense opposition. Like the proclamation of a crucified messiah, the testimony of victims is disturbing because it upsets many of our assumptions about ourselves, our world, and God. These testimonies compel us to see ourselves and God in a radically different light.

The witness of Hamer also reminds us that the prayer of lament, in its many different forms and many different contexts, has a place in a ministry of justice and reconciliation. The prayer of lament is a cry for justice, truth, and the fullness of life in the midst of injustice, deceit, and death. That cry is heard not only in churches, hospitals, and private homes, but also in the public arena when people enter into costly struggle for justice. Indeed, the cry for justice, freedom, and peace is sometimes more courageously and passionately voiced outside the institutional church than within it. Such a voice was that of Fannie Lou Hamer.

Finally, the witness of Hamer reminds us that the prayer of lament is not a prayer for vengeance but, at least within the context of the Christian gospel, a prayer for the coming of justice, reconciliation, and peace throughout God's creation. Hamer's ministry of "tough love," nurtured by the gospel story and the songs of lament and hope of the African American church, is evidence that lament, protest, and anger, when prayed after the manner of the psalmists and Jesus, do not lead to a spirit of vengeance and retaliation for harms suffered, but point in the direction of universal justice and reconciliation.

THE PRACTICE OF THEOLOGICAL REFLECTION IN CONGREGATIONS

In a course on the book of Job taught by a very creative young professor of Old Testament at a Presbyterian seminary, the entire class takes part in a trial of God. One student is appointed the prosecutor and another the defense attorney; many others are called as witnesses for the defense or prosecution. Someone is even appointed to play the part of the judge, who decides the final verdict. Instructor and students report that this event in the course has proved to be a remarkably effective way of helping participants enter into the minds and hearts of people who cry to God from the depths.

When texts like the book of Job and the psalms of lament are studied and discussed in local congregations, the participants are no longer playing roles. They are people finding a voice, perhaps for the first time and from their own sacred texts, to express the deep hurt and ask the hard questions that they have longed to ask but have always thought off limits for a believer. Honest conversations around these hard texts of the Bible can be an extraordinary growing experience for all involved.

Gerald Janzen, an Old Testament scholar, tells of teaching the book of Job over a two-week period to a small group of Canadian Inuit. The culture of the Inuit, like that of native peoples in many parts of the world, has been severely shaken by the relentless impact of the ethos and technology of modernity. As a result, the Inuit have experienced substance abuse, domestic abuse, vandalism, and most ominous of all, a high rate of suicide among the young. The sense of belonging to a community with a future and of having a place and purpose within it has been dangerously weakened, and the temptation to lose heart and act in self-destructive ways is very great.

At the end of the course, the professor asked the three students in the class whether they thought the traditional description of Job as an exemplar of the virtue of patience was correct. Was Job really patient? "The two older Inuit—Iola Metuq and Paul Idlout (who last year was the first to be consecrated a bishop)—agreed: no, the biblical Job was not patient. But the youngest of them, Norman Anikina, still in his early twenties, held out that the biblical Job was indeed patient. I asked him why he thought so. . . . Norman said simply, 'Because he didn't kill himself.' "[30]

Norman's answer is a breathtaking but honest response to the book of Job as it intersected his own life and that of his people. The response of the two older Inuit was not wrong: The Job of the Bible is far from passive and resigned to his fate. He protests, resists, and like Rachel mourning her lost children, refuses consolation. He is indeed very impatient. But Norman was right, too, and his answer brings home the message of the book of Job in a powerful, paradoxical way: Job really was patient "because he didn't kill himself." In fact, the temptation of self-destruction is set before Job early in the book (2:9) and his struggle thereafter can be read as part of his refusal to give in to that temptation. Norman's answer thus represented a deep, experientially based understanding of the meaning of trust in God and hope in God's promises. In times when the forces of death and destruction seem overwhelming, the patience of faith is expressed not in passive acquiescence to the way things are but rather, in Janzen's words, "the stubborn determination to keep going on, until somewhere, sometime, somehow, we encounter the divine compassion at the heart of things that will bring truth to light and comfort to the soul."[31]

An important part of the work of ministry in congregations is to help people like Norman Anikina and his friends grow in the capacity to relate Christian faith to all aspects of life. Theological reflection is not an esoteric activity restricted to seminary professors; it is an essential component of Christian discipleship. The life of faith seeks understanding; "theology matters" in our personal, congregational, and public life.

While all human experience is capable of prompting questions about the fulfillment of God's purposes in our own lives and in all creation, the experiences of tragedy and suffering compel such questions. Our faith is profoundly challenged when we encounter severe suffering and radical evil; familiar ways of thinking and speaking about God are interrupted. As we have seen, the Bible is full of testimonies of people who find themselves compelled to struggle with God, resist consolation, and ask agonizing questions: from Jacob who wrestled with God at the river Jabbok; to Rachel, who refused to be comforted because her children were no more; to Jesus, who cried to God in abandonment on the cross.

When faith is shaken by experiences of suffering, abuse, or injustice, old understandings of God may crumble and new understandings gradually emerge. C. S. Lewis, we remember, describes how he discovered his theological assumptions to be a "house of cards" that fell apart when his wife died of cancer. Similar testimonies are given by Ann Weems and Nicholas Wolterstorff, cited in earlier chapters. With countless others, Weems and Wolterstorff discovered help and healing in the lament prayer tradition. Their impulse to lament, question, and even rage was validated and transformed by such prayer. Their questions were not a denial of faith, but the honest expressions of a wounded faith.

We believe that while many church members have a wounded faith, they may long ago have given up any expectation that they might pursue their troubling questions in the context of Christian community, prayer, and worship. In such cases there has been a failure in the church's ministry. Local congregations are often the only places where people have the opportunity to enter into serious theological conversation about experiences of negativity, failure, sickness, injustice, and death in their own lives and in the lives of others. Whether such opportunities are offered depends in large part on the leadership of the congregation. It depends, too, on whether the faith and spirituality of a congregation have an understanding of prayer that by definition excludes lament and protest or that knows and includes the lament prayer tradition and draws upon it as a rich resource.

Carol Lakey Hess speaks of the need of all members of congregations to cultivate "hard dialogue and deep connections" with each other, with Scripture, and with God. Talk about God becomes contrived and artificial talk rather than "real talk" when it brackets out those life experiences that cause us to question and refuse consolation. "It is our privilege, our right, even our responsibility as the people of God to lament and question when the fullness of life is denied to some persons. We do bad theology when we justify suffering or find only redemptive elements in suffering and thus refrain from questioning God and ourselves."[32]

Hess offers a number of guidelines for "hard dialogue and deep connections" with the Bible and Christian faith in the local congregation. We will not list all of her guidelines but will adopt a few and add some of our own that seem especially pertinent to the use of the lament prayer tradition as an occasion for serious theological conversation in local congregations.

First, "hard dialogue and deep connections" with the biblical witness need not mean argumentation in which there are winners and losers. Instead, it can and should mean the shared struggle and common search of the people of God for deeper understanding. As mentioned earlier, the older Inuit were right in saying that Job was not patient because he resisted the view that his sufferings were the consequence of his sin; and the younger Inuit Norman was right in arguing that Job was patient because he did not give up and destroy himself. We do not have to choose; the two responses are not mutually exclusive, but say the same thing in different ways. Hard dialogue and deep connections can mean mutual enrichment in the faith rather than scoring debating points.

Second, "hard dialogue and deep connections" with the Bible and the Christian faith that we share does not mean rarefied theological reflection that separates intellect from feeling and thought from practice. Good theology refuses to accept these dichotomies. Theology in congregations will be passionate and practical theological reflection; it will not be divorced from strong affections of love of God and neighbor, from the passion for justice and peace, from the desire for salvation and healing. Of course, good theology cannot be reduced to feelings or experiences, certainly not to my feelings or experiences. But theological reflection that does not relate critically and continuously to actual life experience is moribund.

Third, "hard dialogue and deep connections" will involve "stretching the conversational canopy" in our effort to understand the biblical witness. It is especially important to hear the voices of those who have experienced profound suffering or who have been silenced or marginalized by the dominant culture, as was Norman Anikina, or by the events of tragic accident or disease. Instead of assuming that our own interpretations of biblical texts exhaust their meaning (an assumption Hess calls "false universalizing"), pastors and other leaders in congregations should encourage the speaking and hearing of different voices. "New and different truths are revealed when new and different conversation partners are welcomed."[33]

Fourth, "hard dialogue and deep connections" involves the willingness to challenge familiar but inadequate ways of thinking of God, ourselves, our community, and our society. Theological reflection in Christian congregations must be critical and imaginative, exploring fresh understandings of the witness of Scripture and employing new images to convey the message of Scripture to our own time. We recall the witness of Nicholas Wolterstorff regarding his theological struggle after the death of his son in a mountainclimbing accident. Wolterstorff tells us he had known since childhood that God was a caring God, not an unchanging and unresponsive deity, as suggested by some philosophers and theologians. When shaken by the death of his son, however, Wolterstorff was compelled to relate to God in the unfamiliar mode of the prayer of lament. In the process he learned that "God is not only the God of sufferers but the God who suffers."

Instead of explaining our suffering God shares it. But I never saw it. Though I confessed that the man of sorrows was God himself, I never saw the God of sorrows. Though I confessed that the man bleeding on the cross was the redeeming God, I never saw God himself on the cross, blood from sword and thorn and nail dripping healing into the world's wounds. What does this mean for life, that God suffers? I'm only beginning to learn.[34]

"Beginning to learn" to speak anew of God and to God is the fruit of hard dialogue and deep connections that people of faith have, in the midst of a suffering world, with Scripture, with one another, with strangers, and with God.

HOLISTIC CHRISTIAN PRAYER AND HOLISTIC CHRISTIAN MINISTRY

Our emphasis in this chapter, and throughout this study, has been on the wholeness of Christian prayer and the wholeness of Christian life and practice. We have given special attention to the prayer of lament because we see it as an important, though neglected, dimension of authentic prayer. We have argued that it has its place alongside praise, thanksgiving, confession, and intercession in a holistic understanding of prayer. As long as the purposes of God are not yet completely realized, as long as there is an abyss between the fullness of life promised in the gospel and the lived experience of women and men, there is a need for the prayer of lament. The ministry and prayer of the church cannot be whole and wholesome unless it makes room for this prayer in its pastoral care, worship, work for justice, and theological study.

The vignettes of ministry recounted in this chapter are far from exhaustive. They have at best a suggestive and heuristic value. Even so, we are perhaps able to discern in them certain common factors that will be present in any serious recovery of prayer as lamentation in our modern or postmodern world.[35]

First, as our ministry vignettes attest, the prayer of lament arises out of the experience of brokenness and suffering. Shattering experiences need a language adequate to express them. It is not that the pastor somehow is required to make people aware of their pain and suffering, as though such experiences were unknown to them. Rather, the pastoral task is to help the afflicted set their experience within the framework of living faith and honest prayer to God. Prayer that expresses the experience of the absence of God, or even abandonment by God, is one important way in which many people in our violent age can continue to call upon God with authenticity. If such prayer is characterized by a certain excess, that simply corresponds to the excess of jubilation found in a lament prayer like Psalm 22.[36]

Second, it is not to be expected that the prayer of lament will always and only take the form of the biblical texts of lament. The biblical tradition of prayer is a living and seminal tradition, mediated to us over many centuries and practiced in many different contexts. Like all biblical texts, the prayer of lament has a history. It has been enriched by its countless new actualizations and recontexualizations. Fannie Lou Hamer knew the lament tradition primarily through the black heritage of spirituals and songs of sorrow and joy. As sacred texts of a community of faith, the prayers of the Bible have their own historical contexts and yet are not confined to those contexts. Their meaning and use have been enhanced and enriched by the history of reenactment and recontextualization through which they have gone and continue to go.

Third, though few and necessarily sketchy, our ministry vignettes show that the faith that expresses itself in the prayer of lament involves an arduous struggle. An unpredictable but real movement is discernible in these prayers, a movement from lament to praise, from sorrow to joy. This movement is never automatic, never guaranteed, never complete. The struggle continues, as the proclamation of the cross and resurrection of Christ will continue, until the purposes of God for the still groaning creation have been completed.

Finally, at the heart of the lament prayer is a highly paradoxical understanding of God. The prayer of lament is nothing if not a wrestling with God. On the one hand, God is experienced as inscrutable, hidden, beyond our understanding. All systematic theologies and theodicies, especially those that find a supposed explanation of all human suffering in guilt and divine punishment, founder on the rock of the experience of the hiddenness of God. On the other hand, it is to the self-revealed God of the covenant of grace that we lament. Thus Christians confess that God is nowhere more revealed yet hidden, nowhere nearer to us yet further beyond our understanding, than in Jesus—God's gift of Godself for our healing and salvation—who in anguish and abandonment on the cross cried out not to blind fate but to God.

If the triumphalist atheism of modernity found its classical statement in Nietzsche's declaration of the death of God, faith in a postmodern world will find its most compelling expression not in an equally triumphalist theism but in a Christian faith and life centered on the crucified and risen One and in a corresponding understanding and practice of prayer that is strong and bold enough to include the voice of lament. For when addressed to the God who remains ever hidden and free yet is revealed as just and gracious in Jesus, the prayer of lament paradoxically leads to the edges of hope and praise.

Where Lament can show up in Christian Practice
- Worship. Rooted in micro context, but also context of Jesus' redemptive work
- Pastoral Care Body, tentative, full expression
Goal of PC: reform + expand life of Christian piety / Christian framework;
So helping you navigate your framework crisis - and lament has a place in that!
Bc the constant is your relationship with God
Deepening rel. w/ God
Lament reminds that you can survive the disintegration of your old framework!
- Justice + Reconciliation
- Theological Reflections of Congregations

NOTES

1. THE LOSS AND RECOVERY OF THE PRAYER OF LAMENT

1. Kathleen Norris, *The Cloister Walk* (New York: Riverside Books, 1996), 94.

2. Claus Westermann, *Praise and Lament in the Psalms* (Atlanta: John Knox, 1981), 265.

3. See the collection of Brueggemann's writings on the psalms, *The Psalms and the Life of Faith: Walter Brueggemann,* ed. Patrick D. Miller (Minneapolis: Fortress Press, 1995); and Walter Brueggemann, *The Message of the Psalms: A Theological Commentary* (Minneapolis: Augsburg, 1984).

4. See Walter Brueggemann, "The Costly Loss of Lament," in *The Psalms and the Life of Faith,* 98–111.

5. See Patrick Miller, *They Cried to the Lord: The Form and Theology of Biblical Prayer* (Minneapolis: Fortress Press, 1994); Samuel E. Balentine, *Prayer in the Hebrew Bible: The Drama of Divine-Human Dialogue* (Minneapolis: Fortress Press, 1993); Denise Dombkowski Hopkins, *Journey through the Psalms: A Path to Wholeness* (New York: United Church Press, 1990).

6. Balentine, *Prayer in the Hebrew Bible,* 4–5.

7. See Donald Capps, *Biblical Approaches to Pastoral Counseling* (Philadelphia: Westminster Press, 1981); Kenneth Mitchell and Herbert Anderson, *All Our Losses, All Our Griefs: Resources for Pastoral Care* (Philadelphia: Westminster Press, 1983); Eugene Peterson, *Answering God: The Psalms as Tools for Prayer* (San Francisco: Harper & Row, 1989); Denise Ackermann, "On Hearing and Lamenting: Faith and Truth Telling," in *To Remember and to Heal: Theological and Psychological Reflections on Truth and Reconciliation,* ed. H. Russel Botman and Robin M. Petersen (Cape Town: Human & Rousseau, 1996), 47–56; William E. Hulme, *Christian Caregiving: Insights from the Book of Job* (St. Louis: Concordia Publishing House, 1992).

8. See Elaine Ramshaw, *Ritual and Pastoral Care* (Philadelphia: Fortress Press, 1987); David Noel Power, *Worship, Culture, and Theology* (Washington, D.C.: Pastoral Press, 1990).

9. See Karl Rahner and Johann Baptist Metz, *The Courage to Pray* (New York: Crossroad, 1981); Karl Barth, *Church Dogmatics* III/4 (Edinburgh: T. & T. Clark, 1961), 87–115.

10. See *A Troubling in My Soul: Womanist Perspectives on Evil and Suffering,* ed. Emilie M. Townes (Maryknoll, N.Y.: Orbis Books, 1993).

11. See Jürgen Moltmann, *The Crucified God: The Cross of Christ as the Foundation and Criticism of Christian Theology* (New York: Harper & Row, 1974); Hans Urs von Balthasar, *Mysterium Pascale* (Grand Rapids, Mich.: Eerdmans, 1990).

12. See L. Gregory Jones, *Embodying Forgiveness: A Theological Analysis* (Grand Rapids, Mich.: Eerdmans, 1995); Miroslav Volf, *Exclusion and Embrace: A Theological Exploration of Identity, Otherness, and Reconciliation* (Nashville: Abingdon Press, 1996).

13. See Catherine Mowry LaCugna, *God for Us: The Trinity and Christian Life* (New York: HarperCollins, 1991); Elizabeth A. Johnson, *She Who Is: The Mystery of God in Feminist Theological Discourse* (New York: Crossroad, 1992).

14. Ann Weems, *Psalms of Lament* (Louisville: Westminster John Knox Press, 1995), xv.

15. Ibid.

16. Ibid., 20.

17. Ibid., xvi.

18. Ibid.

19. See Botman and Petersen, *To Remember and to Heal.*

20. See Mark Mathabane, "Anger and Amnesty in South Africa," *New York Times,* December 14, 1997.

21. See "A Service of Dedication and Blessing of Commissioners of the Truth and Reconciliation Commission," in *To Remeber and to Heal*, 165–70.

22. See James E. Dittes, *Men at Work* (Louisville: Westminster John Knox Press, 1996). An earlier edition of this work was titled *When Work Goes Sour.*

23. Quoted by Christie Cozad Neuger, "Men's Issues in the Local Church: What Clergymen Have to Say," in *The Care of Men,* ed. Christie Cozad Neuger and James Newton Poling (Nashville: Abingdon, 1997), 50.

24. Robert Wuthnow, *The Crisis in the Churches: Spiritual Malaise, Fiscal Woe* (New York: Oxford University Press, 1997), 115.

25. Ibid., 113.

26. Ibid., 116.

27. Lester Meyer, "A Lack of Laments in the Church's Use of the Psalter," *Lutheran Quarterly* (spring 1993): 67–78.

28. Ibid., 69.

29. Ibid., 70.

30. Ibid., 70–71.

31. See Paul Tillich, *Systematic Theology* (Chicago: University of Chicago Press, 1967), 2:165–66.

32. Ramshaw, *Ritual and Pastoral Care,* 31–32.

33. See Ernst Becker, *The Denial of Death* (New York: Free Press, 1973); Robert J. Lifton and Greg Mitchell, *Hiroshima in America: Fifty Years of Denial* (New York: Putnam's Sons, 1995).

34. See Douglas John Hall, *Lighten Our Darkness: Toward an Indigenous Theology of the Cross* (Philadelphia: Westminster Press, 1976), and *Thinking the Faith: Christian Theology in a North American Context* (Minneapolis: Augsburg, 1989).

35. Walter Brueggemann, *The Hopeful Imagination: Prophetic Voices in Exile* (Philadelphia: Fortress Press, 1986), 41.

36. See Robert Hughes, *The Culture of Complaint: The Fraying of America* (New York: Oxford University Press, 1993).

37. Ibid., 9.

38. Ibid., 10.

39. Walter Brueggemann, "The Friday Voice of Faith," *Reformed Worship* 30 (December 1993): 2–5.

2. THE PRAYER OF LAMENT IN THE BIBLE

1. See Walter Brueggemann, *Theology of the Old Testament: Testimony, Dispute, Advocacy* (Minneapolis: Fortress Press, 1998).

2. Paul Ricoeur, "Toward a Hermeneutic of the Idea of Revelation," in *Essays on Biblical Interpretation,* ed. Lewis S. Mudge (Philadelphia: Fortress Press, 1980), 75.

3. Ibid., 91.

4. Ibid., 92.

5. Paul Ricoeur, "Lamentation as Prayer," in Andre LaCocque and Paul Ricoeur, *Thinking Biblically: Exegetical and Hermeneutical Studies,* trans. David Pellauer (Chicago: University of Chicago Press, 1998), 212.

6. See Hans-Georg Gadamer, *Truth and Method* (New York: Crossroad, 1982), 235–74.

7. Emil Fackenheim, "The Lament of Rachel and the New Covenant," *Crosscurrents* 40 (fall 1990): 345.

8. See David Rhoads, *The Challenge of Diversity: The Witness of Paul and the Gospels* (Minneapolis: Fortress Press, 1997).

9. See Claus Westermann, "The Role of Lament in the Theology of the Old Testament," *Interpretation* 28 (1974): 20–38.

10. Patrick D. Miller, *They Cried to the Lord: The Form and Theology of Biblical Prayer* (Minneapolis: Fortress Press, 1994), 133.

11. See Walter Brueggemann, *The Message of the Psalms: A Theological Commentary* (Minneapolis: Augsburg, 1984).

12. Patrick D. Miller, *Interpreting the Psalms* (Philadelphia: Fortress, 1986), 100.

13. Brueggemann, *Theology of the Old Testament,* 374–81.

14. Westermann, *Praise and Lament in the Psalms*; Erhard Gerstenberger, *Psalms: Part I, with an Introduction to Cultic Poetry* (Grand Rapids, Mich.: Eerdmans, 1988); Miller, *They Cried to the Lord;* Brueggemann, *Message of the Psalms.*

15. Westermann, *Praise and Lament in the Psalms,* 264.

16. Miller, *Interpreting the Psalms,* 9.

17. See Brueggemann, *Theology of the Old Testament,* 378.

18. Walter Brueggemann, "Psalms 9–10: A Counter to Conventional Social Reality," in *The Bible and the Politics of Exegesis,* ed. David Jobling et al. (Cleveland: The Pilgrim Press, 1991), 14.

19. Miller, *Interpreting the Psalms,* 99–100.

20. Dietrich Bonhoeffer, *Psalms: The Prayer Book of the Bible* (Minneapolis: Augsburg, 1970), 60.

21. Westermann, *Praise and Lament in the Psalms,* 266.

22. Ibid., 267.

23. Samuel E. Balentine, *Prayer in the Hebrew Bible* (Minneapolis: Fortress, 1993), 202–3. The citation in this passage is from Walter Brueggemann, *Israel's Praise: Doxology against Idolatry and Ideology* (Philadelphia: Fortress, 1988), xi.

24. Miller, *They Cried to the Lord,* 126.

25. E. S. Gerstenberger and W. Schrage, *Suffering* (Nashville: Abingdon, 1977), 102. See also T. Fretheim, *The Suffering of God* (Philadelphia: Fortress, 1984); Abraham Heschel, *The Prophets,* 2 vols. (New York: Harper & Row, 1962), speaks of the "pathos of God."

26. Walter Brueggemann, "A Shape for Old Testament Theology. II: Embrace of Pain," *Catholic Biblical Quarterly* 47 (1985): 405.

27. For an excellent discussion of prayer in the New Testament, see Miller, *They Cried to the Lord,* 304–35.

28. Westermann, *Praise and Lament in the Psalms,* 265.

29. Karl Barth speaks of the passion expressed in the Lord's Prayer as "a great, unconquerable, permanent, and even dangerous passion." *The Christian Life* (Grand Rapids, Mich.: Eerdmans, 1981), 111.

30. Leonardo Boff, *The Lord's Prayer: The Prayer of Integral Liberation* (Maryknoll, N.Y.: Orbis Books, 1983), 62, 66–67.

31. Brueggemann, "Psalms 9–10," 13.

32. Miller, *Interpreting the Psalms,* 110.

33. Eugene H. Peterson, *Answering God: The Psalms as Tools for Prayer* (New York: Harper, 1989), 102.

34. Susan Lockrie Graham, "Silent Voices: Women in the Gospel of Mark," *Semeia* 54 (1991): 145–58.

35. Gail R. O'Day, "Surprised by Faith: Jesus and the Canaanite Woman," *Listening* 24 (fall 1989): 294.

36. Miller, *Interpreting the Psalms,* 110.

37. To mention only a few: Karl Barth, *Church Dogmatics* IV/1 (Edinburgh: T. & T. Clark, 1956); Hans Urs von Balthasar, *Mysterium Paschale* (Grand Rapids, Mich.: Eerdmans, 1990); Jürgen Moltmann, *The Crucified God: The Cross of Christ as the Foundation and Criticism of Christian Theology* (New York: Harper & Row, 1974); Jon Sobrino, *Christology at the Crossroads: A Latin American Approach* (Maryknoll, N.Y.: Orbis Books, 1978); Elizabeth Johnson, *She Who Is: The Mystery of God in Feminist Theological Discourse* (New York: Crossroad, 1992).

38. See Miller, *They Cried to the Lord,* 324.

39. See Belden C. Lane, "Arguing with God: Blasphemy and the Prayer of Lament in Judaism and Other Faith 'Traditions,'" in *Remembering for the Future,* vol. 3, *The Impact of the Holocaust and Genocide on Jews and Christians* (Oxford: Pergamon Press, 1989), 2543–57.

40. Anson Laytner, *Arguing with God: A Jewish Tradition* (Northvale, N.J.: J. Aronson, 1990), xxii.

41. Ibid., 116.

42. Ibid., 245.

43. Kadia Molodowsky, "God of Mercy," in *A Treasury of Yiddish Poetry,* ed. I. Howe and E. Greenberg (New York: Holt, Rinehart and Winston, 1969), quoted by Laytner, *Arguing with God,* 208–9.

44. Elie Wiesel, *The Trial of God* (New York: Random House, 1979).

45. Elie Wiesel, "A Prayer for the Days of Awe," *New York Times,* October 2, 1997.

46. Brueggemann, "The Friday Voice of Faith," *Reformed Worship* 30 (December 1993): 2.

47. Ulrike Bail, "Vernimm, Gott, Mein Gebet: Psalm 55 und Gewalt gegen Frauen," in *Feministische Hermeneutik und Erstes Testament,* ed. Hedwig Jahnow et al. (Stuttgart: Verlag W. Kohlhammer, 1994), 67–84.

48. For the following account we are indebted to Patrick D. Miller, "Dietrich Bonhoeffer and the Psalms," *Princeton Seminary Bulletin* 15 (November 1994): 274–82.

49. The English translation of the German text of the verses from Psalm 74 is Miller's.

3. THE PRAYER OF LAMENT IN THE CHRISTIAN THEOLOGICAL TRADITION

1. Nicholas Wolterstorff, "If God Is Good and Sovereign, Why Lament?" (lecture given at Calvin College, April 1996).

2. Augustine, *Confessions and Enchiridion,* Library of Christian Classics, ed. Albert C. Outler (Philadelphia: Westminster Press, 1955), 7:81–2.

3. Ibid., 57.

4. Ibid., 175.

5. Ibid., 196.

6. See Wolterstorff, "If God Is Good and Sovereign, Why Lament?"

7. Peter Brown, *Augustine of Hippo* (Berkeley: University of California Press, 1967), 174.

8. *St. Augustine on the Psalms,* trans. Dame Scholastica Hebgin and Dame Felicitas Corrigan (Westminster, Md.: Newman Press, 1960), 1:151–52.

9. Ibid., 200–201.

10. Ibid., 201.

11. Augustine, *Expositions on the Book of Psalms,* vol. 8, Nicene and Post-Nicene Fathers (Grand Rapids, Mich.: Eerdmans, 1956), 428.

12. Ibid., 630–32.

13. *St. Augustine on the Psalms,* 1:201.

14. Ibid., 275.

15. William Werpehowski, "Weeping at the Death of Dido: Sorrow, Virtue, and Augustine's Confessions," *Journal of Religious Ethics* 19 (1991): 186.

16. Robert Kirschner, "Two Responses: Augustine and the Rabbis on Psalm 137," *Vigiliae Christianae* 44 (1990): 242–62.

17. Augustine, *Confessions,* 63.

18. James E. Dittes, "Augustine: Search for a Fail-Safe God to Trust," *Journal for the Scientific Study of Religion* 25 (1986): 61–62.

19. Nicholas Wolterstorff, "Suffering Love," in *Philosophy and the Christian Faith,* ed. Thomas V. Morris (Notre Dame, Ind.: University of Notre Dame Press, 1988), 231.

20. See Martin E. Lehmann, *Luther and Prayer* (Milwaukee: Northwestern Publishing House, 1985); Rudolf Damerau, *Luthers Gebetslehre,* 1515–1546, Zweiter Teil; Studien zu den Grundlagen der Reformation, 14 (Marburg: Im Selbstverlag, 1977).

21. *Luther's Works,* ed. Jaroslav Pelikan (St. Louis: *Concordia Publishing House,* 1958), 14:141.

22. Ibid., 142.

23. Ibid., 145.

24. Ibid.

25. *Luthers Psalmen-Auslegung* (Gottingen: Vanderhoeck & Ruprecht, 1959–65), 1:187.

26. *Luther's Works,* 12:124.

27. Quoted by Mary M. Solberg, *Compelling Knowledge: A Feminist Proposal for an Epistemology of the Cross* (Albany: State University of New York Press, 1997), 57.

28. Heidelberg Disputation, 21, in *Martin Luther's Basic Theological Writings,* ed. Timothy F. Lull (Minneapolis: Fortress, 1989), 31.

29. *Luther's Works,* 14:152.

30. *Martin Luther's Complete Commentary on the First Twenty-Two Psalms,* trans. Henry Cole (London: W. Simpkin and R. Marshall, 1826), 357, 365.

31. Gerhard O. Forde, *On Being a Theologian of the Cross: Reflections on Luther's Heidelberg Disputation, 1518* (Grand Rapids, Mich.: Eerdmans, 1997), 91 n. 21.

32. See Ernst Kutsch, "Deus humiliat et exaltat: Zu Luthers Übersetzung von Psalm 118,21 und Psalm 18,36," *Zeitschrift für Theologie und Kirche* 61 (1964): 193–220; Horst Beintker, "Gottverlassenheit und Transitus durch den Glauben: Eine Erschliessung der Anfechtungen des Menschen Jesus nach Luthers Auglegungen der Psalmen 8 und 22," *Evangelische Theologie* 45 (1985): 108–23.

33. See David P. Scaer, "The Concept of Anfechtung in Luther's Thought," *Concordia Theological Quarterly* 47 (1983): 15–30; Robert A. Kelly, "Oratio, Meditatio, Tentatio Faciunt Theologum: Luther's Piety and the Formation of Theologians," *Consensus* 19 (1993): 9–27.

34. See Martin E. Lehmann, *Luther and Prayer,* 136–37.

35. See Heiko A. Oberman, *Luther: Man between God and the Devil* (New Haven, Conn.: Yale University Press, 1989), 311.

36. *Luther's Works,* 51:232.

37. Martin Luther, *Letters of Spiritual Counsel,* Library of Christian Classics (Philadelphia: Westminster Press, 1955), 18:61.

38. Ibid., 62.

39. *Luther's Works,* 51:234.

40. Luther, *Letters of Spiritual Counsel,* 18:58.

41. Kenneth R. Mitchell and Herbert Anderson, *All Our Losses, All Our Griefs: Resources for Pastoral Care* (Philadelphia: Westminster Press, 1983), 90.

42. *Luther's Works,* 54:7.

43. Ibid., 46:29, 35.

44. Solberg, *Compelling Knowledge,* 159.

45. William Bouwsma, *John Calvin: A Sixteenth-Century Portrait* (New York: Oxford University Press, 1988), 23.

46. Ibid.

47. John Calvin, *Commentary on the Book of the Psalms,* trans. James Anderson (Grand Rapids, Mich.: Baker Book House, 1989), 1:xxxix.

48. John Calvin, *Institutes of the Christian Religion,* Library of Christian Classics, 20–21, ed. John T. McNeill (Philadelphia: Westminster Press, 1960), III.xx.4.

49. Ibid., III.xx.4–12.

50. Calvin, *Psalms,* I:xxxvii. See James A. De Jong, "'An Anatomy of All Parts of the Soul': Insights into Calvin's Spirituality from His Psalms Commentary," in *Calvinus sacrae scripturae professor,* ed. W. Neuser (Grand Rapids, Mich.: Eerdmans, 1994), 1–14.

51. De Jong, "'An Anatomy,'" 9.

52. Ibid., 5.

53. Calvin, *Institutes,* III.xx.11.

54. Calvin, *Psalms,* I:xxxix.

55. Ibid., V:189.

56. Ibid., I:182.

57. Ibid., III:416.

58. Calvin, *Institutes,* I.xvi.3.

59. Susan E. Schreiner, "'Through a Mirror Dimly': Calvin's Sermons on Job," *Calvin Theological Journal* 21 (1985): 179. Quoted by David J. A. Clines, "Job and the Spirituality of the Reformation," in *The Bible, the Reformation, and the Church,* ed. W. P. Stephens, 66.

60. From Calvin's sermons on Job quoted by Clines, "Job and the Spirituality of the Reformation," 67.

61. Bouwsma, *John Calvin,* 86.

62. De Jong, "'An Anatomy,'" 14.

63. Calvin, *Institutes,* I.xvii.7.

64. Ibid., I.xvii.3.

65. For the following, see Daniel Migliore, "Freedom to Pray: Karl Barth's Theology of Prayer," in *Spirituality and Theology: Essays in Honor of Diogenes Allen,* ed. Eric O. Springsted (Louisville: Westminster John Knox Press, 1998), 112–23.

66. For one of many passages where Barth emphasizes that "prayer is decisively petition," see *Church Dogmatics* III/4 (Edinburgh: T. & T. Clark, 1961), 97 ff.

67. Ibid., III/3, 277.

68. Ibid., III/4, 108.

69. Friedrich Schleiermacher, *The Christian Faith,* ed. H. R. Mackintosh and J. S. Stewart (Edinburgh: T. & T. Clark, 1989), 673.

70. Barth, *Church Dogmatics,* III/4, 109.

71. Ibid., III/3, 285.

72. Ibid., IV/2, 357.

73. Ibid., III/2, 592.

74. Karl Barth, *Predigten 1935–1967,* hrsg. Hartmut Spieker und Hinrich Stoevesandt; Gesamtausgabe, Abteil I (Zürich: Theologischer Verlag, 1996), 85–93.

75. Ibid., 89.

76. Ibid.

77. Ibid., 92–93.

78. See Barth, *Church Dogmatics,* IV/3.1, 383–88; 398–408; 421–34; 453–61.

79. In a public conversation held in 1966 in which he was asked about the legitimacy of lament, Barth emphasized that Job not only vigorously complained to God but also made accusations against God. Under certain conditions, a person of faith can even be an accuser of God "provided one goes to the right address." See Karl Barth, *Gesprache,* 1964–1968, ed. Eberhard Busch; Gesamtausgabe, Abteil IV (Zürich: Theologischer Verlag, 1997), 291–92.

80. Barth, *Church Dogmatics,* II/1, 374.

81. Ibid., 373.

82. Barth, *Church Dogmatics,* IV/2, 168.

83. Ibid., 251.

84. Ibid., 487.

85. Ibid.

86. Barth, *Predigten 1935–1967,* 223–31.

87. Ibid., 225.

88. Ibid., 229.

89. Ibid., 230.

90. Ibid., 231.

91. Barth, *Church Dogmatics,* II/1, 374.

92. Ibid., 374.

93. Barth, *Deliverance to the Captives* (New York: Harper & Brothers, 1961), 105.

94. Jürgen Moltmann, "Wrestling with God: A Personal Meditation," in *The Source of Life: The Holy Spirit and the Theology of Life* (Minneapolis: Fortress, 1997), 2.

95. Ibid., 4–5.

96. Jürgen Moltmann, *The Passion for Life: A Messianic Lifestyle* (Philadelphia: Fortress, 1978), 22.

97. Ibid., 23.

98. Jürgen Moltmann, *The Theology of Hope* (New York: Harper & Row, 1967), 21.

99. Jürgen Moltmann, *The Crucified God: The Cross of Christ as the Foundation and Criticism of Christian Theology* (New York: Harper & Row, 1974), 153.

100. Jürgen Moltmann, *The Way of Jesus Christ: Christology in Messianic Dimensions* (San Francisco: Harper, 1990), 152.

101. Moltmann, *The Crucified God,* 150.

102. Ibid., 151.

103. Ibid., 236.

104. Ibid., 243.

105. Ibid., 314.

106. Elizabeth Johnson, *She Who Is* (New York: Crossroad, 1992), 255.

107. Ibid., 259.

108. Ibid.

109. Ibid., 262.

110. Ibid., 263.

111. Ibid., 254.

112. Ibid., 270.

113. Ibid.

114. Alice Walker, *In Search of Our Mothers' Gardens: Womanist Prose* (San Diego: Harcourt Brace Jovanovich, 1983), xi.

115. Clarice Martin, "Biblical Theodicy and Black Women's Spiritual Autobiography: The Miry Bog, the Desolate Pit, a New Song in My Mouth," in *A Troubling in My Soul,* ed. E. Townes (Maryknoll, N.Y.: Orbis Books, 1993), 31.

116. Kathleen Farmer, "Psalms," in *The Women's Bible Commentary* (Louisville: Westminster/John Knox Press, 1992), 144.

117. Ibid.

4. THE PRAYER OF LAMENT IN RECENT PASTORAL THEOLOGY

1. For historical overviews of the history of pastoral care in the church, see John T. McNeill, *A History of the Cure of Souls* (New York: Harper & Brothers, 1951); William A. Clebsch and Charles R. Jaekle, *Pastoral Care in Historical Perspective* (Englewood Cliffs, N.J.: Prentice-Hall, 1964); and Charles V. Gerkin, *An Introduction to Pastoral Care* (Nashville: Abingdon Press, 1997), 23–95.

2. The term "pastoral theology" has been used in a variety of ways over the long course of its history and there is still diversity in the way the term is used today. Thomas Oden retains a classical understanding of pastoral theology as "that branch of Christian theology that deals with the office and functions of a pastor" (see Thomas Oden, *Pastoral Theology* [San Francisco: Harper & Row, 1983], x). Since the mid-twentieth century pastoral theology has been identified as a subdiscipline of practical theology that has as its focus the caring ministries of the church and its representatives (see Seward Hiltner, *Preface to Pastoral Theology* [Nashville: Abingdon Press, 1959]). For an excellent overview of the contemporary status of pastoral theology, see Bonnie J. Miller-McLemore, "The Living Web: Pastoral Theology at the Turn of the Century," in *Through the Eyes of Women: Insights for Pastoral Care,* ed. Jeanne Stevenson Moessner (Minneapolis: Fortress Press, 1996), 9–26.

3. Seward Hiltner, Carroll Wise, and Wayne Oates use the psalms as a primary resource in discussing the relationship between the Bible and pastoral care. A lament psalm, Psalm 38, has particular relevance for this discussion. See Donald Capps's treatment of the lament psalms in pastoral theology in *Biblical Approaches to Pastoral Counseling* (Philadelphia: Westminster Press, 1981), 47–59. Works cited in Capps are Seward Hiltner, *Pastoral Counseling* (Nashville: Abingdon Press, 1949); Carroll A. Wise, *Psychiatry and the Bible* (San Francisco: Harper & Brothers, 1956); and Wayne Oates, *The Bible and Pastoral Care* (Philadelphia: Westminster Press, 1953). More recent works in pastoral theology that include discussions of the biblical lament psalms and lament tradition include Elaine Ramshaw's *Ritual and Pastoral Care* (Minneapolis: Fortress Press, 1987), Carroll Saussy's *The Gift of Anger: A Call to Faithful Action* (Louisville: Westminster John Knox Press, 1995), and "The Healing Power of Anger," by Carroll Saussy and Barbara J. Clarke, in *Through the Eyes of Women,* 112–14.

4. Wayne E. Oates, *The Presence of God in Pastoral Counseling* (Waco, Tex.: Word Books, 1986), 103–16.

5. Ibid., 107.

6. Ibid., 113.

7. Ibid., 115.

8. Ibid., 112.

9. Ibid., 114.

10. Ibid., 116.

11. William E. Hulme, *Pastoral Care and Counseling* (Minneapolis: Augsburg Publishing House, 1981), 118.

12. Ibid.

13. William and Lucy Hulme, *Wrestling with Depression* (Minneapolis: Augsburg, 1995), 72–73, 105–7.

14. Ibid., 105.

15. James D. Whitehead and Evelyn Eaton Whitehead, *Shadows of the Heart: A Spirituality of the Negative Emotions* (New York: Crossroad, 1994).

16. Ibid., 167–68.

17. William V. Arnold, *Introduction to Pastoral Care* (Philadelphia: Westminster Press, 1982), 162.

18. Ibid., 163.

19. Kenneth R. Mitchell and Herbert Anderson, *All Our Losses, All Our Griefs: Resources for Pastoral Care* (Philadelphia: Westminster Press, 1983), 79.

20. Ibid., 124.

21. Herbert Anderson, "Men and Grief: The Hidden Sea of Tears without Outlet," in *The Care of Men,* ed. Christie Cozad Neuger and James Newton Poling (Nashville: Abingdon, 1997), 203–26.

22. Ibid., 225.

23. Ibid.

24. Capps, *Biblical Approaches to Pastoral Counseling,* 47–97.

25. Ibid., 90. In describing the structure of the psalm of lament, Capps follows the outline of Bernhard W. Anderson in *Out of the Depths: The Psalms Speak for Us Today* (Philadelphia: Westminster Press, 1974), 54–56.

26. Eugene H. Peterson, *Five Smooth Stones for Pastoral Work* (Atlanta: John Knox Press, 1980).

27. Eugene H. Peterson, *Answering God: The Psalms as a Tool for Prayer* (San Francisco: Harper, 1989).

28. Peterson, *Five Smooth Stones for Pastoral Work,* 97–100.

29. Peterson, *Answering God,* 121.

30. Ibid., 98.

31. See Thomas Long's review of Nigel Robb's *A Time to Die and a Time to Live: A Guidebook for Those Who Care for the Grieving* (St. Andrews, Scotland: Blake Publications, 1996), *Princeton Seminary Bulletin,* n.s., 18, no. 2 (1977): 240.

32. Our discussion of Freud will draw largely from Ester Shapiro, *Grief as a Family Process* (New York: Guilford Press, 1994). Freud's essay "Mourning and Melancholia" may be found in *The Standard Edition of the Complete Works of Sigmund Freud* (New York: Norton, 1957), 14:239–60.

33. Shapiro, *Grief as a Family Process,* 27–28.

34. Mitchell and Anderson, *All Our Losses, All Our Griefs,* 56–57.

35. Ibid., 23–25.

36. Ibid., 28.

37. R. Scott Sullender, *Grief and Growth: Pastoral Resources for Emotional and Spiritual Growth* (Mahwah, N.J.: Paulist Press, 1985), 60.

38. Mitchell and Anderson, *All Our Losses, All Our Griefs,* 56–57.

39. Ibid., 20.

40. Ibid., 29.

41. Ibid., 29–30.

42. Ibid., 90.

43. Ibid.

44. Ibid., 30.

45. Ibid., 58.

46. Ibid., 81–82.

47. Ibid., 124.

48. Elisabeth Kübler-Ross, *On Death and Dying* (New York: Macmillan, 1969). According to Kübler-Ross, the stages are denial, anger, bargaining, depression, and acceptance.

49. Ann Weems, *Psalms of Lament* (Louisville: Westminster John Knox Press, 1995), 22.

50. See Brueggemann, "The Formfulness of Grief," *Interpretation* 31 (1977): 263–75.

51. Capps, "The Use of Psalms and Grief Counseling," in *Biblical Approaches to Pastoral Counseling,* 73–77.

52. Ibid., 88.

53. Ibid., 78.

54. Ibid.

55. Ibid., 88.

56. Ibid., 79–80.

57. Ibid., 88.

58. Ibid., 80.

59. Ibid., 88.

60. Ibid., 89–90.

61. Ibid., 92.

62. Ibid.

63. Ibid.

64. Ibid., 77.

65. Eugene Peterson, *Five Smooth Stones for Pastoral Work,* 142.

66. Hulme, *Pastoral Care and Counseling,* 153.

67. Peterson, *Five Smooth Stones for Pastoral Work,* 143.

68. Ibid., 144.

69. Ibid., 145.

70. Ramshaw, *Ritual and Pastoral Care,* 33.

71. For an extended discussion of the ways that ritual responds to human need, see Ramshaw, *Ritual and Pastoral Care,* 22–35.

72. Nancy Ramsay, "Compassionate Resistance: An Ethic for Pastoral Care and Counseling" (inaugural address given at Louisville Presbyterian Seminary, September 11, 1997), 2. Her address is drawn from *Counseling Survivors of Child Sexual Abuse,* to be published by Westminster John Knox Press in 1999.

73. See James Poling, *Deliver Us from Evil: Resisting Racial and Gender Oppression* (Minneapolis: Fortress Press, 1996).

74. James Poling, "Resisting Violence in the Name of Jesus," *Journal of Pastoral Theology* 7 (summer 1997): 15–22.

75. James Poling, *The Abuse of Power: A Theological Problem* (Nashville: Abingdon, 1991), 14–15.

76. Poling, "Resisting Violence in the Name of Jesus," 20.

77. This psalm, written by Karen Doudt, was originally published in Poling, *Abuse of Power,* 37–38.

78. Poling, "Resisting Violence in the Name of Jesus," 20–21.

79. Ibid.

80. Denise Ackermann, "On Hearing and Lamenting: Faith and Truth-Telling," in *To Remember and to Heal: Theological and Psychological Reflections on Truth and Reconciliation,* ed. H. Russel Botman and Robin M. Petersen (Cape Town: Human & Rousseau, 1996), 47–56.

81. Ibid., 47.

82. Ibid., 52.

83. Ibid., 53.

84. Ibid., 53, 55.

85. Adrienne Rich, quoted in Ackermann, "On Hearing and Lamenting," 49.

86. Ibid.

87. Ibid., 55.

88. Larry Kent Graham, *Discovering Images of God: Narratives of Care among Lesbians and Gays* (Louisville: Westminster John Knox Press, 1997).

89. Ibid., 11.

90. See Mary Ballou and Nancy W. Gabalac, *A Feminist Position on Mental Health* (Springfield, Ill.: Charles C. Thomas, 1985), 69–97, for a well-developed model of how women internalize damaging self-understandings from their social environment. See also Archie C. Smith, *The Relational Self: Ethics and Therapy from a Black Church Perspective* (Nashville: Abingdon Press, 1982), 156–86.

91. Ibid., 182.

92. Ibid.

93. We are grateful to Larry Graham for a conversation we shared about lament in which he spoke about the community-forming crises of the AIDS epidemic and the Stonewall Revolution and made the observation: "Lament forms community."

94. Seward Hiltner, *Pastoral Counseling* (Nashville: Abingdon Press, 1949), 19.

95. Ibid., 27–28.

96. Smith, *The Relational Self.*

97. Theresa Snorton, "The Legacy of the African-American Matriarch: New Perspectives for Pastoral Care," in *Through the Eyes of Women,* 50–65.

98. Ibid., 50.

99. Ibid., 58.

100. Ibid.

101. Ibid., 58–59. The 1997 movie *Soul Food* provides a powerful portrayal of the power and influence of the legacy of this spiritual strength.

102. Ibid., 62.

103. Ibid., 50, 59.

104. Ibid., 59.

105. Ibid., 60, 63.

106. Ibid., 60.

107. Ibid., 50.

108. Ibid., 60.

109. Ibid., 61–62.

110. Ibid., 61.

111. Ibid., 60.

112. Christie Cozad Neuger, "Pastoral Counseling as an Art of Personal Political Activism," in *The Arts of Ministry: Feminist-Womanist Approaches,* ed. Christie Cozad Neuger (Louisville: Westminster John Knox Press, 1996), 110. The theme, which begins in the section "Coming to Voice," continues throughout the essay.

113. Ibid., 93.

114. Ibid.

115. Ibid., 88.

116. Ibid., 105.

117. Ibid., 103–4.

118. Ibid., 105.

119. See Rebecca S. Chopp, "Theology and the Poetics of Testimony," *Criterion* (winter 1998): 2–12.

5. TOWARD A PASTORAL THEOLOGY OF THE PRAYER OF LAMENT

1. C. S. Lewis, *A Grief Observed* (New York: Seabury Press, 1961), 31.

2. Nicholas Wolterstorff, *Lament for a Son* (Grand Rapids, Mich.: Eerdmans, 1987), 70.

3. See Patrick D. Miller, "The Psalms and Pastoral Care," *Reformed Liturgy and Music* (summer 1990): 131. Miller refers to the work of Elaine Scarry, *The Body in Pain* (New York: Oxford University Press, 1985). We acknowledge our indebtedness to Miller's article in developing some of the themes of this chapter.

4. Scarry, *Body in Pain,* 4.

5. Elie Wiesel, "Jenseits des Schweigens," in *Das Gegenteil von Gleichgultigkeit Ist Erinnerung,* ed. Dagmar Mensink und Reinhold Boschki (Mainz: Matthias-Grunewald Verlag, 1995), 12.

6. James Poling, *The Abuse of Power: A Theological Problem* (Nashville: Abingdon, 1991), 35–48.

7. There is much controversy surrounding the recovery of traumatic memories and much new research being done about the memory and how it functions. For those interested in a sensitive treatment of the complex issues involved in recovering traumatic memories, see Lenore Terr, *Unchained Memories: True Stories of Traumatic Memories, Lost and Found* (New York: HarperCollins Basic Books, 1994).

8. Karl Rahner and Johann Baptist Metz, *The Courage to Pray* (New York: Crossroad, 1981), 18.

9. Ibid.

10. Miller, "The Psalms and Pastoral Care," 131.

11. Lewis, *A Grief Observed,* 1.

12. Kenneth Mitchell and Herbert Anderson, *All Our Losses, All Our Griefs* (Philadelphia: Westminster Press, 1983), 81–82.

13. Scarry, *Body in Pain,* 216.

14. See Larry Graham, *Care for Persons, Care for the World: A Psychosystems Approach to Pastoral Care and Counseling* (Nashville: Abingdon Press, 1992).

15. Eberhard Bethge, *Dietrich Bonhoeffer: Man of Vision, Man of Courage* (New York: Harper & Row, 1979), 512.

16. Snorton, "The Legacy of the African-American Matriarch," 60.

17. See David Tracy, "The Hidden God: The Divine Other of Liberation," *Cross Currents* (spring 1996): 5–16.

18. Wolterstorff, *Lament for a Son,* 71.

19. Tracy, "The Hidden God," 7.

20. Ibid., 13.

21. Karl Barth, *Church Dogmatics,* III/4 (Edinburgh: T. & T. Clark, 1961), 108.

22. Patrick D. Miller, *They Cried to the Lord: The Form and Theology of Biblical Prayer* (Minneapolis: Fortress, 1994), 126.

23. Elizabeth Johnson, *She Who Is: The Mystery of God in Feminist Theological Discourse* (New York: Crossroad, 1992), 266.

24. See Harold S. Kushner, *When Bad Things Happen to Good People* (New York: Avon Books, 1981).

25. David R. Blumenthal, *Facing the Abusing God: A Theology of Protest* (Louisville: Westminster/John Knox Press, 1993), 267.

26. These are questions that Wendy Farley asks of Blumenthal in their illuminating conversations. See chapter 13 of Blumenthal, *Facing the Abusing God.*

27. Walter Brueggemann, "The Costly Loss of Lament," in *The Psalms and the Life of Faith: Walter Brueggemann,* ed. Patrick D. Miller (Minneapolis: Fortress, 1995), 59.

28. Revisiting Luther's famous theology of the cross, David Tracy calls for a retrieval of the awareness of a twofold hiddenness of God: the hiddenness of God in the suffering of the cross on the one hand, and the hiddenness of God that prompts the sense of the utter inscrutability of God on the other. Only a dialectical grasp of these two understandings of the hiddenness of God is able to do justice to the complexity and ambiguity of the biblical witness and much human experience of God. See Tracy, "The Hidden God."

29. Paul Ricoeur, "Lamentation as Prayer," in Andre LaCocque and Paul Ricoeur, *Thinking Biblically,* 218.

30. Johnson, *She Who Is,* 212.

31. Catherine Mowry LaCugna, *God for Us: The Trinity and Christian Life* (San Francisco: Harper, 1991), 1.

32. For a "pastoral exegesis" of the doctrine of the Trinity, see Ellen Charry, "Spiritual Formation by the Doctrine of the Trinity," *Theology Today* 54, no. 3 (October 1997): 367–80.

33. Johnson, *She Who Is*, 222.

34. Ibid., 254.

35. Jacquelyn Grant, "The Sin of Servanthood," in *A Troubling in My Soul: Womanist Perspectives on Evil and Suffering*, ed. Emilie M. Townes (Maryknoll, N.Y.: Orbis Books, 1993), 199–218.

36. Rahner and Metz, *The Courage to Pray*, 26.

37. J. B. Metz, *Faith in History and Society: Toward a Practical Fundamental Theology* (New York: Seabury Press, 1980), 111.

38. David Tracy, "The Hidden God," 14.

39. Ibid., 20.

40. A. Yarbro Collins, "Persecution and Vengeance in the Book of Revelation," in *Apocalypticism in the Mediterranean World* (Tübingen: Mohr, 1983), 746–47.

41. Carroll Saussy and Barbara J. Clarke, "The Healing Power of Anger," in *Through the Eyes of Women*, 107–22.

42. Therese A. Rando, *Treatment of Complicated Mourning* (Champaign, Ill.: Research Press, 1993), 466.

43. Miroslav Volf, *Exclusion and Embrace: A Theological Exploration of Identity, Otherness, and Reconciliation* (Nashville: Abingdon, 1996), 124.

44. Walter Brueggemann, *The Message of the Psalms: A Theological Commentary* (Minneapolis: Augsburg, 1984), 85 ff.

45. See Denise Dombkowski Hopkins, *Journey through the Psalms: A Path to Wholeness* (New York: United Church Press, 1990), 68–69; and Patrick Miller, *Interpreting the Psalms* (Philadelphia: Fortress, 1986), 150–53.

46. Dietrich Bonhoeffer, "Sermon on a Psalm of Vengeance," *Theology Today* 38 (1981): 469.

47. Hopkins, *Journey through the Psalms*, 69.

48. See John Patton, *Is Human Forgiveness Possible?* (Nashville: Abingdon, 1985).

49. "Most of us where we are victims need to repent of what the perpetrators do to our soul. Victims need to repent of the fact that all too often they mimic the behavior of the oppressor, let themselves be shaped in the mirror image of the enemy." Volf, *Exclusion and Embrace*, 117.

50. Our reflections in this section owe much to Miroslav Volf's powerful work, *Exclusion and Embrace*.

51. "Crazy Mary Katherine," in Martin Bell, *Nenshu and the Tiger* (New York: Seabury Press, 1975), 51–55.

52. Gustavo Gutiérrez, *On Job: God-Talk and the Suffering of the Innocent* (Maryknoll, N.Y.: Orbis Books, 1985), 29.

53. Ibid., 31.

54. Ibid., 32.

55. Wolterstorff, *Lament for a Son*, 72.

56. See Geoffrey Wainwright, *Doxology: The Praise of God in Worship, Doctrine, and Life* (New York: Oxford University Press, 1980).

57. See Walter Brueggemann, *Hopeful Imagination: Prophetic Voices in Exile* (Philadelphia: Fortress, 1986), and the collection of Brueggemann's essays on the psalms, *The Psalms and the Life of Faith: Walter Brueggemann*, ed. Patrick D. Miller (Minneapolis: Fortress, 1995).

58. Hopkins, *Journey through the Psalms*, 12.

59. See Hopkins, *Journey through the Psalms,* chapter 2: "Your Hallelujahs Don't Have to Be Hollow Anymore."

60. Brueggemann, "Praise and the Psalms: A Politics of Glad Abandonment," in Miller, *The Psalms and the Life of Faith,* 116–17.

61. Samuel E. Balentine, "Enthroned on the Praises and Laments of Israel," in *The Lord's Prayer,* ed. Daniel L. Migliore (Grand Rapids, Mich.: Eerdmans, 1993), 34.

62. See William Lynch, *Images of Hope: Imagination as Healer of the Hopeless* (New York: Mentor-Omega, 1965).

63. Cecil Williams, *No Hiding Place: Empowerment and Recovery for Our Troubled Communities* (San Francisco: Harper, 1992), 9.

64. Andrew D. Lester, *Hope in Pastoral Care and Counseling* (Louisville: Westminster John Knox Press, 1995), 85.

65. LaCugna, *God for Us: The Trinity and Christian Life,* 341.

66. Ibid., 342.

6. THE PRAYER OF LAMENT AND THE PRACTICE OF MINISTRY

1. A number of recent works in pastoral theology and practical theology employ the imagery of midwifery. See Kathleen D. Billman, "Integrating Theology and Pastoral Care in Ministry," *Currents in Theology and Mission* 19, no. 5 (June 1992): 165–73; Elaine Ramshaw, *Ritual and Pastoral Care* (Philadelphia: Fortress Press, 1987), 22; Carol Hess, "Becoming Midwives to Justice: A Feminist Approach to Practical Theology," in *Liberating Faith Practices: Feminist Practical Theologies in Context,* ed. Denise M. Ackermann and Riet Bons-Storm (Leuven: Peeters, 1998).

2. See Bruno Bettelheim, *Freud and Man's Soul: Man of Vision, Man of Courage* (New York: Knopf, 1983).

3. For insightful descriptions of Christian life as involving the learning of specific habits and practices, see L. Gregory Jones, *Embodying Forgiveness: A Theological Analysis* (Grand Rapids, Mich.: Eerdmans, 1995); *Practicing Our Faith,* ed. Dorothy C. Bass (San Francisco: Jossey-Bass, 1997); *Liberating Faith Practices,* ed. Denise M. Ackermann and Riet Bons-Storm; Martha Ellen Stortz, "Practicing Christians: Prayer as Formation," in *The Promise of Lutheran Ethics,* ed. Karen L. Bloomquist and John R. Stumme (Minneapolis: Fortress Press, 1998).

4. The story told in the following paragraphs is constructed from a taped interview with The Rev. Lydia Villanueva on January 18, 1996, and from participation in the All Saints' Day liturgy she created. Used with the written permission of Reverend Villanueva.

5. Interview with Villanueva on January 18, 1996.

6. From a speech delivered by Walter Brueggemann at the Professional Leadership Conference, Lutheran School of Theology at Chicago, February 1998.

7. "What a Friend We Have in Jesus," text by Joseph Scriven, 1820–1886.

8. J. Frank Henderson, *Liturgies of Lament* (Chicago: Liturgy Training Publications, 1994), 13–21. This helpful resource includes principles for preparing the liturgy, sample liturgies for special occasions, and resources (scriptures, prayers, and other liturgical texts). For prayers and liturgies commemorating the Holocaust, see *Liturgies on the Holocaust: An Interfaith Anthology,* ed. Marcia Sachs Littell and Sharon Weissman (Harrisburg, Pa.: Trinity Press International, 1998).

9. Ibid.

10. See Christie Cozad Neuger, ed., *The Arts of Ministry: Feminist-Womanist Approaches* (Louisville: Westminster John Knox Press, 1996).

11. Walter Brueggemann, "The Psalms and the Life of Faith," in *The Psalms and the Life of Faith: Walter Brueggemann,* ed. Patrick D. Miller (Minneapolis: Fortress Press, 1995), 5.

12. Donald Capps, *The Poet's Gift* (Louisville: Westminster/John Knox Press, 1993). See especially chapter 2, "Pastoral Conversation as Embodied Language."

13. See Rebecca Chopp, "Theology and the Poetics of Testimony," *Criterion* 17, no. 1 (winter 1998): 2.

14. Ibid.

15. Bill Williams, *Naked before God: The Return of a Broken Disciple* (Harrisburg, Pa.: Morehouse, 1998), 309.

16. For a good biography of Hamer, see Kay Mills, *This Little Light of Mine: The Life of Fannie Lou Hamer* (New York: Dutton, 1993).

17. See Charles Marsh, *God's Long Summer: Stories of Faith and Civil Rights* (Princeton, N.J.: Princeton University Press, 1997), 42–43.

18. Ibid., 45.

19. Ibid., 26.

20. Ibid., 27.

21. Jacquelyn Grant, "Womanist Theology: Black Women's Experience as a Source for Doing Theology, with Special Reference to Christology," in *Constructive Christian Theology in the Worldwide Church,* ed. William R. Barr (Grand Rapids, Mich.: Eerdmans, 1997), 346.

22. Jacquelyn Grant, "Womanist Jesus and the Mutual Struggle for Liberation," in *The Recovery of Black Presence: An Interdisciplinary Exploration,* ed. Randall C. Bailey and Jacquelyn Grant (Nashville: Abingdon, 1995), 139.

23. Grant, "Womanist Theology," 349.

24. Grant, "Womanist Jesus," 140.

25. Marsh, *God's Long Summer,* 45.

26. Ibid., 46.

27. Ibid., 25.

28. Ibid., 213, n. 98.

29. Mills, *This Little Light of Mine,* 313.

30. J. Gerald Janzen, "Lust for Life and the Bitterness of Job," *Theology Today* 55, no. 2 (July 1998): 161–62.

31. Ibid., 162.

32. Carol Hess, *Caretakers of Our Mothers' Gardens* (Nashville: Abingdon, 1997), 210. The phrase "hard dialogue and deep connections" is taken from chapter 6 of this lively and engaging volume. The author's analysis of "conversational education," while focusing on conversations among women, provides a model for dialogue among all members of congregations.

33. Ibid., 206.

34. Nicholas Wolterstorff, *Lament for a Son* (Grand Rapids, Mich.: Eerdmans, 1987), 81–82.

35. The following reflections are indebted to Paul Ricoeur's essay "Lamentation as Prayer," 211–32.

36. See Ricoeur, "Lamentation as Prayer."

GENERAL INDEX

SCRIPTURE INDEX

OLD TESTAMENT

NEW TESTAMENT

1 Corinthians
13:12   59, 64, 66

2 Corinthians
11:23 ff.   35
12:7 ff.   35
12:8   37

Ephesians
4:25   120

James
5:7–18   40

Revelation
6:9   36